John Ozoga's
WHITETAIL INTRIGUE

Scientific Insights for
White-tailed Deer Hunters

Edited by Patrick Durkin

Book design by Allen West, Krause Publications.

Cover Photo Credits:
Front Cover: Charles J. Alsheimer
Back Cover: Len Rue Jr. (bottom), Mark Raycroft (top)

Published by

700 E. State St. • Iola, WI 54990-0001

Please call or write for our free catalog of publications. Our toll-free number to
place an order or to obtain a free catalog is (800) 258-0929. Please use our regular
business telephone (715) 445-2214 for editorial comment and further information.
Library of Congress Catalog Number: 99-68133
ISBN: 0-87341-881-6
Printed in the United States of America

To my very special Janice:
this family's guiding light.

Bill Kinney

CONTENTS

FOREWORD

One of my most satisfying moments as editor of *Deer & Deer Hunting* was the day in November 1993 when John Ozoga agreed to write "Deer Research" as a regular column in our magazine.

Even though his articles appeared at times in the magazine in the late 1980s, his work was absent from *D&DH* in the early 1990s because someone in the Michigan Department of Natural Resources believed outside writing constituted a conflict of interest for agency personnel.

John explained his situation to me shortly after the magazine hired me in January 1991. Even though John couldn't write for us, I often called him to discuss various aspects of deer behavior, or to compare notes on deer politics in whitetail country. In effect, John became one of my technical advisers as I edited the magazine and spliced his insights into the text of other people's articles.

Nearly every time we spoke, I reminded John there would always be room for his writings in *D&DH*; all he had to do was give the word. As John inched closer toward his pending retirement in early 1994, we began talking about the type of research findings he would like to share with the magazine's readers.

Still, it wasn't until I assigned John his first article and manuscript deadline that I allowed myself to celebrate the magazine's coup. Finally, after four years of courting this venerable researcher and talented writer, we actually had an agreement! When I hung up the phone after making that verbal pact, I pumped a fist and then typed "John J. Ozoga, Research Editor" into the magazine's masthead.

Never has John disappointed me since that day. Though retired from his career as a research biologist, he has continued to stay atop deer research. It's obvious from our conversations and the articles he submits that he still pores over scientific papers on whitetails, always adding his own insights into what his fellow researchers across North America report.

Bill Lea

Before long, John became a staple of the *D&DH* editorial diet. Then, a couple of years ago, while editing *D&DH*'s 20th anniversary book, *The Deer Hunters*, I struggled to decide which of John's articles to include. I eventually chose "Should You Doctor Scrapes?," which is also on Page 72 of this book. That article was first published in the November 1994 issue of *D&DH*. In the meantime, however, I had mentioned my dilemma to Charlie Alsheimer, the magazine's Northern field editor. Charlie suggested the obvious answer: "You really should do a full-color book with all of John's *Deer & Deer Hunting* articles." That idea came to fruition in 1999 when we started compiling and editing the book that follows.

So, here we go.

One of the many qualities that

always impresses our readers is John's objective yet heartfelt fascination with whitetails. Despite more than 30 years of working with hundreds of individual deer, John is ever the scientist. Never does he let himself fall victim to naming deer or referring to them by anything other than an ID number. These are wild animals after all, and his respect for them runs so deep that he refuses to domesticate them in any way.

John's studied detachment allows him to explore the whitetail's incredible ability to adjust and adapt to its ever-changing world and habitat. He refuses to romanticize the creature or offer off-hand explanations for various deer behaviors or adaptations. He more likely will list several possibilities, and note that even with exhaustive research, the ways of whitetails will always contain just enough mystery to defy easy explanation.

Despite his no-nonsense approach to whitetail research, there's another side to John that's not always apparent in his writing. While he simply won't draw conclusions about deer without the requisite research and academic peer review, he isn't judgmental when he hears layman's interpretations. If anything, he encourages the observations and explanations offered by the regular deer hunter. He might say some of them are a bit "cheeky" with their opinions, but he still offers encouragement and often agrees they might be onto something.

It's John's ability to connect with deer hunters that makes his writings so accessible to deer hunting's masses. While other researchers might have just as many insights to offer, few are his equal in presenting information in clear, concise, easily understood terms. That's why I always consider John J. Ozoga to be the deer hunter's biologist. The only thing that might equal his passion for the whitetail is his respect for the deer hunter.

Charles J. Alsheimer

Let's hope this mutual admiration continues for many deer seasons to come.

— *Patrick Durkin*
Editor, Deer & Deer Hunting
February 2000

INTRODUCTION

Ask any writer, and they'll say one of their deepest fears is working with an editor who doesn't have a good feel for the subject matter or an appreciation for the way the writer presents it.

The writer-editor relationship doesn't grow overnight. It usually requires years of work in which the writer delivers a stream of manuscripts and then holds his breath, almost dreading to see what remains of his efforts when the articles appear in print. If trust doesn't take root and grow, the editor-writer relationship never progresses beyond the uneasy, dysfunctional relationship based solely on paychecks.

I like to think John Ozoga's relationship with the editors of *Deer & Deer Hunting* magazine skipped most of the growing pains. John always seemed to believe *D&DH* was the magazine that fit him best — almost as if he had a hand in its creation.

While John might not have conceived *D&DH*, he has helped shape its purpose and long-term vision since coming aboard in 1994 as the magazine's research editor. And when Krause Publications — the parent company of *D&DH* — approached John about compiling his many articles into a hardcover book, he quickly agreed.

John then gave the magazine's editors the ultimate compliment by trusting us to organize his first 34 "Deer Research" articles into a defining outline for the book. Even so, we told him we would put something down on paper and send it past him for approval.

This brings me to the role Jennifer Pillath, associate editor for *D&DH*, played in pulling this book together. Jennifer's work on *Whitetail Intrigue* began with the mundane task of cataloging all the Xerox copies of John's articles, and putting them into a loose-leaf binder. Then, after reading the articles and discussing the book's overall theme with me, she began dividing the articles into four more specific themes to help shape the book's focus.

That might sound like a simple job, but try it sometime with somebody's body of work. You can't begin to organize anything until you thoroughly understand the writer's guiding philosophy and the principles that serve as that philosophy's foundation. And you certainly can't know either of those things until you've read, even studied, the material that will make up the book.

Jennifer performed that task flawlessly. After she outlined her plan and I offered some ideas for fine-tuning the outline, we soon had a framework to present to John. Our goal was to satisfy his desire for a book that captured the essence of his work for *Deer & Deer Hunting* magazine.

Here's what we came up with:

Part 1 is called "The Deer Society: Finding a Place in the Social Arena." This section includes seven chapters in which John outlines the well-defined differences and roles of the sexes among whitetails, and the sexes' sometimes disparate preferences in habitat, "territory" and companions.

Part 2 is called "The Herd's Communication: How Deer Speak Without Words." This section includes nine chapters in which John discusses the whitetail's heavy dependence on scents, odors and visual cues to communicate.

Part 3 is called "Survival of the Herd: A Combat with Nature." This section includes 10 chapters in which John discusses the many dangers and stress factors that deer encounter daily and seasonally, as well as some of the freakish biological occurrences that afflict individual deer.

Part 4 is called "The Herd's Future: A Joint Effort." John uses the eight chapters in this section to discuss how the challenges facing whitetails can be caused or cured by the way people manage deer herds. Many of the herds' stressors, of course, result from excessive deer numbers, which are often caused by a reluctance to pursue aggressive deer-harvest programs.

Of course, no matter how clear the writing or the book's overall focus, the material can't be fully enjoyed and appreciated unless it's presented in a clean, well-crafted format. Again we called on Jennifer to assist in this area. She worked with our longtime *D&DH* artist, Al West, to design a layout that best complemented John's text with a wide array of color photography. As you read or flip through the pages of this book, I think you'll agree Al and Jennifer did a fine job executing that crucial task.

Enough said. We hope you'll enjoy this treasury of John Ozoga's work, and that it leads to a deeper appreciation of North America's most popular big-game animal.

— *Patrick Durkin*
Iola, Wis.

ACKNOWLEDGMENTS

I've researched and written about this intriguing creature called the white-tailed deer for nearly four decades. Along the way, I've had help from a lot of people.

But one person stands out above the rest. If not for my wife, Janice, and her continual coaxing, I never would have written up my research findings for magazines and newspapers, nor produced a book such as this. Thanks again, Jan, for pointing me in the right direction.

Certainly, I'm pleased, and thankful that Krause Publications considered my contributions to *Deer & Deer Hunting* magazine worthy of being put into book form. In that regard, I'm profoundly grateful to Editor Patrick Durkin for encouraging this effort, for smoothing out my sometimes rough prose, and for providing the introductory material for this book.

I'm also indebted to Al Hofacker for the instrumental role he played in getting me started writing for *D&DH*. In the early 1980s, many magazine editors considered my writings "too technical," "too educational," and "lacking pizzazz." Meanwhile, Al was in the forefront. He understood deer hunters and knew what they wanted. Today, many magazines have followed Hofacker's lead by providing their readers with scientifically sound information — something I refer to as "soft science." Deer biology in outdoor magazines has become commonplace, but it was Al Hofacker and

D&DH that paved the way.

Having worked for the Michigan Department of Natural Resources for more than 33 years, I'm indebted to many of its employees. I'd especially like to recognize Carl Bennett, Craig Bienz, Rodney Clute, Pete Davis, Dan DeLisle, Robert Doepker, Dick Dover, Harry Hill, Ed Langenau, Jeff Lukowski, Leo Perry, Bruce Veneberg and Louis Verme. They all provided valuable assistance in one way or another. I couldn't have accomplished the research I did without their input.

Nonetheless, one doesn't compile the information printed on the pages of this book solely from personal experience. In addition, I've relied heavily on the works of Anthony and George Bubenik, Valerius Geist, George Goss, David Guynn, Harry Jacobson, Larry Marchinton, Karl Miller, Aaron Moen, Dietland Muller-Schwarze, Duane Ullrey and many other scientists like them. These are some of the people who have contributed to our understanding of whitetails so that books like this are possible.

Last, but certainly not least, I greatly appreciate the support of my mother and father, daughter Holly, and sons John, Mark and Keith. They're not all deer hunters, but each has come to appreciate this amazing critter — the white-tailed deer — as much as I do. And I know Mom would have liked to see this book, too.

— *John J. Ozoga*
Munising, Mich.

Charles J. Alsheimer.

The Deer Society

FINDING A PLACE IN THE SOCIAL ARENA

Much like a loosely knit town, the whitetail's society works together to fit into myriad habitats across North America. Roles within the deer herd are earned, assigned, assumed, challenged and reassigned year-round and throughout a deer's lifetime.

What affects a deer's status? Its age, sex, size, strength and health are just a few of the factors that help determine each deer's role in the herd's often-mysterious social structure.

A deer's status within the herd not only affects its own life, but possibly the life of its offspring — especially among the herd's doe population. But whether a mature doe is choosing a woodlot for fawning or a buck is competing for breeding rights, a deer's standing within the herd's hierarchy helps determine its health and day-to-day life.

Chapter 1

A DIVIDED HOUSEHOLD:

Segregation of the Sexes

Does select habitat that is best suited for rearing offspring, which means diversified food and cover arrangements with ample hiding cover for mother and young. This serves as a predator defense during the critical stage of early fawn-rearing. By comparison, bucks tend to select areas where nutrition is superb, which allows for maximum body growth to attain a high dominance rank and improved breeding success.

In white-tailed deer, the adult sexes live separately during much of the year, just as do mule deer, red deer, elk, moose, bighorn sheep and other ungulates. Scientists refer to this social and spatial separation — which is pronounced during the non-breeding months — as sexual segregation or niche separation of the sexes.

Related female whitetails live in a matriarchal society, composed of mothers, daughters, grandmothers, great-grandmothers and so forth. Adult bucks, on the other hand, form fraternal or bachelor groups generally composed of unrelated males. In either case, the size of the social group and the degree of social complexity varies, depending on many factors that influence the herd's sex-age composition and density.

As a result, while the typical (non-migratory) female whitetail might spend her entire life on a relatively small ancestral range, the male is inclined to disperse to new range. Therefore, at some point, the young male must leave one societal unit and join the other if he is to someday become a successful breeder.

Unfortunately, adaptive advantages of the different lifestyles of ungulate sexes are still hotly debated by the world's researchers. Equally unfortunate is that seasonal differences in food, cover and social requirements of the two sexes are seldom considered in deer-management plans. Given the potential significance of those differences, some of us researchers question whether current deer habitat and herd-management strategies adequately serve both sexes. Are we more often bound to systems that strive to produce an abundance — and sometimes an overabundance — of whitetails for political reasons, regardless of the herd's condition?

The Male's Role

In many parts of North America, antlered bucks are harvested so intensively that true buck groups are virtually non-existent. From the standpoint of the whitetail's social evolution, groups of yearling bucks, in the absence of older bucks, do not represent true fraternal groups. Groups of yearling deer tend to represent transitory, summertime social groups and might even include yearling females, thus being quite different from exclusive, age-structured groups of bucks 2½ years of age and older. Yearling social groups are distinct groups that can include both sexes. Just seeing a number of yearling bucks in a group does not make it a bachelor group.

Because relatively few dominant white-tailed bucks do most of the breeding, Dale McCullough (1979) points out: "A young male can only hope to become a dominant male by engaging in hierarchical competition over a long period. The achievement of dominant status by young males requires outliving older, stronger males and dominating males of similar age. It is not enough to maintain position. To succeed, the young male must continually strive to move up in position. This requires that he associate not only with animals of lower rank, but also with those of higher rank." McCullough emphasizes that in an age-structured male society, a high rank is not easily attained; it requires experience and the learning of competitive skills. "Success, as in any contest of strength, skill, and endurance, comes from long and diligent training," McCullough states. "A young male, choosing not to join all-male groups would not be able to obtain the necessary skills to compete successfully."

Considering that the white-tailed buck's chances of breeding are largely determined by his rank in the male dominance hierarchy, it seems the young buck has little choice but to associate with other males. Although tightly linked to the mother-young system early in life, he must eventually break those bonds. When sexually mature, the buck must seek out and interact with older males, achieve male group membership, and rise in dominance rank. If he doesn't, and instead chooses to remain with female relatives, it's my guess he will become a hen-pecked "psychological castrate," never achieving respected breeder-status.

Why the Difference?

It should also be obvious, even to the casual observer, that as with any behavioral trait, the whitetail's social organization — sexual segregation included — is an adaptation. It evolved in response to numerous environmental stresses, including predators, diseases, climate, habitat conditions and hunting by American Indians. And, as with any adaptation, the whitetail's social organization is genetically linked, inherited and essential for the species' existence. It promotes social order, genetic selection and physical fitness.

Considering that the white-tailed buck's chances of breeding are largely determined by his rank in the male dominance hierarchy, it seems as though the young buck has little choice but to associate with other males.

Pardon the complex reasoning involved here, but because the whitetail sexes differ in many aspects of physiology, behavior and anatomy, they must have evolved differently. For example, bucks and does differ in size, shape, growth rate, metabolic rate, life span, food and cover requirements, and in many aspects of physiology and biochemistry that result in behavioral traits that differ. Based on intensive behavioral investigations at southern Michigan's George Reserve, McCullough and his co-workers (1989) concluded that — because of sex differences in food, cover and use of space — bucks and does do not compete equally for the necessities of life on a year-round basis.

One might carry this logic one step further. That is, if bucks and does evolved differently, they must also respond differently to environmental change. As a result, habitat-management practices that benefit female deer might not necessarily benefit bucks equally, or sometimes might even be detrimental to bucks.

Also, harvest-management strategies that inflict unnatural patterns of mortality (such as buck-only shooting) and create herds with abnormal sex and age composition — thereby altering important aspects of the whitetail's social environment — could affect the welfare of one sex, favorably or otherwise, more so than the other. Based largely on my telemetry research of whitetails in upper Michigan's square-mile Cusino enclosure, researcher Lou Verme (1988) reopened this can of worms by proposing that biosocial factors were more important than nutrition in explaining the seasonal niche separation of the adult sexes.

Biosocial Factors

Even within the confines of the Cusino enclosure, we could see bucks and does separate during the non-breeding period. While growing antlers, adult bucks concentrated in the hilly hardwoods that covered the area's northern portion. In contrast, does avoided that sector, and raised fawns in brushy areas more interspersed with openings in southern parts of the enclosure. Verme hypothesized: "It is imperative that (1) bachelor buck groups occupy habitat that enables them to see one another readily so as to continually assess their dominance position on the hierarchy, and (2) the area selected must afford the best possible skulking and escape cover while antlers are in the stage most vulnerable to disfigurement, if not severe injury."

You'll note that Verme's thesis revolves around the

Charles J. Alsheimer

idea that bucks select habitat they prefer; the impetus being that female deer then occupy whatever habitat the males ignore. That is debatable because the reverse might also prevail. That is, females might choose first, and the males take what's left.

When examining historical records of the Cusino enclosure, however, one finds different patterns of buck-habitat use prevailed during the early years of study. Telemetry locations of radio-collared bucks in 1966 and field observations made in 1977, for example, revealed that adult males commonly, if not more frequently, inhabited brushy portions of the enclosure during antler growth when deer density was relatively low. Further, records for nearly 200 antlered bucks revealed yearling bucks were no more prone to velvet-antler damage than older bucks, even though younger bucks stayed in more brushy cover.

Therefore, although adult bucks living in the Cusino enclosure seemed to develop traditional summertime use of certain areas, and biosocial factors might have been involved, there is no basis for the implied long-term nature of adult-buck habitat occupation nor historical support for Verme's hypothesis.

Oregon State University researchers Martin Main and Bruce Coblentz (1990) also disagreed with Verme's thesis when they reviewed five major hypotheses investigators proposed to explain sexual segregation among ungulates. According to Main and Coblentz, a major weakness in Verme's hypothesis is the implication that cervids living in open habitats need not segregate. However, other investigators have reported sexual segregation for mule deer in open desert, shrubsteppe and meadows; for red deer in grass and moorlands; and for

Biosocial factors are just as important as nutritional factors when discussing sexual segregation. During the vulnerable antler-development phase, bucks will seek areas that offer protection and escape cover to avoid antler injury.

barren-ground caribou in the arctic tundra. Probably the most compelling argument against Verme's hypothesis is that the protection of antlers cannot be used to explain sexual segregation among horned ungulates. Main and Coblentz concluded that Verme "attempted to fit a unique explanation to a single species when the behavior described is common among polygynous ungulates."

Main and Coblentz also rejected the hypothesis that males voluntarily leave superior range to minimize competition with females, their young and potential future offspring. In that regard, the researchers point out that relatively few dominant bucks do most of the breeding. As a result, "because breeding opportunities are not equally distributed among males, non-breeding males would gain nothing and lose much by segregating to areas with reduced forage opportunities."

Segregation for Protection

Sexual segregation as an anti-predator strategy has also been proposed to explain such behavior among males immediately after the rut and preceding antler shedding. Although some investigators suggest antler shedding serves as a form of "female mimicry" that enables males to rejoin females while minimizing the risk of being selectively preyed upon, Main and Coblentz note: "This explanation fails to address segregation prior to the breeding period or among bovids." Also, adult male ungulates frequently occupy habitat of greater predator density, and studies indicate that predation tends to be higher on adult males than on adult females, especially in winter.

Others have proposed that adult males segregate from females during the non-breeding period to minimize sexually motivated aggression among males when breeding is not possible. But there seems little support for this hypothesis, because hormonal control of reproduction and related male aggression among Northern-temperate ungulates tends to be tightly regulated by seasonal changes in photoperiod.

If winter range were reasonably good, pregnant females would emerge in somewhat better condition than adult bucks, who depleted their energy reserves during the previous rut and entered winter in comparatively poor condition.

As an alternative explanation to Verme's hypothesis, Main and Coblentz suggest that "bachelor groups may form as a consequence of males seeking similar forage resources while increasing their individual security by feeding as a group.

"Furthermore, occurrence of solitary adult males during nonbreeding periods has been reported for white-tailed deer, and a dominant floater — i.e., a mature buck with high social ranking that associates with different groups throughout the year and utilizes a large home range — has been reported for white-tailed deer by Brown (1974)."

Fawn-Rearing Habitat

According to the Oregon researchers, the one hypothesis that seems to address sexual segregation among ungulates most adequately is that "sexual segregation occurs as a result of differing energetic and reproductive strategies." That is, they propose females select habitat that is best suited for rearing offspring. Normally, that means diversified food and cover arrangements with ample hiding cover for mother and young. This serves as a predator defense during the critical stage of early fawn-rearing. By comparison, males tend to select areas where nutrition is superb, which allows for maximum body growth to attain high dominance rank and improved breeding success.

Generally speaking, male and female whitetails subsist on relatively low-quality forage in winter, and leave the winter range in depleted, poor physical condition. I suspect, however, if winter range was reasonably good, pregnant females would emerge in somewhat better condition than adult bucks, who depleted their energy reserves during the previous rut and entered winter in

comparatively poor condition.

Forage and environmental conditions are normally better in spring and summer, allowing deer to fairly rapidly replenish their energy reserves. All Northern-temperate ungulates give birth during this period, when conditions are most favorable for rearing young. And this is when the reproductive patterns of the adult sexes differ the most, and when bucks and does show the greatest separation.

Admittedly, studies aimed at evaluating habitat quality and determining dietary differences between the deer sexes have been largely inconclusive, and the results sometimes contradictory. However, the widely differing results often were caused by differences in study methods, data collection, and/or interpretation. Most researchers acknowledge the subject deserves further study.

In summary, Main and Coblentz suggest "habitat selection by females may be influenced by specific needs such as water requirements during lactation, presence of localized and persistent forage resources such as perennial browse, and predator avoidance.

"Predator avoidance may further be responsible for use of steep slopes or proximity to escape cover. As offspring become older and better able to escape predators, behavior and patterns of habitat use might be expected to change.

"During winter, protection of offspring might be of less concern than satisfying dietary needs because of the reproductive trade-off between caring for present young and future offspring. Results from studies of winter diets suggest females feed more selectively than males, presumably because of their smaller size and the protein requirements of gestation. Males may have a greater need for digestible energy than for protein during winter, especially when rutting activities result in substantial weight loss."

A Study of Contradictions

The Oregon researchers emphasize that the male's mating success is influenced by his body size, physical strength, and general body condition, as is winter survival. Therefore, the "replenishment of energy reserves should coincide with major growing seasons, and optimization of forage resources by males should be most evident during these periods as they prepare for rut. Optimal foraging by males may require avoidance of heavily grazed areas or adoption of foraging patterns that exploit temporal resources of high quality. The importance of maximizing body condition for males apparently exceeds even increased risk of predation."

My observations (Ozoga 1989) indicate that, at least on Northern range, adult bucks intensively scent-mark their favored summer habitat as soon as they return to it in spring, probably as a means of reclaiming range they vacated for about four months. As a result, I've suggested that such marking, which is done primarily on overhead limbs, could serve to intimidate other deer, including pregnant females that require solitude for fawn-rearing, and thereby assist in distributing the herd more evenly and segregating the sexes during the non-breeding period.

Studies conducted by Floyd Weckerly and John Nelson (1990), in mixed deciduous forest-agricultural habitats in Tennessee, demonstrated diet differences between sexes in whitetails only in October. They concluded, because of the lack of consistent differences in diets between sexes in their study, partitioning might not be the same for Southern populations of white-tailed deer as for Northern populations.

Nonetheless, despite their contradictory findings, it's interesting to note the Tennessee investigators recommended that, until more is learned about resource use and demography of white-tailed deer in Southeastern habitats, "populations in these habitats be managed assuming resource partitioning as shown for the (Northern) George Reserve deer herd."

In McCullough's words: "Resource partitioning between the sexes in white-tailed deer adds a new dimension to the role of social behavior as it relates the animal to its environment." Indeed, if bucks differ from does in their use of space, food and cover resources on a seasonal basis, then deer herd and habitat management considera-

tions take on an entirely new level of complexity.

McCullough warns that this complex issue should be carefully considered, especially when determining deer-harvest management strategies: "Unbalancing populations toward females intuitively would be expected to increase productivity, but in practice seldom does in moderate- to high-density populations."

Conclusion

Clearly, poor growth rates among young deer and reproductive failure among adult does — when associated with food competition and malnutrition — invariably are the result of too many female deer, not because of too many bucks.

Main probably hit the proverbial nail on the head when he criticized traditional deer management practices that expand female groups, especially predator-control efforts and buck-only harvesting. These practices run counter to how the white-tailed deer's social system evolved. Wherever high newborn fawn survival and inadequate female deer harvest contributes to abnormally high densities of females and young, overbrowsing and range forage depletion is likely. In turn, this excludes bucks from using such habitat.

Conversely, female groups might be prevented from becoming established in areas used by males where predation or other factors reduce fawn-rearing success. In other words, Main suggests white-tailed bucks often occupy certain habitat strictly by default — areas where few or no does live. When the doe density is high, such habitat is likely to be of especially poor nutritional quality; in all likelihood it will produce small-bodied bucks sporting undersized antlers.

References

Brown, B.A. 1974. *Social organization in male groups of white-tailed deer. Pages 436-446 in V. Geist and F. Walther, eds. The behavior of ungulates and its relation to management. IUCN Morges, Switzerland.*

Main, M.B., and B.E. Coblentz. 1990. *Sexual segregation among ungulates: A critique.* Wildlife Society Bulletin. 18:204-210.

McCullough, D.R. 1979. *The George Reserve deer herd: Population ecology of a K-selected species. University Michigan Press, Ann Arbor. 271 pages.*

McCullough, D.R., D.H. Hirth, and S.J. Newhouse.

1989. *Resource partitioning between the sexes in white-tailed deer.* Journal of Wildlife Management. 53:277-283.

Ozoga, J.J. 1989. *Temporal pattern of scraping behavior in white-tailed deer.* Journal of Mammalogy. 70:633-636.

Verme, L.J. 1988. *Niche selection by male white-tailed deer: An alternative hypothesis.* Wildlife Society Bulletin. 16:448-451.

Weckerly, F.W., and J.P. Nelson Jr. 1990. *Age and sex differences of white-tailed deer diet composition, quality and calcium.* Journal of Wildlife Management. 54:532-538.

Charles J. Alsheimer

Chapter 2

SOCIAL STRUCTURE:

Life in the Female Society

The whitetail's female society evolved primarily to maximize reproductive success, even in the presence of effective predators. The society also evolved to make efficient use of food and cover, which probably changed suddenly and frequently during primitive times.

The white-tailed deer's social organization evolved in response to predators, disease, habitat, climate, hunting by American Indians and other constantly changing pressures. The deer's social system is geared toward providing the basic necessities of life, including mating, predator avoidance, exploitation of resources (food, cover and water), and the rearing of young. Clearly, this system is an adaptation — genetically linked and inherited — critical to the species' healthy existence.

Ironically, until only a couple of decades ago, we knew little about the intricate details of the white-tailed deer's social behavior. And even today — except where quality deer management is practiced — the species' social requirements are seldom considered when setting deer harvest objectives.

European big-game managers, on the other hand, emphasize the importance of understanding a species' social structure. They strive to maintain populations that are in social and nutritional balance. Such a management philosophy — based on sociobiological principles — rests on the premise that social harmony minimizes tension and strife, promotes an orderly way of life, encourages genetic selection and assures physical fitness within the population.

Conversely, according to European philosophy, improper deer harvesting can lead to social disorder and chaos, which spawns excitement and hyperactivity. In turn, this contributes to higher-than-normal food requirements, poor physical condition, low productivity, increased mortality and severe habitat damage.

Overharvest of prime-age ungulates, in particular, tends to upset a given population's so-called agonistic, or competitive, balance, which leads to social disruption. When mature animals are too few to dampen the aggressiveness of younger members, then strife, excitement and confusion can become dangerously intense and energetically costly to the society. Such an unhealthy social structure can only be remedied through selec-

USING X-RAYS IN REPRODUCTIVE STUDIES

Researchers use many techniques to determine reproductive performance in white-tailed deer. It's a simple procedure to examine dead deer — especially those killed in spring on highways — to count, age and determine the sex of fetuses inside pregnant does. This has also been done in many states to monitor annual changes in deer herd productivity.

But gathering such information from live, free-ranging deer can be difficult. Two techniques sometimes used in reproductive studies involve laparoscopy and laparotomy, which both require minor surgery. An incision is made in the abdominal area to insert an instrument called an *endoscope*, which allows a visual examination of the ovaries and uterus.

At Michigan's Cusino Wildlife Research Station in the early 1960s, we developed X-ray procedures to determine pregnancy in live deer. Although we routinely X-rayed female deer as part of our studies, I'm unaware of many other uses for this technique in deer research.

The X-ray technique has several limitations in reproductive studies in whitetails, but it can be a valuable tool in some cases. Most deer fetuses (which develop for about 200 days) can only be detected with certainty after they are about 85 days old. This means deer in northern Michigan, for example, must be examined in March or April. At that time they're still restricted by snow cover, which makes them easier to trap. However, it's still late enough to assure detection of unusually young fetuses.

Given the prolonged severe winters along Lake Superior, we seldom had serious problems live-trapping the enclosure's herd within the imposed time limits. We also tested blood samples, in conjunction with X-rays, to identify non-breeders. Most adults in our studies, however, carried fetuses ranging in age from 90 to 130 days old.

When live-trapping and transferring the deer to the station for X-rays, it was necessary to anesthetize them to minimize their movements. If not, the X-rays were blurred.

There is no reason to believe the low levels of radiation harmed the doe or her fetuses. In fact, our most frequently X-rayed doe successfully raised 31 of her 32 fawns, and was the most prolific whitetail ever reported in scientific literature.

At first we relied heavily on X-rays to document expected fawn production and to determine newborn-fawn mortality rates. We could even detect malformed or dead fetuses on the radiographs. Later, we developed more precise techniques to accurately estimate the age of fetuses.

The size and clarity of the fetus's bones on the X-rays increases dramatically with age. For example, an 85-day-old fetus is about 6 inches long, and only the base of its skull, vertebral column and some leg bones can be identified on X-rays. By 110 days, however, the fetus measures about 10 inches, and many of its skeletal parts and teeth are discernible.

We learned how to measure fetus skeletons to determine their age and predict their fawning dates. We could predict 66 percent of the fawning dates within five days, and 93 percent within nine days of the calculated arrival. As I recall, that was

Janice Ozoga

X-raying female deer in March allowed researchers to determine the number of fetuses each doe carried. Fawns were later captured and identified to measure each doe's reproductive performance and to provide information on the whitetail's matriarchal society.

considerably closer than the predictions made by the doctor who helped bring my four children into the world.

It's important to note that deer in our studies were in excellent condition because of their superb diet. X-rays might not determine a fetus's age very well in malnourished deer because the growth could be retarded.

Therefore, the X-ray technique allowed us to determine when does bred, how many fawns each conceived, and when the fawns should be born. Through subsequent field observations, we determined each doe's fawn-rearing success. Such information proved especially valuable when tracking the reproductive history of individual does as they advanced socially.

— *John J. Ozoga*

tive harvesting of individuals in each sex-age class.

Separate Quarters

Adult male and female whitetails live separately much of the year, just as they do in elk, moose, mule deer, red deer, bighorn sheep and other ungulate species. Females live in a matriarchal society of related individuals, while bucks — generally unrelated — live in all-male groups in a fraternal society. Hence, each sex lives by the rules of its own society, but each must also interact and communicate effectively with the other.

Also, a key factor in the female whitetail's social behavior is the tendency for adults to aggressively defend a fawn-rearing territory for about one month. Such behavior results in sharp seasonal changes in female sociability. For example, this behavior restricts the number of does within a given area during the fawning season, and it also determines how deer will distribute themselves at that time of year. (See "Defending Ground: How Territorial are Whitetails?" on Page 46)

Members of mammal societies do not interact at random. Each member has an identity. Individuals communicate, recognize each other and function cooperatively. Their relationships are highly ordered, giving way to social classes — or social infrastructure — wherein individuals advance according to levels of physical, physiological and behavioral maturity.

The Whitetail's Hierarchy

In ungulates, social class structure tends to be hierarchical in nature, with the most immature individuals occupying the lower classes, and the most mature occupying the upper classes. As a result, competition and dominant-submissive relationships have a suppressor effect within the female and male societies. This means the reproductive performance of animals in lower social classes is restricted by pressure from individuals of higher social standing.

According to work by Anthony Bubenik and other predominately European researchers, most ungulates demonstrate five maturity classes within a society: kids, pre-teens, teens, primes and seniors. Males and females can generally be assigned to one of these classes within their respective society based on their level of maturity. In a smoothly operating and well-structured society, a long-lived individual advances from a young (pre-pubertal) state to peak productivity at prime age, and onto senility at advanced age.

It is important to note, however, that an animal's age alone does not determine its social standing. Nutrition, social relationships, reproductive success, herd composition and density, and a host of other factors might interact to determine an individual's rate of development and social rank. Also, the sexes differ greatly with regard to factors that determine their social growth and status within their respective societies.

A Case Example

While working with deer in Michigan's square-mile Cusino enclosure, I was able to investigate the social life of whitetails with detail and control enjoyed by few other investigators. During the course of those studies, all deer within the enclosure were annually live-trapped, blood-sampled, measured, weighed and marked for individual identification. But by far, the most valuable data were gathered by X-raying the does in March to determine fetus numbers and age. Subsequent field observations allowed us to mark and identify the fawns, and determine their mothers through intensive observation. As a result, these data produced a fairly complete picture of each doe's reproductive performance, and provided considerable insight into the workings of the matriarchal society.

My studies indicate female whitetails can be assigned to specific social maturity classes. The assignment is based largely on their reproductive performance. Although my interpretation differs from what's reported in European literature, I suggest the whitetail's female society consists of five classes: kids, teens, dispersers, matriarchs (two subclasses) and seniors. My observations for a healthy, expanding white-tailed deer female society follow.

Class 1: Kids

Female whitetails remain in the kid class at least one year, some even longer, depending on their rate of maturity and achievement of puberty. This is determined largely by such things as birth date, nutrition and social pressure. These young animals are immature in all respects, and still highly dependent on older females for leadership. They are the population's most subordinate animals, and are likely to suffer severe consequences without adult female guidance, especially during winter in Northern migratory herds. They do not breed during their first autumn.

When 1 year old, female and male whitetails might band together, or temporarily link up with older non-productive female relatives, while their mothers raise new fawns. However, they reunite with their mothers as soon as possible.

When nutrition is extremely poor, or the herd's density is exceptionally high, some females might remain in Class 1 several years. Typically, animals in this class are highly susceptible to predation, malnutrition and other natural mortality.

Class 2: Teens

I consider first-time mothers as teens, which probably agrees with the European classification system. Most does will be 2 years old when they produce their first offspring, but they could be younger or older. They will not be fully grown. Teens are dominated by older females. If they fail to raise their fawns, they revert to behavior typical of younger females. They seek their mother's companionship as soon as possible, and behave more like younger females. They do not advance beyond this class until they raise at least one fawn.

As a social class, they would have been the last does to breed during the previous rut. One-year-olds in this class will normally breed and conceive single fawns in December. However, at least in a Northern environment, they only breed under the most ideal nutritional conditions. Even then, they tend to breed only when the female society is structured heavily toward young females. This condition generally results from intensive antlerless harvesting. In my studies, only one of 208 yearling females produced a fawn, despite optimal nutrition. This was likely caused by domination of older members in this society.

In this class, 2- and 3-year-olds conceive an average of about 1.4 and 1.7 fetuses, respectively. In my studies, those that failed to achieve threshold body weights of 130 pounds before breeding (remember, my subjects were the large *borealis* subspecies) seldom conceived twins, and no does in this class conceived triplets. Regardless of their age, Class 2 does tended to produce a preponderance (about 60 percent) of male offspring.

These are the poorest mothers, more likely to abandon fawns than defend them against predators. That's probably because of their incomplete physiological development and maternal inexperience. They will establish fawning territories adjacent to their mothers and, in some cases, benefit from the elder doe's predator defense.

As a group, they usually give birth a few days to several weeks later than older does. Even when well-nourished, they are likely to lose 20 percent of their newborns. And when severely crowded with 100 deer per square-mile or more, or exposed to intense predation, they might lose more than half of their fawns within a few weeks.

Even under the most ideal nutritional circumstances, Class 2 does produce the smallest male fawns at weaning age, regardless of litter size. Interestingly, when well-fed, their single female fawns will be as large as those produced by older does.

Class 3: Dispersers

Does in this class are second-time mothers. Depending on habitat availability and herd composition, they are likely to shift their fawn-rearing areas a quarter-mile or more from their birth location. This serves to expand the ancestral range during good times, that is, when food and cover resources are ideal and related females are increasing in number. However, if older females are removed from the population at a high rate, for whatever reason, thereby leaving voids within the ancestral range, few second-time mothers disperse.

Dispersal is risky because the doe might settle in poor fawning habitat or attempt to usurp the area of a more dominant doe. Depending on conditions, dispersers might lose 20 percent or more of their newborns, but they could lose half of them when predators are abundant.

When well-nourished, Class 3 does will breed earlier than Class 2 does, and at about the same time as older, prime-age does. They conceive an average of about 1.8 fawns each, and are unique in that they produce a preponderance of female fawns (nearly 60 percent). This production of excess female offspring by dispersing does is probably an adaptive trait. Why? Because it allows for more rapid growth of a growing kinship group when circumstances favor population growth.

Although female progeny produced by does in this class tend to be as large as those reared by older females, male offspring (even singletons) are generally smaller than those produced by more mature does. The reasons for such a size difference among these fawns are highly speculative. However, it could be caused by the benefits some female fawns receive from being associated with female relatives other than the mother. Researchers call this benefit social facilitation. On the other hand, male fawns raised by dispersers might not have as many female relatives to associate with, and might be more behaviorally restricted in their feeding and movements.

Class 4: Matriarchs

Matriarchs are prime-age, maternally experienced females, generally 4 to 10 years of age. They are mature in all aspects of physical, physiological and psychological development. They represent the epitome of health and physical fitness. They are the survivors, the hardiest and finest female stock of their species. Matriarchs are the reproductive machines that permit a population to grow at a maximum rate. They also serve as the social governors of the female society.

Matriarchs are clan leaders by virtue of their long life and ability to produce daughters that also survive. However, based on my enclosure data, I divide this class into two subclasses: secondary and primary matriarchs. This is based on the complexity of the matriarchies.

Secondary Matriarchs

Secondary matriarchs are females who successfully dispersed within the past year or two. In all likelihood they are grandmothers. In a rapidly growing deer population, they could be young, possibly only 4 or 5 years old. They might serve as leaders for small subgroups of no more than two or three daughters and their offspring.

Secondary matriarchs usually breed early in the rut, and conceive an average of about 1.9 fawns per doe, equally split between males and females. They are successful mothers, rarely losing more than 10 percent of their newborn fawns, even when threatened by predators. At weaning age, their fawns are superior to those produced by younger does, and almost on par with those reared by older established matriarchs.

Primary Matriarchs

In whitetails, primary matriarchs are the true clan leaders. They are great-grandmothers or older, ranging from 6 to 10 years of age. Given excellent nutrition and a stable social environment, some might hold their superior social position until the ripe old age of 12 or more. They tend to be extremely aggressive, dominating one or more secondary matriarchal daughters. They travel freely over a large ancestral range.

Healthy primary matriarchs are generally the first to breed, and usually conceive twins or triplets, and tend to produce a slight excess (about 55 percent) of male progeny. Because they control the best fawn-rearing habitat, and are vigilant and protective mothers, rarely losing more than 10 percent of their newborns. At weaning age, male offspring of these does tend to be the population's largest young-of-the-year. They also might be enormous for their age if litter mate(s) died early in life.

Class 5: Seniors

Most senior females will be 12 years or older, depending on the climate's severity, their nutritional level and probably the deer's reproductive history. These does are no longer physically fit, might exhibit hormonal imbalances, tend to lose their high dominance rank, breed later than prime-age does, and more likely conceive single males. Because their milk production tends to decline, and their fawns are born later than normal, their offspring (especially twins) might be inferior to those raised by prime-age does. Also, because of their late fawning date and loss of dominance, some senior females might be forced to seek new fawning grounds. Beyond 16 years of age, some does might fail to breed altogether, especially on poor range.

In Northern areas, where winters are severe, senior females might represent a high proportion of the malnutrition-related winter deaths. This is especially true in areas with minimal antlerless harvests. However, given favorable circumstances, even in the wild, some senior females might live to be 20 years old.

Overview

It should be understood that my sketch of the whitetail's female society is that of a well-nourished (supplementally fed) and rapidly expanding Northern deer herd living in forest habitat. Also, my study populations were well-structured, with a good representation of deer in all sex and age classes. These were populations I considered socially and nutritionally balanced, but living at high densities. Obviously, deer populations in different climates or habitats, those distorted by human-induced mortality, or extremely under-nourished populations, probably respond differently.

Nonetheless, the system I describe probably operates in most natural environments when habitat conditions are favorable and white-tailed deer populations are expanding. Regardless of the environment, it is largely the female whitetail's reproductive success and longevity that determine the individual's rate of social growth and, ultimately, the complexity of the female society.

Any factors that decrease reproductive success, or cause excessive female mortality, will likely slow development of the female society. Poor nutrition, along with extreme social pressure from overly abundant mature females, will suppress reproductive output of younger females, hence delaying their rate of social maturity. The opposite effects — an advanced rate of social maturity — might be expected for young female whitetails when faced with minimal social pressure but bountiful food and cover resources.

In my view, the whitetail's female society evolved primarily to maximize reproductive success, even in the presence of effective predators. The society also evolved to make efficient use of food and cover resources, which probably changed suddenly and frequently during primeval times. Certainly, fires, floods, windstorms and similar calamities periodically devastated mature forests, set back vegetation succession, and produced patches of ideal habitat for whitetails. I believe the female whitetail's social system evolved primarily to cope with such environmental change, and allows the species to take quick advantage of such opportunity.

Even seemingly subtle things such as breeding date, sex ratio of progeny, location of fawning sites with respect to those of female relatives, and so forth — which change with social class — are highly important when it comes to maintaining social order and allowing whitetails to exploit food and cover resources in the most harmonious manner possible.

And, as mentioned earlier, the female society must work in concert with the male society. Even the prevailing structure of the male society could have considerable influence on the social development and well-being of female whitetails — especially if the females demonstrate mate selection, and/or male pheromones function to stimulate and synchronize breeding, as some researchers believe.

References

Ozoga, J.J., 1987. *Maximum fecundity in supplementally fed Northern Michigan white-tailed deer.* Journal of Mammalogy 68:878879.

Ozoga, J.J., and L.J. Verme. 1985. *Determining fetus age in live white-tailed does by X-ray.* Journal of Wildlife Management 49:372-374.

Verme, L.J., L.D. Fay, and U.V. Mostosky. 1962. *Use of X-ray in determining pregnancy in deer.* Journal of Wildlife Management 26:409-411.

Bill Kinney

Chapter 3

THE ESTROUS CYCLE:

Following Doe Activity During the Rut

Herd density and sex-age composition, which are often determined by the timing and intensity of the buck kill, will greatly influence the stability and predictability of deer behavior during the rut.

If you hunt whitetails during their breeding season — as most of us do — but don't understand the breedable doe's behavior, you could be in trouble.

Like it or not, the buck you hunt is at the mercy of the estrous doe. Or is he?

Plotting out-of-season buck movements, monitoring weather conditions, determining food sources, calculating moon phases, and so on, might be important and can contribute to success. No doubt a host of factors might provide clues about a buck's travel patterns. But all too often, the estrous doe is the most potent force in determining a buck's whereabouts, behavior and vulnerability. All your careful plotting and meticulous strategies will likely go down the tube if the estrous doe unexpectedly appears in the wrong place at the right time.

The Energy Balance

Wildlife managers are concerned about deer activity, especially during the breeding season, but for different reasons from the hunter. With regard to a deer's welfare, there is a definite relationship between the amount of energy taken in (food) vs. the amount spent (activity). A negative energy balance during autumn, for whatever reason, can hurt the deer's physical condition, interfere with reproduction, and lower survival rates during the critical winter months.

The rut is characterized by greatly increased movement among all deer, but especially by bucks. Therefore, the rut demands that deer spend a lot of energy. Sometimes, greatly increased buck activity can be linked to higher-than-normal buck mortality during winter.

The Price of an Energy Deficit

Mounting evidence also suggests a negative energy balance during autumn can diminish the doe's physical condition and her breeding success. This means the rut's social stress can have the same damaging effects as nutritional stress on deer. Increased social, or behavioral, stress can cause increased activity, depressed physical condition, delayed breeding, lower conception rates, increased foraging and damage to the environment. Ultimately, such factors lead to poor quality or, possibly, no offspring. These so-called sociobiological relationships have not been thoroughly studied. However, given their potential importance, we need to better understand such seemingly subtle things as the estrous doe's activity rhythms.

Michigan researcher Lou Verme and I explored the activity patterns of estrous whitetails more than 20 years ago. Consequently, I was captivated by a recent article in the *Journal of Mammalogy* by Rick Relyea and Stephen Demarais (1994), titled, "Activity of Desert Mule Deer During the Breeding Season." I was somewhat dismayed, however, to learn that, after an extensive literature search, these mule deer researchers could only find two studies that quantified ungulate behavioral changes during the breeding season. Both of the investigations involved whitetails: Ozoga and Verme 1975 and Holzenbein and Schwede 1989. Clearly, this is a topic in need of more study.

Most studies show that female whitetails move shorter distances per day and concentrate their activities on a smaller portion of their range during the rut.

Using motion-sensitive radio-collars, Relyea and Demarais found activity for mule deer bucks and does increased from pre-rut to post-rut. They also observed that bucks were most active around sunrise and sunset (crepuscular) during pre-rut and post-rut, but that female mule deer shifted their normal daily rhythm from being most active during twilight hours in pre-rut to constant during peak rut, followed by low levels of crepuscular activity during post-rut.

Relyea and Demarais speculated that changes in daily activity patterns of females could be caused by harassment of females by males. In their words: "Assuming our radio-collared females were bred during peak rut and a male could not differentiate a bred female from an unbred female until he approached her closely, pregnant females could reduce interactions with males by becoming less active during times of greatest activity of males and more active during times of lowest activity of males."

Because the behavior of mule deer differs quite markedly from that of whitetails during the breeding season, certain species differences in activity patterns during the rut are expected. For one thing, white-tailed bucks also move outside of their normal home range, but only during peak rut, not normally throughout the pre-rut to post-rut period as with mule deer.

Most studies show that white-tailed does move shorter distances per day and concentrate their activities on a smaller portion of their range during the rut. During peak rut, females become more active, but tend to crisscross in a smaller area. The advantage of this is that the doe's urinary signals are concentrated during the breeding period, thereby enhancing doe-to-buck communication during the doe's relatively short receptive period.

That means whitetails are most active during peak rut because bucks are traveling outside their home range searching for does, and does are walking intensively in a small area to attract bucks. Such behavior stops after the breeding period, and activity returns to pre-rut levels.

The Restless Doe

While monitoring activity patterns of penned whitetails in the early 1970s (using an elaborate array of wiring, microswitches and event-recorders), I accidentally discovered that does became restless and began pacing in their pen shortly before mating. This observation led to a more intensive investigation of doe activity patterns during estrus, which was later published in the *Journal of Wildlife Management* (Ozoga and Verme 1975). Ultimately, we used a measure of the doe's activity as a means of predicting estrus. That information proved valuable in other reproductive studies and during some sophisticated studies of blood hormone changes around the doe's estrus period.

Our studies with penned does revealed that a doe will accept a buck only during a 24- to 36-hour period at peak estrus. However, we observed that in the absence of a tending buck, the doe became about 28 times more active than normal one to two nights before estrus. This restlessness coincides with increased ovarian production of estrogen, the female hormone that precipitates a doe's mating urge. In fact, we calculated that one doe walked more than 20 miles the night before she mated. Based on our findings, we theorized that such an increase in doe travel would be adaptive, in that the estrous doe would then be more likely to find a mate if one were not nearby.

Stefan Holzenbein and George Schwede (1989) tested our theory by monitoring the activities of eight radio-collared does at the National Zoo's Conservation and Research Center in Front Royal, Va. Instead of wandering extensively, however, seven of the does they tracked restricted their movements to core areas of their home range around at the time of estrus. Bucks were apparently readily available and quick to locate does as they came into estrus. Presumably, all seven does were bred within core areas of their normal range. It's interesting to note, however, that one doe suddenly started wandering, and left her home range shortly before her estrous period, probably because she had not been located quickly by a potential mate.

Holzenbein and Schwede concluded that female whitetails usually make their location predictable by restricting their movements before becoming receptive, making it relatively easy for a buck to find them. Also, such a concentration of doe activity likely accounts for a buck's tendency to cluster his scrapes in certain locations where he might attract the greatest attention from prospective mates.

However, if a doe attains estrus without being found by a buck, she might wander extensively in search of a mate. Some researchers suggest that estrus among all but the youngest of related reproducing females should be synchronous, because estrus can be induced by male-produced pheromones.

If so, it's also conceivable that females compete for the attention of choice mates. Subordination tends to have a strong suppressor effect on a doe's reproductive performance. Older, maternally experienced does within a clan are most dominant; they also control the most favorable habitat, maintain the best physical condition, and usually breed first. Therefore, if a dominant and subordinate doe come into estrus at the same time, the dominant doe might displace the subordinate and copulate first. If this is the case, subordinate does are more likely to delay mating, mate with a subordinate male and go searching for mates.

Selective Breeders

There is some experimental evidence that suggests does are indeed mate selective, thereby responding more positively to one suitor than another. In our studies at the Cusino enclosure in northern Michigan, for example, we found that does were more receptive to bucks similar to them in age. That is, mature does preferred to be courted by mature, rut-experienced bucks, while yearling does seemed intimidated by the real monarchs. Hence, a good deal of testing and chasing of females by males during the rut is likely in most herds.

As researchers Larry Marchinton and Karl Miller note: "The whole process of chasing and courtship is a very visible one that exposes participants to risk from predators, both human and otherwise. This is the only time of the year when white-tailed deer, particularly bucks, forsake cover and put themselves into vulnerable positions." Marchinton and Miller emphasize that such seemingly neurotic behavior has strong selective values. "It allows the doe to be bred by the most physically superior buck in the area. She dashes around — in anthropomorphic terms, making quite a spectacle of herself — so that the local bucks become aware of her impending receptivity and join her entourage, at least until they are displaced by the largest buck. This competition among suitors usually assures that her offspring will be sired by the best buck she can find."

On the other hand, if adult females of a clan regroup during the breeding period, several females might come into estrus in the same general area within relatively few days. If several socially regrouped females come into estrus only a day or two apart, a dominant buck might remain with the clan a few days and breed several does within fairly rapid succession. In such cases, a potential trophy might be pretty well anchored in some distant location for a period of days, leaving you to ponder the reasons for his sudden departure from an otherwise predictable daily routine.

Differences by Region

Keep in mind that many factors can account for differences in the estrous doe's behavior from one area to the next, which might have a strong bearing on buck behavior and hunting success. The timing, length and intensity of the breeding season, as well as the estrous doe's behavior, might differ sharply from North to South, in particular. Important factors such as herd density and sex-age composition, which are often determined by the timing and intensity of buck harvesting, will greatly influence the stability and predictability of deer behavior during the rut.

In the North, the rut tends to be short but intense where we also see distinct regrouping of related does during pre-rut, especially in moderate- to high-density populations. The North's hunting seasons also tend to be held later, usually during or shortly after peak rut. In contrast, many Southern states have early deer seasons, sometimes resulting in a high buck harvest before peak rut. In some cases, buck harvesting might be so extreme that a buck shortage develops during peak breeding. This can produce erratic behavior by estrous does searching for mates.

The Role of Herd Composition

One thing that has always impressed me about whitetails is their high degree of social order and elaborate communication during the rut, especially when mature bucks are present. On the other hand, chaotic rut behavior prevails when intensive buck harvesting leaves only yearling bucks to fill the role of herd sires.

You'll find that the seek-and-chase style of courtship among yearling bucks differs greatly from the more ritualized soliciting of attention demonstrated by rut-experienced mature bucks. If you hunt a socially unbalanced deer herd, where mature sires are absent or in short supply, expect local does to exhibit peculiar behavior during that brief period when they are in rut.

References

Holzenbein, S., and G. Schwede. 1989. *Activity and movement of female white-tailed deer during the rut.* Journal of Wildlife Management. 53:219-223.

Marchinton, R.L., and K.V. Miller. The Rut. Pages 109-121, in D. Gerlach, S. Atwater, and J. Schnell, eds. Deer. Stackpole Books, Mechanicsburg, Pa. 384 pages.

Ozoga, J.J., and L.J. Verme. 1975. *Activity patterns of white-tailed deer during estrus.* Journal of Wildlife Management. 39:679-683.

Relyea, R.A., and S. Demarais. 1994. *Activity of desert mule deer during the breeding season.* Journal of Mammalogy. 75:940-949.

Chapter 4

SOCIAL STRUCTURE:

Life in the Male Society

In natural deer populations, only superior bucks reach the pinnacle role of herd sires. While many are called, few are chosen. This breeding system assures the perpetuation of adaptive traits and physical fitness within the whitetail's population.

Sexual segregation among white-tailed deer means adult bucks and does live separately — spatially and socially — except during the rut. In fact, white-tailed bucks and does differ so dramatically in so many aspects that one must wonder how such differences occurred in the first place.

A female whitetail might spend her entire life in association with related females in a close-knit society on familiar ancestral range. At some point, however, the male must sever ties with his mother and other female relatives. When sexually mature, the young buck is harassed, dominated and rejected by his female relatives. He has little choice but to seek, interact and achieve compatible associations with other males if he is to someday become a herd sire.

Although some of my colleagues might disagree with my word choice, I refer to the whitetail's separate matriarchal and fraternal units as societies. I broadly define a society as a group of individuals belonging to the same species and organized in a cooperative manner. In my view, society members communicate, interact and recognize each other.

It is also important to note that puberty in white-tailed bucks recurs annually. That is, bucks are fairly docile, highly sociable, and almost frail-looking critters most of the year when not in breeding condition. Each autumn, however, they become hormonally charged, weapon-wielding masses of muscle. They become unpredictable beasts of amazing strength, stamina and determination.

The Developing Male

A white-tailed buck requires about six years to reach his maximum body size. During the interim, he becomes somewhat stronger each autumn while growing larger in body and antlers. He's a little wiser, too. He advances accordingly in the male society, gaining social status each year as he matures and rises in rank over his peers. In other words, with each fall's resurgence of rutting behavior, the buck develops physically, physiologically and psychologically in a step-wise fashion. Such a pattern produces social maturity classes among males that are more pronounced than those of female whitetails.

Anyone who spends much time hunting or watching whitetails recognizes the differences in physical appearance and behavior among bucks of different age. Young, sexually inexperienced bucks, for example, are not only smaller in body and antlers, but they are amateurish in their rut-season behavior. When compared to more mature bucks, these youngsters scurry about, spar and chase in a disoriented, almost comical, fashion.

By comparison, the finesse and ritualistic behavior of a rut-experienced mature buck with massive antlers and a rut-swollen neck is a sight to behold. Granted, much of the buck's behavior is instinctive, but his rutting skills — including his sign-posting behavior — steadily improve with experience. In addition, his physical size and strength are extremely important in determining his ultimate social rank.

As I discussed earlier (see "Social Structure: Life in the Female Society" on Page 18), European researchers recognize five social maturity classes among ungulates: kids, pre-teens, teens, primes and seniors. (These terms are taken from human social science, and apply to both sexes.) Animals at the same level of physical, physiological and behavioral development belong to the same class, and serve a distinct role within the society. Therefore, besides its physical and psychological growth, an animal is also growing socially with advancing age to hold higher and more prominent ranks within the society.

Social Growth and Maturity

The only paper I've seen that refers to specific social maturity classes in white-tailed deer was written by Bennet A. Brown Jr. It's titled "Social Organization in Male Groups of White-tailed Deer," and it appeared in *The Behavior of Ungulates and Its Relation to Management*, which was edited by V. Geist and F. Walther (1974). The paper was presented at the International Union for the Conservation of Nature and Natural Resources Conference, held in Morges, Switzerland.

The paper was based on studies by Brown in 1969 and 1970 on the Rob and Bessie Welder Refuge in Texas. Brown used radio-telemetry and direct observation to identify four primary association patterns in white-tailed bucks. Brown described the four groups as immature, subdominant floaters, group core members, and dominant floaters. I used the same terms when discussing the bucks' social organization in *Deer*, a 1994 book edited by Gerlach, Atwater and Schnell.

From information available in scientific literature, and based on my own studies in Cusino's square-mile deer enclosure in Michigan, it's obvious that white-tailed bucks have distinct social classes when they're allowed to mature into natural, age-balanced populations. With some modification of Brown's classification system, I suggest the whitetail's male society consists of five classes: kids, subdominant floaters, fraternal group members (two subclasses), dominant floaters and seniors.

Class 1: Kids

I use the term *kids* because it more accurately describes young bucks than Brown's term, *immature*. That is, bucks in subsequent classes might be sexually active, but they aren't necessarily full-grown or behaviorally mature. Male whitetails normally remain in the kid class with their female siblings for at least 12 months. Even at a young age, male whitetails are inherently more independent, active and inquisitive than female deer. Therefore, after weaning, Class 1 males might socialize frequently with female relatives other than their mother, or possibly with young bucks.

Most buck fawns (kids) presumably do not achieve puberty. However, if polished button antlers signify puberty — and they probably do — then some populations produce more sexually active buck fawns than others. In the Cusino enclosure studies, for example, when we fed deer nutritious supplemental rations, 84 percent of buck fawns grew polished infant antlers. For a brief period toward the end of the rut, precocious males might exhibit rutty behavior, and will sometimes spar with each other. They seem to take special interest in scrapes and rubs made by older bucks, and might occasionally scent-mark overhead limbs.

Although some buck fawns (generally 6 to 8 months old) are capable of breeding in captivity or in highly disturbed populations where older bucks are scarce or absent, it's unlikely that many of them breed in balanced, natural populations. That's because in a age- and gender-balanced population, buck fawns will be dominated by older males and female relatives. After their first, relatively short burst of puberty, they seek adult female companionship and remain part of the traditional family group through winter.

Class 1 whitetails of both sexes are driven away by their mothers when fawns are born the following year. The yearling groups then band together in summer and travel the corridors between fawn-rearing territories on familiar ancestral range. If the mother loses her fawns, however, she allows her yearling offspring to rejoin her within a few days.

Class 2: Subdominant Floaters

Subdominant floaters are young bucks that left their family's social unit. They are in some stage of dispersal, but have yet to earn membership into a male group. Most of them are between 1 and 2 years old.

Normally, only about 20 percent of bucks disperse from their birth range when 1 year old. Most leave when they're about 16 months old, shortly before breeding starts in autumn. Probably less than 10 percent of Class 2 males are 2½ years old, meaning they remained with the family group one extra year.

Class 2 males tend to shed their antler velvet somewhat later than older bucks, but soon after seem compelled to seek and interact with other males, generally in late

September in the northern Midwest. Initially, they spar with other bucks in a congenial and highly ritualistic fashion, which is probably essential in the formation and maintenance of male social bonds. Before the rut, however, the subdominant floater is likely to travel extensively and interact with various male and female groups.

Subdominant floaters are immature in all aspects of physical, physiological and psychological development. Although they might have accomplished much of their skeletal growth, even the largest tend to be a third smaller in body weight, and carry small antlers (some might only have spikes), as compared to more mature bucks. Physiologically, Class 2 bucks are capable of breeding, but they lag behind older bucks in sex-organ development, attain lower threshold levels of testosterone, and enter breeding condition later than older males.

These young bucks tend to be inquisitive. They readily investigate signposts created by older bucks, but they do minimal scent-marking themselves. Depending on their social environment, they make less than half as many antler rubs as older bucks, and probably make no scrapes when older bucks are present.

In a highly structured male society, Class 2 bucks are dominated by older males. This suppressor effect reduces the young buck's aggressiveness and libido, thereby helping to maintain social order during the breeding season. The behaviorally suppressed young buck also expends less energy, experiences less weight loss during the rut, and therefore grows to a greater size at maturity before assuming a herd sire role.

I don't know of any detailed study regarding fraternal group formation, but my observations indicate that most subdominant floaters achieve social bonds with other males during sparring matches before the rut, and then spend the winter with them. Some do not find male companions, however. Instead, they reunite with female relatives for the winter, becoming 2½-year-old subdominant floaters the next year.

Class 3: Fraternal Group Members

Brown suggests the real stability of the whitetail's male society rests within fraternal groups formed by two to four core members that achieve true social bonds. Generally, these core members are young bucks, probably 2½ to 4½ years old, who have not achieved their maximum body and antler size. However, depending on herd density and composition, some fraternal group members might be as young as 1½ years or as old as 5½ years.

Most true fraternal groups probably have fewer than six members, but members from neighboring groups might share a common range while growing antlers. During late summer and early autumn, in particular, subdominant floaters and bucks from neighboring groups might occasionally intermingle to form much larger, but temporary, male groups.

Although group members frequently spar among themselves and with subdominant floaters, serious aggression among socially bonded members is generally subdued and infrequent. These middle-class bucks seem to engage in much of the sparring with subdominant floaters and members of neighboring fraternal groups, thus somewhat buffering the older, alpha bucks from excessive, unnecessary energy drain during the pre-rut. Although fraternal group members separate and become solitary travelers during the rut, they quickly regroup after the breeding season to spend the winter together, probably in areas near concentrations of does and fawns.

Because bucks within established fraternal groups differ so much in physical attributes and behavior, I divided this class into two subclasses: secondary and primary members.

Secondary Group Members

Secondary group members are males that achieved group membership within the past year. They are normally 2½ years old during the rut, but could include 1½-year-old bucks that dispersed from their natal range when 12 months old. However, they could also be 3½-year-olds who delayed dispersing. They tend to be superior in body size and antler development to Class 2 bucks, but they still are not fully grown and remain submissive to older bucks. Their antlers are normally branched (most will have eight points) and larger than those of most younger bucks. Still, their antlers are rarely equal to those of older bucks.

Because these secondary group members are so psychologically suppressed by older bucks, they do minimal scent-marking, have low testosterone levels and are normally inactive during the rut. As a result, they lose little weight during the rut and tend to carry their antlers longer than any other bucks (at least on Northern range). In a structured male society, they are readily identifiable during the rut by their decent antlers but lack of neck swelling, which is a result of low testosterone. They have almost no opportunity to breed in a socially structured population.

Primary Group Members

Most primary fraternal group members will be 3½ and 4½ years old, but some in high-density herds could be older and difficult to distinguish from the alpha (Class 4) bucks. Although they will have achieved their full skeletal size, their body weight, rut-season neck measurements, and antler size are likely to increase in subsequent years.

Within a fraternal group, pairs of bucks in this subclass tend to develop close social bonds, and can generally be found together during the summer. They might even begin to wander together out of their normal summer range on brief, exploratory jaunts. Bucks in this subclass also readily engage in ritualistic sparring matches that eventually lead to a strict dominance hierarchy in advance of the primary breeding season. However, they become

DO SOME BIG BUCKS DECLINE TO RUT?

We normally assume that all sexually mature white-tailed bucks compete aggressively to breed as many does as possible. Is there any evidence that some big bucks, while otherwise physically and physiologically normal, opt not to compete for breeding privileges? Until reading Valerius Geist's opinion in *Deer* (1994) that some big mule deer bucks choose not to partake in the rut's frenzy, I had not deeply pondered the question.

Geist suggests the "non-participants" are generally large muleys with huge antlers. Also, they tend to stick to heavy cover and do not socialize with other large bucks. Therefore, presumably, they are not part of a structured male society.

At least one of the bucks Geist studied was a middle-age animal that behaved normally until the "old master buck" thoroughly trounced him in battle. Afterward, the vanquished buck did not rut for several years. Later, however, after the population declined and virtually all the large bucks died, this buck became the alpha buck, a status he held for three consecutive years.

Geist wrote: "The opting-out strategy works when there is a die-off, as can happen in a severe winter.

When the large bucks, exhausted by the rut, may die, he is more likely to survive, having spent the fall feeding and resting. Not only does opting out preserve the buck's fat reserves, which he may then draw on to survive lean times, but it also gives him a head start for growth the following spring and summer.

"This in turn increases his chances for survival and his ultimate body size, and thus his ability to fight during the next rut. Moreover, following a population crash and the concomitant decline in sexual competition, a huge master buck may now breed a greater number of females. That buck thereby increases his genes disproportionately in the herd."

In reviewing more than 20 years of data from my Cusino deer enclosure studies, I recall one white-tailed buck that also used the opting-out strategy successfully. Although I seldom observed this buck (M-5), he did not associate with other bucks and apparently did not compete for breeding rights. He, too, grew to a large size, but held a low dominance rank when we live-trapped him annually and placed him in a holding pen with the rest of the herd.

Most interestingly, when we examined M-5's blood, we found he had unusually high plasma progesterone values (typically regarded as a female hormone, but produced in quantity by the adrenal gland when animals are stressed). However, when the alpha buck was later poached, M-5 immediately assumed the top position on the dominance hierarchy, and his progesterone values dropped to a normal level. He held his alpha rank for the next three years before he was removed from the population.

Geist observes, however, that the opting-out strategy doesn't always pay off. The largest buck he studied, for example, also chose not to participate in the rut, but died before a population decline and probably never did breed. Granted, white-tailed bucks probably only opt out of the rut when populations are high, and only when other mature bucks are present.

They probably aren't common, either. But maybe this behavior explains why, every now and then, some monster buck just seems to materialize out of nowhere.

— *John J. Ozoga*

---

extremely hormonally charged, making them rutty, aggressive and unpredictable during the breeding season.

They are physiologically and psychologically well-equipped in all aspects of ritualistic breeding behavior. They are likely to make as many antler rubs and scrapes as older alpha bucks, and will compete readily but cautiously for breeding privileges. Bucks in this subclass probably do considerable breeding when the alpha buck is not available. That is especially true where the breeding window is narrow, as it is on the whitetail's Northern range, where most does breed during a couple of weeks in November.

Whenever violent buck fights erupt, primary fraternal group members are probably involved. They're less likely to fight with alpha bucks, and more likely to engage in battle with primary group members from neighboring

fraternal groups. Winners of such battles become psychologically high and physiologically stimulated. If their physical attributes match their psyche, they are likely on their way to assuming the prominent role of dominant floaters in the years ahead. If not, the next battle might lead to their demise.

Class 4: Dominant Floaters

Dominant floaters — a term most aptly coined by Brown — are the alpha bucks. These are the most dominant males in the population, and the true social governors of the male society.

In a socially well-balanced society, they are generally 5½ to 9½ years old, fully grown and mature in all aspects. Typically, they are superb physical specimens. They are the largest-bodied, largest-antlered and most physically fit males of their species. They possess highly polished competitive skills that were gained through years of sparring, and fighting when necessary. Most importantly, alpha bucks exhibit finely tuned, ritualistic threat patterns and dominance displays, and have elaborate signposting capabilities. Such talents frequently enable them to bluff and intimidate younger bucks, thereby eliminating the need to risk injury by physically proving their superiority.

Dominant bucks tend to be wide-ranging travelers. They move freely, and float uncontested over a relatively large breeding range occupied by several fraternal groups, whose members are dominated year-round by the alpha male through stereotyped threat patterns. The dominant floater is a master at producing numerous, strategically located rubs and scrapes to advertise and communicate his superior social rank and presence to other bucks and does. These scent-marked signposts convey long-lasting messages that carry the maker's distinct odor and special pheromones, which have strong suppressor effects on younger bucks, while being highly attractive to estrous females.

The longevity of a dominant floater depends on many factors, but hinges primarily on his general health and the amount of competition from up-and-coming bucks. Should he become injured, show weakness or falter in the least when attempting to confirm his supreme social rank during the pre-rut or rut, he will likely be challenged repeatedly by younger bucks. These repetitive challenges will probably terminate his superior status. Even under optimal conditions, I doubt any buck can hold the alpha rank beyond 10½ years of age when faced with competition from prime-age bucks.

Class 5: Seniors

Seniors are aged bucks who are past their physical prime. Some might be as young as 8½ or 9½ years old, but most will be 10½ years or older. Obviously, few bucks achieve this old age in hunted populations. I once calculated that less than one buck in 360,000 ever reaches such an old age in heavily hunted lower Michigan.

In some ungulate species, senior males reportedly retreat from society, and no longer compete with other males for social rank or breeding opportunities. They live out their final years peaceably as hermits. Having observed white-tailed bucks for many years, however, I find it difficult to believe that an alpha buck will relinquish his supreme social position so graciously. Bucks who struggle unsuccessfully to hold their dominance generally enter winter in wretched physical condition and die before winter's end. Others might not even survive the onslaught of competition from younger bucks during the rut.

Some senior white-tailed bucks can survive for a few years where the climate is not so severe. However, they show their age. Their faces become gray, and they lose the firm, well-rounded bodies they had in their prime. Senior bucks also exhibit decreased testosterone secretion, and they're more likely to grow stunted and malformed antlers.

The oldest free-ranging buck I know of was 17 years old when he was live-captured in northern Minnesota. Few bucks live beyond 12½ years, however, because most old deer suffer from arthritis and badly worn teeth. They normally die of malnutrition or predation during winter.

Conclusion

Within the whitetail's female society, social rank is primarily determined by age and reproductive history. Nearly every female will breed when sexually mature. Compared to females, the male's climb on the social ladder is a much more prolonged and tenuous struggle. For one thing, it takes a male longer to reach his maximum body size. Also, in an age-structured male society — which likely evolved naturally — the immature buck first serves as an obedient subordinate in an apprentice role, where he grows, learns and matures in all aspects.

For obvious reasons, few hunted deer populations today exhibit the detailed male social organization as I've outlined here. Instead, in most areas, the annual harvest of bucks is so excessive that yearling (Class 2) bucks must prematurely assume herd sire roles and do most of the breeding. In the absence of mature, dominant bucks — the social governors — the rut becomes a chaotic scramble among young bucks to breed any estrous doe, thus eliminating any selectivity for adaptive traits.

In many respects, the whitetail's male society seems more complex than the female society, because it is more rigid, ritualistic and dominance-oriented. To be dominant, however, a buck must be mature, physically superior and have exceptionally good communicative skills. In natural deer populations, only superior bucks reach the pinnacle role of herd sires. While many are called, few are chosen. This breeding system assures the perpetuation of adaptive traits and physical fitness within the population.

Lance Krueger

BEAUTY OR BRAWN:

Do Antlers Have a True Function?

Biologists are baffled by deer antlers. While coveted for their beauty, antlers serve many other functions in the wild. However, determining an antler's primary purpose is a difficult task, and one that has produced a handful of theories.

Deer antlers rank among the most bizarre structures in the animal kingdom. Their annual death and regrowth makes them the only mammalian appendages capable of complete regeneration. Further, they grow more rapidly than tumors, and sometimes display unusual outgrowths resembling cancer.

The late Dr. Richard Goss, one of the world's leading authorities on deer antler regeneration, function and evolution, referred to antlers as "an extravagance of nature," comparing them to other "biological luxuries," such as flowers, butterfly wings and peacock tails.

He also said deer antlers are so improbable, "... that if they had not evolved in the first place they would never have been conceived even in the wildest fantasies of the most imaginative biologists ... not even in the annals of science fiction."

How and why antlers evolved continues to baffle biologists. Many theories abound, increasing the belief worldwide that antlers are more than aesthetic wonders.

Thermal Radiators

Noting that bucks increase food consumption and metabolism during summer to build fat reserves and strengthen themselves for the rut, one investigator proposed that velvet antlers serve as thermal radiators, releasing excess body heat.

Growing antlers are the only appendages in the animal kingdom that have a temperature equal to the body's core. They are almost hot to touch. The branched nature of antlers increases surface area, and the copious blood flow to velvet antlers dissipates heat during hot weather. Logically, then, as the antlers harden and lose velvet in autumn, energy loss is minimized during winter when energy conservation is important.

Goss points out, however, that reindeer, or caribou, typically grow antlers in spring when the Arctic climate is more like winter than summer. For them, the adaptive thermoregulatory theory makes no sense.

Roe deer and Pere David's deer also counter the thermal radiator theory. These are species that mate during

Charles J. Alsheimer

A sparring match often begins when one buck approaches another, lowers its head and presents its antlers. At least during early autumn, soon after velvet shedding, the second buck usually accepts the invitation to spar. Seldom do sparring matches between youngsters turn violent. One buck usually tucks tail and runs at the first sign of real aggression.

summer and grow antlers in the winter.

As plausible as the thermoregulatory theory might be, most scientists doubt antlers evolved for that reason. If they had, many argue, female deer would also frequently grow antlers, and tropical species would be expected to grow the largest antlers, which is not the case.

Scent Communication

The late Dr. Anthony Bubenik, famous for his work in deer sociobiology, proposed that velvet antlers secrete an oily substance containing pheromones that serve an important function in scent-marking.

In each hair follicle of the velvet antler is a sebaceous gland that produces an oily secretion called sebum. This sebum causes the velvet antler's shiny appearance and becomes most obvious as the velvet shrinks. Bubenik suggested that bucks smear the sebum over their bodies, and then onto vegetation located at head-height, "leaving a strong scent track."

My studies indicate that velvet-antlered whitetails considerably mark overhead branches throughout their summer range. However, it is not clear what secretions are deposited.

A buck's hardened antlers are especially important for scent-marking rubs before and during the rut. If you closely examine the antlers of a mature buck, you'll note that the basal portion of the main antler beam is quite rough, a condition referred to as pearling. This feature makes the antler a rasp-like tool, which is effective for stripping bark from small trees and shrubs when bucks form scented signposts. The antlers naturally become scented with forehead secretions while making antler rubs.

According to Bubenik, some species even use antlers for scent-marking after the velvet has been shed by spraying the antlers with urine, rubbing them on tarsal glands or thrashing them in urine-soaked wallows.

Secondary Sex Characters

Despite many theories about antler function, it's important to recognize that deer antlers are secondary sex characters. They evolved hand-in-hand with certain aspects of the whitetail's breeding behavior.

After considerable research, deer scientist Valerius Geist concluded that horns and antlers evolved to function as weapons — allowing opponents to participate in shoving matches and tests of strength — and as display organs for intimidation.

It is more than coincidence that antlers harden and mature just before breeding season. Because velvet is shed at the end of the growing season, when antlers turn into solid bone, this suggests antlers are used primarily for aggressive rituals during the mating season.

Because antlers are branched structures, they're ideal for defense while sparring or fighting. A wide, multi-tined rack protects the head and eyes. It serves effectively as a basket to catch and hold the antlers of a challenger.

The shape is more conducive for pushing and wrestling than for killing.

Skill Sparring

Soon after shedding velvet, bucks tend to meet in open areas and engage in highly ritualized sparring. All bucks partake in such contests, which might involve deer evenly matched or mismatched in age, body size or antler form. The yearling buck, for example, seems compelled to provoke antler contact with other, often older, bucks.

According to Bubenik, sparring is not always a decisive contest, but it can be. Sometimes there is a winner and loser. Bubenik suggests sparring serves two special purposes: skill and demonstrative sparring.

I believe early-season sparring is as essential in the formation of social bonds among males as mutual grooming is for female whitetails. If a male is to achieve a social rank before the breeding season, he must interact with other males of any size.

A sparring match often begins when one buck approaches another, lowers his head and presents his antlers. At least during early autumn, soon after velvet shedding, the second buck usually accepts the invitation to spar.

In skill sparring, a buck gains knowledge of the size of his antlers and they relate to those of other bucks. These bouts tend to be gentle, almost congenial in nature. Bucks merely click their antlers together with minimal pushing and shoving.

When two grossly mismatched bucks engage in skill sparring, the large-antlered buck might merely lower his head, sometimes offering only one side of his rack. He'll stand still and only offer resistance, tolerating the persistent attention of the smaller buck.

Demonstrative Sparring

Even a friendly match of skill sparring might turn into a bout of demonstrative sparring, however, as primary breeding season approaches. The purpose of these more serious encounters is to assess and establish social rank. These are true tests of physical strength.

In demonstrative sparring, bucks push and shove with all their strength. With antlers clinched together, contestants grapple with one another, indulge in skillful neck twisting and use other maneuvers to force their opponents off balance. There is always a winner and a loser, resulting in a dominant-submissive relationship.

Over the period of a few weeks, bucks repeatedly test one another. They gradually assess one another's strength with minimal risk of serious injury. In the process, each buck will secure a certain social rank and learn his position on the dominance-hierarchy scale before the onset of breeding.

Through experience, then, each buck learns which of its associates are stronger and must be avoided, and which are weaker and can be intimidated. The rank each buck earns during demonstrative sparring governs his behavior, and determines how other deer respond to him and what his chances of breeding in the weeks ahead will be.

This creates social order, minimizes unnecessary fighting, helps conserve energy, encourages selective mating by physically superior sires and ensures genetic fitness within the herd.

Fighting

Violent dominance fighting is rare among whitetails, and differs markedly from sparring. True fights can lead to serious injury and even death. Such aggressive interactions usually occur only among evenly matched prime-aged bucks.

The frequency and intensity of fighting depends upon many factors — hormone-charged prime-age bucks are totally unpredictable — but it tends to be situational in nature.

Generally, more fighting occurs when deer are abundant, when the adult sex ratio is closely balanced, and when a high proportion of bucks are 3½ years or older. Most fighting occurs about the time the first does come into breeding, which is when testosterone levels normally peak in prime-age bucks. In addition, combatants need not be strangers, and serious fighting might occur anytime during the breeding season.

While fighting, bucks keep their bodies close to the ground. Their antlers are clinched together, but periodically, they forcefully twist them to throw their opponents off balance. Their rapid forward thrusts and complex twisting movements are surprisingly swift and vicious.

Most fighting bouts last only a minute or less. Broken antler tines, gouged eyes and torn ears are tell-tale signs of such combat. But sex-crazed bucks might fight for hours, resulting in serious injuries and occasionally in the death of one or both contestants. Locked antlers and death from exhaustion sometimes occur.

Should a dominant buck lose a fight and show signs of weakness, he is likely to be challenged by other bucks looking to rise a notch or two on the hierarchy scale. Such repeated attacks might leave the dethroned monarch exhausted and in poor physical condition. Few fallen monarchs survive the rigors of the harsh winter season.

Intimidation

An equally appealing theory is that antlers might have evolved more for display purposes than for head-to-head combat, a hypothesis Bubenik endorsed. Large antlers are showy structures and serve as status symbols. They permit mature bucks to display and advertise themselves.

Bubenik noted considerable species variation in male

response to antlers of different size. Mature bull moose, for example, ignored a dummy equipped with small antlers, but responded aggressively toward the dummy when it carried large antlers. Caribou even attacked the dummy while Bubenik carried it.

Typically, a buck's body size, antler size, dominance rank and his chance of breeding increase with age and peak when he's between 4½ and 8½ years old. These prime-age bucks have the largest, strongest and most optimally designed antlers. They also possess highly developed competitive skills.

Along with ritual threat patterns and dominance displays, the rut-experienced buck can use his large antlers to intimidate and bluff smaller bucks into submission without wasting energy or risking injury in demonstrative sparring or fighting.

Along with ritual threat patterns and dominance displays, the rut-experienced buck can use his large antlers to intimidate and bluff smaller bucks into submission without wasting energy or risking injury in demonstrative sparring or fighting.

Younger bucks are at a distinct disadvantage physically, physiologically and behaviorally when contesting dominance. Young bucks lack the tremendous sex hormone surge of mature bucks. As a result, they never achieve the psychological high of older bucks, and are more easily bluffed into submission.

This suppressor effect reduces the young buck's libido aggressiveness. This means he also expends less energy, experiences less weight loss during the rut, and therefore grows to a greater size at maturity.

The Deception Strategy

Some cervid males, including white-tailed deer, purposely attempt to deceive their opponents by changing the configuration and increasing the size of their antlers with vines, grasses, reeds or brush.

According to Bubenik, males sometimes thrash their antlers in vegetation and do not try to rid themselves of the debris. Instead, "they parade with the debris as if they are aware of its effect on other males ... having antlers full of the plant debris, he will re-enter the sparring arena with obvious intention to continue sparring. If the opponent is still there, he will be approached frontally in an unritualized and threatening way. In none of these cases have I observed the attacked male to stand his ground."

However, only the mature antlers of older animals serve as "social semaphores," as Goss calls them. This also might explain why highly dominant bucks sometimes lose their superior rank if their antlers are broken.

Attractiveness

While large antlers on mature bucks can be intimidat-

ing, especially when combined with aggression, the opposite might also be true. During the skill-sparring stage, younger bucks seem to associate and interact with large dominant bucks possessing large antlers.

Based on extensive whitetail research conducted in southern Michigan's George Reserve, Dr. Dale McCullough suggests this: "A young male can only hope to become a dominant male by engaging in hierarchical competition over a long time period ... It is not enough to maintain position; to succeed, the young male must continually strive to move up in position. This requires that he associate not only with animals of lower rank, but also with those of higher rank."

Therefore, the young buck must not only seek out and associate with other older bucks, he must also be accepted by them before settling in an area. To achieve a compatible relationship with a large-antlered buck would almost ensure the yearling's membership in an established fraternal group.

Mate Selection

During the rut, mature does avoid the sexual advances of young, related, reproductively active males. This can be viewed as a form of mate selection, because suitor rejection can determine with whom a doe will mate.

Except during the rut, does tend to avoid contact with mature bucks. However, I've witnessed females avoiding the sexual advances of mature males, suggesting that does might sometimes give unfavorable, and favorable, visual signals to bucks.

For example, a female might flee even at the distant sight of a particular buck. Other times, however, she might run a tight circle around him, or run back and forth in front of the buck before leaving the scene. Although both scenarios demonstrate avoidance, they seem to convey different messages.

Some evidence suggests that females of certain deer species prefer large-antlered males as mates. Because dominance, large antlers and a large body generally go together, such a partner would more than likely possess the most suitable genes.

Bubenik's studies using dummy heads, for example, showed that female elk, caribou, moose and red deer were always attracted by large antlers. Even when accompanied by a bull, female caribou and moose were ready to switch partners if the dummy possessed larger antlers.

Even so, mate selection relative to antler size has not been studied extensively. Most efforts have been inconclusive.

One of the more extensive studies concerning male preference in cervids was conducted on Eld's deer by Dr. Chris Wemmer of the National Zoological Park, Front Royal, Va.

"In general, we found there's no male deer type that has a 'John Travolta' effect on estrous does," Wemmer wrote. "Females showed choice in our experimental set-up, but each differed. One male was slightly more popular than the others, but he was somewhat 'runty' and reminded me of Montgomery Clift!"

Conclusion

Antlers might be many things to many deer. Occasionally, they're even used as tools to knock down apples or acorns or dig wallows, and they serve as good back-scratchers. The problem, of course, is deciding which functions are primary and which are secondary. The answer, however, is inescapable. Although they are used skillfully for many functions, especially during the breeding season, the antlers of white-tailed deer must have evolved first as instruments of aggression.

References

Brown, R.D., Ed. 1988. Antler development in Cervidae. *Caesar Kleberg Wildlife Research Institute., Kingsville, Texas. 480 pages.*

Chapman, D.I. 1975. Antlers — bones of contention. Mammal Review, *Volume 5, No. 4, pages 121-172.*

Goss, R.J. 1983. Deer Antlers: regeneration, function, and evolution. *Academic Press, NY. 316 pages.*

Chapter 6

SIGNPOSTING:

When Do Whitetails Make Scrapes?

If you find many scrapes in late September or early October, it might signal competitive scraping by several mature bucks. In contrast, an absence of scraping before mid-October probably indicates a shortage or absence of older bucks.

Nothing seems to stir the deer hunter's imagination more — or raise his expectations higher — than the sight of a freshly pawed scrape.

And no other subject has generated more hype and abuse in recent white-tailed deer hunting literature. Separating the scientific facts of scrapes from testimonial fiction, however, is never easy.

Scrapes are exciting, and can be good places to hunt for a couple of reasons. For one, most bonafide scrapes are made by mature, dominant bucks. And two, the maker sometimes returns to check some of his scrapes. A dominant buck's scrapes also tend to serve as social centers of deer activity, because they are attractive to other deer.

Complex Signposts

Scientific literature tells us that scrapes are highly complex signposts, involving visual and olfactory signals. A full scrape sequence includes three major components:

✓Overhead limb mutilation and scent-marking.

✓Ground pawing.

✓Urination, sometimes combined with tarsal gland rubbing (referred to as rub-urination). The precise chemical signals deposited at the scrape, however, remain subject to debate.

Adult bucks exhibit limb-marking, ground-pawing and rub-urination — independently or in combination — year-round, but the act of pawing and overhead limb mutilation occurs most frequently when bucks carry hardened antlers. I've observed some scraping during each month of the year. Aside from a slight flurry of springtime scraping, however, most full-fledged scraping occurs during the rut each autumn. Such behavior tends to be associated with the male's testicle enlargement, high levels of testosterone in the buck's blood, heightened aggression, the formation of a dominance hierarchy, and, ultimately, breeding.

Although does might occasionally paw areas where they urinate, to my knowledge, they've never been seen marking overhead limbs in association with their pawed areas. For that reason, females fail to exhibit the full scrape sequence.

Because the scrape is such a highly complex signpost, researchers speculate that many messages are involved, and that the messages likely change seasonally. Even during autumn, factors such as scrape size, location, scraping intensity, re-use patterns, visitation rates and a host of other influences change weekly, and the reasons for the changes aren't always clear. Knowing how and why scraping intensity changes as autumn progresses won't guarantee you hunting success. However, a better understanding of seasonal scraping patterns could help put you in the right place at the right time.

Scrapes probably serve two primary purposes. First, they are an aggressive expression of dominance directed at other males. Second, they allow the buck to communicate to females his presence, superior status and readiness to breed.

thing to note is that most scraping activity precedes breeding, and scraping largely stops once breeding is completed. This means, of course, that the duration of scraping activity probably varies with the breeding season's length. Therefore, one could expect extended scraping activity in Southern areas where the whitetail's breeding season is prolonged. Likewise, a resurgence of scraping might occur in December in parts of the Midwest where many doe fawns reach puberty and breed.

Although some mature bucks fail to scrape in captivity, I doubt that happens often in the wild. Most mature, dominant bucks strive to breed as many does as possible, and the scrape serves as an important tool for communicating such intentions.

The Importance of Buck Age

Scraping is undoubtedly an inherited trait. Therefore, given the opportunity and motivation, all sexually active bucks, regardless of their age, probably possess the innate ability to make scrapes. However, research indicates that a buck's scraping ability improves markedly with age and experience — as he becomes behaviorally and physiologically mature. While working with captive deer at the University of Georgia, Professor Karl Miller and his co-workers found that a buck's scraping ability was related to his age, dominance rank and testosterone level.

Although some mature subordinate bucks scraped infrequently, only mature, dominant deer produced a significant number of scrapes. Yearling and 2½-year-old bucks were not observed making scrapes even when they were dominant. However, they made scrapes in subsequent years when their testosterone levels rose. And although subordinate bucks regularly visited and scent-marked overhead limbs at scrapes made by dominant bucks, subordinate bucks did not paw or urinate at the scrape site.

My investigations, conducted in the square-mile Cusino enclosure in Upper Michigan produced somewhat different results. In the absence of older bucks, even yearling bucks in my studies made scrapes. However, the yearlings made only 15 percent as many scrapes as mature bucks. Also, the enclosure's yearling bucks commenced scraping about six weeks later than mature bucks. Even so, both age classes exhibited peak scraping activity each year for a relatively brief period during the last week of October and first week of November, about two weeks before peak breeding. Once breeding began, scrape activity rapidly declined.

This basic seasonal rhythm has been observed in other studies across the United States. The important

Scrape Visitation

Scrapes probably serve two primary purposes. First, they are an aggressive expression of dominance directed at other males. Second, they allow the buck to communicate to females his presence, superior status and readiness to breed. This means that scrapes convey information to deer of both sexes and all ages. It also means subordinate bucks and does might differ in their responses to scrapes.

I investigated seasonal aspects of scrape visitation in the Cusino enclosure in May 1986 by locating and marking 26 scrapes that had been pawed the previous autumn. I then raked each scrape lightly with a small hand tiller to loosen the soil — which made track detection easier — and then covered each with leaf litter except for a central circular area 10 inches in diameter. I then examined the sites through December for evidence of deer tracks or active pawing.

In all, 17 of the 26 scrapes, or 65 percent, pawed in 1985 were also pawed in 1986. Meanwhile, I found deer tracks in 25 of the 26 scrapes, or 95 percent. Consistent pawing of the scrapes did not begin until late September, but rose sharply thereafter and peaked during the first week of November, about two weeks before peak breeding. Nearly 80 percent of the scraping occurred before the first female bred on Nov. 8. The rate of scrape re-use recorded in this study was somewhat higher than I detected in previous or subsequent studies, and was considerably higher than most other investigators had reported. Also, more scraping occurred before breeding than usual. Normally, about 50 percent to 60 percent of the scraping occurred before the enclosure's first doe bred.

Deer tracks, without evidence of pawing, were detected in the test scrape sites throughout summer and autumn, but the number of tracked scrapes rose sharply and peaked in mid-November during the time of peak breeding. Based on variations in deer track size, I concluded that deer of both sexes and all ages apparently visited the scrapes. It's interesting to note, however, that even during the height of the rut in mid-November, 65 percent of the scrapes were not pawed or closely visited by deer during a given 24-hour period.

In subsequent studies using remote sensing cameras (see "The Overhead Limb: Is it a Sign Only Bucks Understand" on Page 92), photographic evidence indicated that the number of bucks, does and fawns visiting scrapes was roughly proportionate to the number of each in the population. That means scrapes attract all deer, and the deer hunter who watches a scrape is likely to see many deer besides the maker.

Studies conducted by Grant Woods, who used heat-sensors and video cameras to record activity and behavioral patterns of wild deer at scrape sites in Missouri, produced results similar to mine. Woods reported that about 70 percent of the deer he photographed at scrapes were does. He also concluded that does frequently visit and scent-mark scrapes.

Woods, however, found that does paid more attention to overhead limbs than to pawed areas. Using essentially the same methods, my data showed the reverse response: Does paid more attention to scraped areas, but rarely checked overhead limbs. Although I've not examined my data closely, it's obvious that much of the deer activity at scrapes occurs during darkness. Even so, based on observations, Woods suggests deer exhibit peak periods of daytime scrape visitation. In his studies, he noted that most daytime deer visits occurred between 8:45 a.m. and 10:15 a.m. The second peak of activity occurred from 3:45 p.m. to 5:15 p.m. The weakest peak occurred from 11:45 a.m. to 1:15 p.m. (Deer tend to exhibit five prominent peaks of activity, probably year-round: early morning, midday, sunset and twice during the night.)

Scrape Location

Research conducted by Terry Kile, Tom Litchfield and Larry Marchinton in Georgia revealed that antler rubs and scrapes were not randomly distributed. Rubs were concentrated in areas with many small saplings. More scrapes, on the other hand, occurred in upland hard-woods where the understory was relatively open, and in conspicuous places, such as along game trails, old roads or the edges of openings.

Most scrapes are found along deer travel ways or clustered in areas of high deer activity where they will draw the most response from other deer, especially does. For that reason, the location of a buck's scrapes could change during the course of the rut, depending on weather, food sources or other factors that might cause a shift in deer travel or concentration patterns.

Other than the maker, most deer probably do not go far out of their way to visit scrapes. Deer are more likely to inspect scrapes they encounter during their travels, those strategically located in their path.

Other than the maker, most deer probably do not go far out of their way to visit scrapes. Deer are more likely to inspect scrapes they encounter during their travels, those strategically located in their path.

Based on my research, I concluded that the best scrape sites were those with:

✓Concentrated deer activity

✓Open understory vegetation (not brushy or sod-bound)

✓Relatively level ground

✓Moderately dry and easily exposed soil (not water-logged or rocky)

✓A suitable overhead limb

Also, given otherwise favorable circumstances, I found that bucks could be easily induced to scrape beneath artificially positioned limbs. In fact, the absence of a good overhead limb largely prevents deer from scraping in many potentially hot spots.

Changes in scrape location might also occur each year. Forest cuttings, changing farming practices, differences in mast crop production, weather differences or changes in the deer herd's sex-age composition are some important factors that can account for sharp annual changes in scrape location and intensity. But under stable conditions, some favored scrape sites might show repeated use for generations.

Scrape Patterns

For the same reasons discussed above, the intensity of scrape site re-use from year to year could change drastically. Even under the most favorable and stable conditions, only about half of the scrapes made one year will be used the next. However, should a mature buck survive, he will likely reopen scrapes he used the previous year, providing doe activity patterns did not change much between years.

In my studies, about half of the scrapes made by bucks were reopened during the same season, compared to a 15 percent re-use rate reported by Litchfield. The reasons for these differences are unknown, but could be caused by the location of food sources and doe visitation rates, buck ages, mortality of bucks from hunting or many other factors. Litchfield reported that 88 percent of reused scrapes in his study were near a deer trail or along the edge of an opening. In my studies, bucks more frequently reopened those scrapes where the limbs above them had been scent-marked by bucks during the summer.

For whatever reason, some scrapes will be periodically reopened for as long as three months. In fact, some scrapes might be reopened daily for five or six consecutive days, but then remain unused for several weeks. Others might only receive occasional hit-and-miss attention. Few scrapes are reopened daily for several weeks.

It's important to note, however, that deer tracks can be found in some scrapes for as long as two or more weeks after the site has been pawed. Also, the dominant buck, and even subordinate bucks, might visit scrapes, scent-mark the overhead limbs, but not paw the site.

Scrape Size

Scrapes are generally circular or slightly oval in shape, but can be of various sizes. Scrape size hinges primarily on the age of the buck who made it, and the frequency with which it's reopened. Typically, scrapes made by young bucks are smaller and less frequently reopened than those made by older bucks. Large scrapes tend to be frequently reopened.

Litchfield reported that 52 scrapes in his study area were oval in shape and averaged about 21 by 31 inches in size. However, reopened scrapes were 61 percent larger than scrapes pawed only once. I measured more than 500 scrapes made by mature bucks in the Cusino enclosure during 1988 and 1990, and found they were about 30 percent larger than those in Litchfield's study. In fact, I found scrapes measuring 3 feet by 5 feet to be fairly common.

In my study, however, scrape size not only increased with re-use, but the average scrape also became larger as the season progressed, primarily because so many scrapes were pawed repeatedly. Generally, I found scrapes were smaller than average before Oct. 25, but larger than average thereafter. Interestingly, however, even those scrapes pawed only once were largest during the period of peak scraping.

Given what research has shown, your best chance of seeing a dominant buck at his scrapes will be before peak breeding — probably during the early morning. However, a buck in rut could show up at his scrapes at any time of the day or night.

Sometimes in my enclosure studies, small scrapes close to each other eventually became one as each scrape was enlarged by repeated pawing. Some of these resultant monstrous scrapes measured 4 feet by 10 feet. Whether that's the work of one buck or several bucks is unknown. In some cases, especially where good scrape locations are limited, several bucks might attempt to make scrapes beneath the same tree. Needless to say, such a location would be exciting to hunt.

Conclusion

For the hunter, the bottom line is that early detection of scraping activity (springtime, or September and early October) signals the presence of a mature buck — one 3½ years of age or older. If you find many scrapes in late September or early October, that might signal competitive scraping by several mature bucks. In contrast, an absence of scraping before mid-October probably indicates a shortage or absence of older bucks.

Even when older bucks are present, scrape-hunting success is likely to vary by region. And it can vary from one week to the next within the same region, depending on the timing of the hunt relative to the primary breeding period. For example, in the Upper Great Lakes region, an archer hunting the last week of October or the first week of November can expect to find good buck activity at choice scrapes with many new scrapes being formed and many old ones being repawed. The gun-hunter hunting the same area in late November, however, might become frustrated if he camps on an individual scrape. He might have better luck hunting in the vicinity of scrape clusters that still show good tracking, even if they're not pawed, providing does have not left the area.

Hunters must be alert to shifts in areas of deer concentration that might occur because of weather, changing food sources or hunting pressure. If changes in deer concentrations occur early in the season, the buck's scrape locations will likely change accordingly. However, if bucks stop using a choice scrape site just because the important overhead limbs break away, simply tie in some new limbs, and you'll probably be back in business.

Given what research has shown, the best chance of seeing a dominant buck at his scrapes will be before peak breeding — probably during the early morning. However, a buck in rut could show up at his scrapes at any time of the day or night. Also, remember that while all bucks might visit and mark limbs above a dominant buck's scrapes, only the dominant individual is likely to paw the scrape or urinate into it. Large scrapes will generally reflect more frequent reopening by the dominant individual, but not necessarily the highest visitation rates.

Despite the claims of some self-proclaimed experts, there is much that researchers admittedly don't know about the white-tailed buck's scraping behavior —

especially when it comes to predicting the maker's visitation schedule. Also, while certain basics apply to the buck's scraping behavior throughout its extensive range, other contrasting results suggest that buck scraping patterns might vary by region.

Therefore, study the subject as best you can, and learn the basics behind scraping behavior, but stay alert to specific scraping patterns that might be unique to the whitetails in your area.

References

Kile, T.L. and R.L. Marchinton. 1977. *White-tailed deer rubs and scrapes: spatial, temporal and physical characteristics and social role.* American Midland Naturalist 97:257-266.

Litchfield, T.R. 1987. *Relationships among white-tailed deer rubbing, scraping and breeding activities.* M.S. Thesis, University of Georgia, Athens, Ga., 49 pages.

Miller, K.V., R.L. Marchinton, and P.B. Bush. 1991. *Signpost communication by white-tailed deer: research since Calgary.* Applied Animal Behavior Science 29:195-204.

Miller, K.V., R.L. Marchinton, K.J. Forand, and K.L. Johansen. 1987. *Dominance, testosterone levels, and scraping activity in a captive herd of white-tailed deer.* Journal of Mammalogy 68:812-817.

Ozoga, J.J. 1989. *Temporal pattern of white-tailed deer scraping behavior.* Journal of Mammalogy 70:633-636.

Ozoga, J.J. 1989. *Induced scraping activity in white-tailed deer.* Journal of Wildlife Management 53:877-880.

Ozoga, J.J., and L.J. Verme. 1985. *Comparative breeding behavior and performance of yearling vs. prime-age white-tailed bucks.* Journal of Wildlife Management 49:364-372.

Woods, G.R., L.W. Robbins, and S. Spence. 1988. *A new look at scrape behavior by using remote infrared sensing cameras.* Southeast Deer Study Group Meeting 11:16 (Abstract).

Chapter 7

DEFENDING GROUND:

How Territorial are Whitetails?

Whitetails become more territorial during certain times of the year. Does aggressively defend preferred fawning sites for about a month, and bucks in rut often defend whatever territory they happen to be in at the moment.

The question seems simple enough: Do whitetails exhibit territorial behavior? The answer, however, is still hotly debated by today's researchers.

Some investigators suggest the concept of territoriality applies to whitetails only under certain circumstances, whereas others are skeptical that free-ranging deer demonstrate such behavior. The problem, at least in part, revolves around the definition of territory.

Many, if not most, species of birds and mammals defend a portion of their total home range against intrusion from other members of their species, at least during certain times of the year. This defended area is called a territory.

Territorial defense usually involves outright aggression by the property owner when boundary lines are crossed by another of its kind. However, other factors might also complicate the issue.

By some definitions, a territory need not be a fixed piece of geography — it can be floating in nature, meaning the animal defends only the area it happens to be in at the moment or during a certain time of the season or day, or both. Other defini-

tions have been equally vague, contributing to confusion of the concept as it applies to deer.

Defining Territory

Floyd Weckerly (1992), in seeking a clearer definition of territoriality, as it might apply to whitetails, suggested that the defended area should have resources that enhance reproductive success. "The defended area," he said, "also should be exclusive because enhancing reproductive success involves excluding conspecifics (other deer). Resources for deer are food, cover, water or fawning sites."

In his definition, Weckerly considers fawning sites as "discrete areas that contain resources (e.g., cover, habitat structure) that enhance survival of neonates." William Graf (1956), observed that territorialistic behavior is usually developed in direct relation to the social development of the animal: "The greater the social development the greater the degree of territorialistic behavior." After extensive study of the social behavior of Roosevelt elk, he observed that cows, in particular, delineate portions of their home range with signposts.

According to Graf, the cow's signposting is highly ritualized, "starting with the careful 'nosing' of a sapling or limb chosen for this operation. The nosing consists of carefully drawing the nose up and down the 'post' as though sniffing it. This may be repeated a half dozen times, more or less. The second step is to scrape the 'post' with the incisors, by drawing them in deliberate vertical strokes from bottom to top of the marked spot on the post and letting the shavings that result from this action, fall to the ground. ... The third step is to carefully rub the sides of the muzzle and chin on the scraped post by deliberate forward horizontal strokes of the head. The fourth step is to rub the sides of muzzle and chin against the flanks, again in the same careful and deliberate manner as in the previous steps. ... The entire series of actions may be repeated over a period of 5 to 15 minutes." Graf notes that adult bulls, with harems, also perform such marking, but only during the rut.

Graf concluded that elk exhibit a high order of territorialism in parts of their range, and speculated that "there are indications of territorialism in other members of North American deer which up to this time have either been overlooked or have been misinterpreted by the observers."

The Influence of Food

Noted scientist Tony Peterle (1975) proposed that deer should have developed certain sociobiological traits that enable them to cope with constantly changing food availability. Such changing food resources must have prevailed prior to man's intrusion into natural environments. When food occurs in unpredictable patches, he observed, "animals tend to seek food in cohesive social groups which facilitate food-finding and utilization. Group size may be a function of the availability of food in a given patch."

"Could it be," Peterle questioned, "that prior to the advent of man — food in white-tailed deer habitat was distributed in patches, and thus ensured a cohesive social organization which may have been involved in population control? Following large-scale removal of mature forests, food became more evenly distributed over available habitat, social systems in deer were disturbed, and any social regulatory mechanism became inoperative. ... Perhaps we will see a return of social systems in deer that, at one time in history, may have been responsible for preventing overpopulation and starvation."

The suggestion of a self-regulating mechanism among whitetails did not set well with several respondents. Christian Smith (1976), from the University of British Columbia, for one, responded negatively to the idea. "If Peterle is correct," he challenged, "we should detect clear evidence of territoriality in the behavior of white-tailed deer. However, no conclusive indication of such behavior exists in all the vast literature on the species." Valerius Geist (1981), a world renowned scientist from the University of Calgary, later coined the term *facultative territoriality* to describe the behavior of mule deer. Under conditions of high and uniform resource availability, Geist found that some family groups of mule deer defend much of their home range as territories.

Carving Out Territory

A territory may also be defined as any area occupied exclusively by an animal or group of animals by means of overt defense or through some sort of advertising, such as signposting or scent-marking. A dominant buck's scrapes and rubs, for example, might quite adequately warn: "Remember our last encounter? Well, I'm still here. So, beware!"

Based on extensive study of white-tailed buck behavior in the Southeast, Larry Marchinton and Tom Atkeson (1985), concluded that Geist's concept of facultative territoriality applied equally well to white-tailed deer. Although not normally considered a territorial species, they suggested that under certain conditions of population density, sex ratio and age structure, breeding-aged white-tailed bucks "establish breeding areas by marking and defending against other males not exhibiting subordinate postures. The outcome of encounters between 'dominant type' individuals depends then on where they meet, which adds a spatial element to the dominance hierarchy. Observations also suggest that, under some circumstances, family groups defend feeding territories."

My studies of whitetail rubbing and scraping behavior, conducted in Upper Michigan's square-mile Cusino deer enclosure, produced findings in general agreement with those of Marchinton and Atkeson. I found, for example, that when given a choice to paw mock scrapes that I had treated with buck urine, or make their own scrape nearby, bucks more readily developed their own new scrapes. Furthermore, although bucks sometimes pawed beneath the limbs I positioned for my fake scrapes, they often pawed their own circular or oval area beside mine, rather than enlarge the one I had made.

How Private Are Scrapes?

Although bucks frequently visit scrapes made by other bucks, and two or more bucks occasionally compete to dominate the same scraped site, I'm convinced that individual bucks are more inclined to make and maintain their own exclusive scrapes. My observations lead me to believe that a buck's scrapes are pretty much his personal property, and scrapes could very well serve as "mini-breeding territories" to attract prospective mates, as proposed by Marchinton and his coworkers.

While following radio-collared bucks in the Cusino enclosure, it was often possible to identify some rather strict signposting patterns among certain deer. In at least

A territory can be defined as any area occupied exclusively by an animal or group of animals by means of overt defense or through some sort of advertising. A dominant buck's scrapes and rubs, for example, might quite adequately warn: "Remember our last encounter? Well, I'm still here. So, beware!"

I had never witnessed before. It looked as though an extensive area had been rototilled — they must have fought for an hour or more.

I have no idea what prompted such a vicious fight. Presumably, however, the subordinate buck, while in his claimed breeding area, chose to fight to the death rather than relinquish such highly prized ground, even to a far superior challenger. Interestingly, that particular scrape line was not maintained the following year.

Is Population a Factor?

Population density might also be important in the expression of territorial behavior in many species, including whitetails. That is, when populations are below the density permitted by the carrying capacity of the environment, territorial defense might be difficult to identify, or it might be temporarily suspended.

I perhaps had one of the most unique opportunities to study the effects of increasing density upon the behavior and population dynamics of whitetails (Ozoga and Verme 1982). Using the herd inside the square-mile Cusino enclosure, I initiated a study in 1972 to evaluate the pros and cons of

one instance, a certain scrape triggered savage fighting between mature bucks.

Each year during the rut, one of the enclosure bucks bedded in a beaver flooding during the day. He then formed an extensive line of scrapes to the nearest feeder less than half a mile away, which he followed during the evening and at night. One morning, I found the 7½-year-old buck along his scrape line, badly beaten and unable to gain his feet. He died a couple of hours later. Inspection of the general area revealed evidence of buck fighting like

supplemental feeding to achieve higher population than the habitat could support naturally. While allowing the herd to increase from 23 to 159 deer over a five-year period, I also looked closely at the species' social organization and examined the consequences of social stress upon deer, independent of nutrition.

Although the resulting herd size, about one deer per four acres, was 10 times the area's normal carrying capacity, we saw no behavioral or clinical signs of an impending population crash. Crowding did not result in dramatic density-dependent changes in deer physiology, as some investigators had proposed for other members of the deer family.

Can a Herd Curb its Growth?

Once the test herd surpassed 100 deer per square-mile, however, we recorded certain subtle changes in reproductive performance, such as delayed breeding and slightly lower fawning rates among young does. But the outstanding change was the steady rise in newborn fawn mortality among young does as deer density increased (Ozoga et al. 1982). Despite unlimited high quality feed, at highest herd density, prime-age does lost only 6 percent of the fawns they carried, and 3-year-old does lost 24 percent. But, first-time mothers (2-year-olds) lost a whopping 63 percent of their fawns.

Indirect evidence suggested that most fawns died shortly after birth and that losses were related to territorial behavior associated with fawn rearing. That is, because does with newborn fawns are extremely antagonistic and defend a territory (10 to 20 acres) for about one month, crowding at peak deer density likely limited fawn-rearing space and disrupted maternal behavior. We concluded that heavy fawn mortality resulted either because of imprinting failure or outright abandonment of otherwise healthy offspring by socially stressed young, inexperienced mothers.

Initially, boundary disputes tend to involve some rather violent, aggressive interactions. This is one time during the year that a doe will readily attack a buck twice her size. Once dominance is achieved, however, some form of scent-marking (possibly via urine and feces) by the dominant doe likely delineates her territory. Whatever the mechanisms involved, subordinate does, and even mature bucks, seem to recognize and avoid crossing such territorial lines.

Young does fawning for the first time will set up and defend an area that borders their mothers' territories. As the family group increases in number, crowding over a period of years causes second-time mothers (usually 3-years-olds) to disperse a quarter-mile or so to establish new fawning grounds. This territorial system yields certain predator defense benefits that enhance fawn-rearing success, and it also provides for an orderly expansion of a given clan's range during times of excellent nutrition.

Territorial History

It's also important to note that an animal's territorial boundaries, as well as the dominance relationships that formed them, might have taken place several years prior. Where certain regions are occupied by whole families, such as is the case with does that live within a matriarchal society, ancestral range might pass onto descen-

Where certain regions are occupied by whole families, such as is the case with female whitetails that live within a matriarchal society, ancestral range might pass onto descendants by tradition, with boundary disputes occurring only once in several generations.

dants by tradition, with boundary disputes occurring only once in several generations.

Although not reported in my original manuscript, it's interesting to note that the dominance rank of a young doe's relatives played a key role in determining her fawn-rearing success in the Cusino enclosure when fawning space was limited. During the final year of study, 2-year-old does from the most dominant family group were able to raise five of seven fawns they carried, whereas does of similar age belonging to more subordinate families raised only 1 of 9 fawns they carried.

There are a number of possible implications here, namely: (1) dominant does tend to produce female offspring that are better able to compete for limited fawning space, possibly by being more aggressive, (2) dominant females are more successful in expanding their ancestral range, and as a result control larger and superior ancestral fawning range, and (3) regardless of their age, does associated with dominant families are less subject to social stress and are more likely to find suitable fawning sites, even when herd density is high.

Dispersal is Risky

Generally, dispersal is risky business, as the dispersing doe incurs considerable competition for space when seeking new fawning grounds. Especially when deer density is high, the disperser might settle in unsuitable fawning habitat or attempt to rear young within another doe's territory. As a result, dispersing does normally experience much higher newborn fawn losses as compared to nondispersers.

Rather unusual dispersal traits were reported by Charles Nixon and his coworkers (1991) for does in intensively farmed areas of Illinois. These areas have excellent nutrition but limited forest cover, thus resulting in a high mortality rate for deer due to hunting. Because suitable fawning space is limited, many young does surviving in refuge areas must disperse long distances in spring to find other isolated pockets of forest cover devoid of deer where they can raise fawns. In such cases, members of a female clan can not merely expand their ancestral range, instead, young does are forced to sever ties with relatives to seek new range.

Can Research Provide Answers?

The topic of dominance and territoriality and their effect on reproductive performance is an area of study most scientists have ignored. And, with good reason. In order to conduct such a comprehensive study, much must be known about the genetic and social relationships of individual animals, the timing and success of their breeding, fawn rearing success, precise area use patterns, and so on. To say the least, these areas are difficult to research with free-ranging whitetails.

Meanwhile, one can debate the cause-and-effect relationships involved, but available evidence strongly suggests social environment might sometimes be just as important as nutrition in determining physical condition and reproductive performance. Even variations in the timing of a doe's breeding and the sex of her progeny can oftentimes be linked to social factors and adaptive breeding strategies. These factors allow the species to maximize available food and cover resources, however limited or luxurious those resources might be.

Granted, most whitetail populations probably succumb to nutritional limitations long before social factors kick in to curtail population growth. However, behaviorisms such as territoriality might account for the otherwise unexpected stability and composition noted in some isolated and/or unhunted whitetail populations.

Indeed, if whitetails do defend certain property, even if only under special circumstances or during certain times of the year, then the animal's social environment and space become limiting factors.

References

Geist, V. 1981. Behavior: adaptive strategies in mule deer. Pages 157-223 in O.C. Wallmo, ed. Mule and black-tailed deer of North America. Univ. Nebraska Press, Lincoln.

Graf, W. 1956. Territorialism in deer. J. Mammal. 37:165-170.

Marchinton, R.L., and T.D. Atkeson. 1985. Plasticity of sociospatial behavior of white-tailed deer and the concept of facultative territoriality. Biol. Deer Production 22:375-377.

Nixon, C.M., L.P. Hansen, P.A. Brewer, and J.E. Chelsvig. 1991. Ecology of white-tailed deer in an intensively farmed region of Illinois. Wildlife Monogr. 118. 77 pages.

Ozoga, J.J., and L.J. Verme. 1982. Physical and reproductive characteristics of a supplementally fed white-tailed deer herd. J. Wildlife Manage. 46:281-301.

Ozoga, J.J., L.J. Verme, and C.S. Bienz. 1982. Parturition behavior and territoriality in white-tailed deer: impact of neonatal mortality. J. Wildlife Manage. 46:1-11.

Peterle, T.J. 1975. Deer sociobiology. Wildlife Soc. Bull. 3:82-83.

Smith, C.A. 1976. Deer sociobiology — Some second thoughts. Wildlife Soc. Bull. 4:181-182.

Weckerly, F.W. 1992. Territoriality in North American Deer: A call for a common definition. Wildlife Soc. Bull. 20:228-231.

Bill Kinney

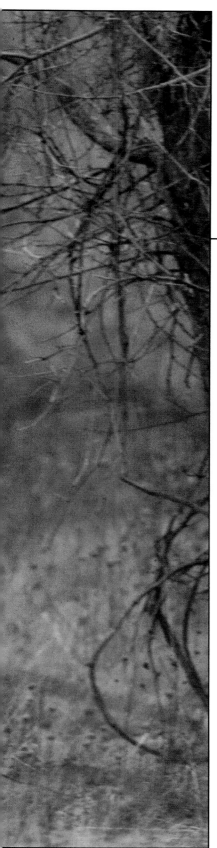

The Herd's Communication

HOW DEER SPEAK WITHOUT WORDS

The relatively silent white-tailed deer that slips across forest clearings and effortlessly leaps woodland streams seldom raises its voice loud enough to be heard by humans, even if they're within 100 yards.

Be assured, however, that the whitetail is constantly communicating its presence in a language of signs and scents. This language is so complex that it perplexes and intrigues humans, begging our long-term investigation.

While rubs, scrapes and overhead limbs or "licking branches" have long fascinated deer hunters, scientists have only recently begun to piece together how deer use these signposts to share information. Even so, we're a long way from unlocking all the mysteries of pheromones, or comprehending the whitetail's incredible olfactory abilities that make such communication possible.

A SUBTLE LANGUAGE:

The Reason Whitetails are Tight-Lipped

Whitetails aren't completely voiceless. They voice sounds that range in tone and volume to communicate an array of socially important information.

According to noted scientist Valerius Geist: "Gregariousness and ornateness tend to go hand-in-hand" in the deer family. But not with whitetails. These deer aren't showy. They lack the prominent body markings and elaborate behaviorisms that are more typical of open-country herding ungulates.

Although whitetails are highly social, they're a solitary species. They live much of their lives alone or in small groups, they prefer dense protective forest cover, and they rely primarily on camouflage coloration to hide from predators.

They aren't especially vocal, either. Instead of relying on complex visual displays and vocalizations for social communication, whitetails make more use of scent-marking.

Silent by Choice

This doesn't mean whitetails lack the ability to communicate vocally. There's scientific evidence that they use several voiced sounds to convey messages. Although most such sounds are subtle and audible to humans only at short distances, certain sounds whitetails make can be heard at great distances.

Using sophisticated electronic gear and sonograms to create graphic pictures of sound waves, Mississippi researchers (C.W. Richardson, et al. 1983) identified seven sounds made by deer. Meanwhile, Georgia investigators (T.D. Atkeson et al. 1988) recorded 12 sounds.

Despite differences in interpreting the studies' data, the sounds made by deer can be grouped into five categories based on the type of message being communicated.

Mother-Newborn Fawn Calls

Five vocalizations made by whitetails involve mothers and their young. Fawns use four different calls when seeking maternal care or when nursing, and mothers call to fawns when searching for them before nursing.

When approaching their fawn's bedding area, does commonly give a maternal grunt. This low-intensity call, which is audible to humans for only a few yards, generally causes the fawn to leave its bed and run to the doe. If a fawn doesn't respond, the doe often grunts even louder.

Does continue to use the maternal grunt to maintain the family group's cohesiveness after fawns are old enough to move around with their mothers. Some evidence suggests the doe's maternal grunt is distinct and recognizable to her fawns.

Young fawns commonly mew in response to the mother's grunt, or when they're hungry or require other maternal attention. I've also heard sibling fawns communicate to each other using similar weak sounds. Fawns also make a louder bleat, especially when they're disturbed, which more intensely solicits care. The mew is a soft sound that can be heard for only a short distance. The bleat, however, is loud enough to be heard by humans, as well as predators, from several hundred feet.

Deer snort by releasing a brief blast of air through their nostrils. Alarm snorts differ, depending on the distance a deer is from the perceived danger.

When nursing, a content fawn often produces a brief, low-intensity nursing whine. Richardson and his co-workers speculate that the fawn's whine helps identify it, reaffirms the maternal bond, transmits pleasure, and encourages more or continued attention.

Mating Calls

After a buck or doe is 1½ years old, it grunts for different reasons. The tending grunt is given by the male while courting an estrous doe, when tending her closely and guarding her from other bucks, or when testing prospective mates to determine if they're approaching estrus. The tending grunt usually lasts longer than other types of grunt calls, and differs in tone from grunts made during competitive encounters.

Bucks infrequently emit sounds called the Flehmen-sniff when investigating female urine. The sound is made when the buck tastes the urine and inhales through pinched nostrils. Researchers note marked differences between bucks in their use of the Flehmen-sniff, but question whether those sounds serve as communication.

Alarm Calls

Deer emit two alarm calls in response to danger. Compared to most calls, alarm sounds tend to be loud. Probably the most common alarm sound made by whitetails is the snort, also called the alert snort.

Deer snort by releasing a brief blast of air through their nostrils. Alarm snorts differ, depending on the distance a deer is from the perceived danger.

When a deer is surprised at close range, it often gives a short, almost explosive, air blast through its nose as it runs off. The startled animal makes an all-out effort to escape as rapidly as possible. The associated noises, including more snorts and reckless crashing through brush, alert other deer in the social group that danger is nearby.

When startled at close range, whitetails normally hold their tails straight out in flight instead of tail-flagging. When danger is detected at greater distances and the situation is obviously not immediately life-threatening, deer more often hide and produce a series of longer snorts. These longer snorts sometimes have more of a whistling quality.

Studies by David Hirth and Dale McCullough revealed that members of doe groups are much more likely to give alarm snorts than members of buck groups. Considering the evolutionary significance of alarm signals, Hirth and McCullough hypothesized that snorting occurs more frequently in mother-and-young groups because it benefits related deer.

Unrelated bucks, however, are more likely to express selfish behavior by slipping away quietly. This increases the likelihood of their own survival at the expense of close competitors for resources and mates.

Injured deer sometimes bawl loudly, just as they do when grasped by a predator or by humans. Severely frightened deer will also bawl sometimes. Young animals tend to emit a high-pitched bawl, while older individuals emit more of a deep roar.

Except for nursing does, deer generally flee the bawl of another deer. But healthy, nursing does readily respond to the bawl of their own fawns. Based on sonographic analysis, researchers determined the structure of each fawn's call tends to be distinctive. Therefore, does might be able to recognize their fawns' bawl, and defend them more readily against predators. However, I've seen as many as three does rush to a single fawn when it bawls. I've also seen does respond to a distant fawn's bawl by running to find their own fawns, and then moving them to new hiding places.

Non-Vocal Communication

Although not a vocalization, hoof-stomping is another alarm signal. It's made, of course, when deer repeatedly stomp a front hoof. It's commonly made in conjunction with the alert snort, and is most often performed by adult females. Adult bucks and fawns of both sexes only occasionally hoof-stomp.

Sometimes, when detecting an unidentifiable object, a deer will stare, cup its ears forward, and raise its tail to expose its white rump patch. This, too, alerts other group members to potential danger. If the deer still can't identify the object, it might stomp its front hoofs to try to make the potential predator move. Even if the object can't be positively identified, the deer might bound away, tail flagging.

Agonistic Calls

Visual displays, in the form of body language, are more important during agonistic encounters, or competitive encounters, between whitetails than vocalizations. However, when competing for dominance, whitetails often grunt, snort and wheeze, which seem to make any display more effective.

The low grunt is considered the least intense, vocally aggressive behavior. Adults of both sexes use this low guttural grunt, and often combine it with other visual displays of aggression throughout the year. According to Atkeson and his co-workers, this sound — which is usually given singularly — "is a voiced sound of low pitch, tonality and intensity, and of brief duration." It can be given with the mouth open or closed.

The grunt-snort includes the basic grunt, plus one to four rapid bursts of air through the nostrils. Does and bucks use the grunt-snort during more intense encounters. While investigating the aggressive behavior of deer at winter cuttings (Ozoga 1972), I found that adult does, in particular, used the grunt-snort during competition for limited food. When combining the grunt-snort with a lunging move, does dominated adult bucks in half of their victories with bucks. Although no physical contact occurred during such contests, the grunt-snort seemed to make aggressive posturing more effective, causing submission with few injury risks.

The grunt-snort-wheeze is only produced by adult bucks during the rut. This sound combines the grunt-snort with a drawn-out wheezing release of air through pinched nostrils. Because the grunt-snort-wheeze often precedes a fight, Miller and Marchinton (1994) consider it the buck's most threatening call.

Atkeson and his Georgia cohorts were the first to document calling between adult does when separated from their family group. They described this as a "voiced grunt of moderate pitch, intensity and tonality." This grunt is longer than the low grunt or maternal grunt, but shorter than the tending grunt. Such calling presumably enables group members to maintain contact when out of view from each other. Contact calling has not been documented among bucks.

Conclusion

It's obvious that whitetails are not completely voiceless. Despite their quiet, secretive nature, they use voiced sounds to communicate an array of socially important information. Their calls range in volume and tone.

The grunt appears to be the primary sound made by adults. Six of the 12 vocalizations identified so far involve grunting, sometimes combined with other sounds and body language, to convey contrasting messages. Three of the grunting calls solicit attention and grouping, while three serve as threats and preludes to aggressive action if ignored.

The quietest voiced sounds occur between the doe and her offspring, although adult does also communicate in low tones.

Most of these sounds have been detected while monitoring captive animals under highly artificial conditions. Therefore, in the wild, it's likely deer use other subtle forms of voice communication yet to be discovered by scientists.

References

Atkeson, T.D., R.L. Marchinton, and K.V. Miller. 1988. *Vocalizations of white-tailed deer.* The American Midland Naturalist *120:194-200.*

Hirth, D.H., and D.R. McCullough. 1977. *Evolution of alarm signals in ungulates with special reference to white-tailed deer.* The American Naturalist. *111:31-42.*

Miller, K.V., and R.L. Marchinton. 1994. *Deer talk: sounds, smells, and postures. in* Deer, eds. Gerlach, D.,

S. Atwater, and J. Schnell, pages 158-168. Stackpole Books, Harrisburg, Pa. 384 pages.

Ozoga, J.J. 1972. *Aggressive behavior of white-tailed deer at winter cuttings.* J. Wildlife Management *36:861-868.*

Richardson, L.W., H.A. Jacobson, R.J. Muncy, and C.J. Perkins. 1983. *Acoustics of white-tailed deer (Odocoileus virginianus).* J. Mammalogy *64:245-252.*

Chapter 2

SCENT TALK:

Why Deer Think With their Noses

Bucks place scent on limb tips with their heads, largely for the benefit of other bucks. But are the secretions produced on the head, or do bucks use their head to transfer secretions from other parts of their body? Deciphering their chemical language isn't easy.

It's difficult to think like a deer, even though we hunters often offer such advice. Why? Because, as with most mammals, deer tend to think through their noses. And, as many people say, when compared to deer, we humans have no noses.

Whitetails have extraordinary, or *macrosmatic*, olfactory capabilities. That means they're able to recognize faint traces of scent, an ability that far exceeds our weak powers of odor detection. They use their noses to test for small, volatile airborne molecules. In addition, they have a specialized vomeronasal system to analyze larger, less volatile molecules in some liquids like urine.

Deer use their super sense of smell to avoid predators and to locate water and nourishing foods. They also employ these powers year-round in conjunction with glandular secretions and body odors — referred to as chemical signals — as their primary means of communication.

With a forest-dwelling animal like the whitetail, which spends most of its time in dense cover, chemical signals are much more important in communication than visual signs and vocalizations. Those methods serve only immediate, short-range purposes. Body odors, however, can be memorized and left on objects in the woods. They can also identify the maker, permit scent-matching of marks with individuals, and produce long-lasting messages that continue to work in the maker's absence.

Visible and Smelly

During the breeding season, bucks produce highly visible signposts in the form of antler rubs and ground scrapes. This helps them express their dominance and attract prospective mates. At that time, scent-marking is accompanied by sometimes violent, aggressive action. Bucks paw the soil like irate bulls, and their antlers thrash brush, rub bark from trees, and break overhead limbs,

Whitetails scent-mark at other times of the year, too, but that's done unaggressively. For instance, bucks judiciously scent-mark overhead limbs on their summer range. They might deposit social odors so subtly that most marking goes unnoticed, at least to a human's comparatively dull senses.

Therefore, the secretions from deer, the ways they present them and the messages they convey likely change with the seasons. The secretions can also go by different names.

Karl Miller, a professor at the University of Georgia, says: "Chemical signals that relay information among animals are called pheromones. This term was originally coined to describe chemical sex attractants in insects, but it has since been expanded to include any chemical produced by one individual that transfers information to another member of the same species. Some researchers reserve 'pheromones' for insects and use 'chemical signals' when referring to mammals."

Whatever the terminology, Miller said, "These signals include releaser pheromones, which evoke an immediate behavioral response; priming pheromones, which result in a physiological response; and informer pheromones, which relay information but generally don't result in behavioral or physiological responses."

As far as we know, the communicative odors produced by deer might include secretions from urine, the vaginal canal, certain skin glands and, probably, saliva. Feces also serve as a means of odor communication in some mammals. This might include whitetails, but it hasn't been documented.

The Seven Glands

Researchers have identified seven types of skin glands in whitetails that likely play a role in scent communication. These include the forehead, preorbital and nasal glands on the head; the tarsal, metatarsal and interdigital glands on the legs; and the preputial gland on the buck's penis sheath. More glands undoubtedly exist.

Studies by Miller and R. Larry Marchinton and their University of Georgia students were among the first to scientifically document scent-marking by whitetails outside the breeding season. The Georgia researchers observed that white-tailed bucks employed the full scrape sequence primarily during the breeding period, but they marked overhead limbs year-round.

In summarizing their findings, Miller said: "Although

A buck's forehead glands are known to produce pheromones that express dominance. When bucks make rubs, they create signposts that are visually attractive and carry the maker's odor, signaling the presence of a dominant animal.

frequencies of overhead branch marking tended to be higher for dominants than subordinates, it occurred frequently among all bucks throughout the year. A scrape sequence is a composite of three separate behavior patterns that also occur independently of each other, suggesting that scrapes might have multiple functions. Perhaps the overhanging branch conveys individual identity and presence, pawing denotes aggressive intent to other bucks, and urine deposited in the scrape might relay social or physiological status to bucks and does."

Although I have not reported my observations in scientific literature, I discussed limb-marking by whitetails in the October 1994 issue of *Deer & Deer Hunting* (see "The Overhead Limb: Is it a Sign Only Bucks Understand?" on Page 92). Using 100 artificially positioned limbs in Michigan's Cusino square-mile deer enclosure, I found that bucks intensively marked their summer ranges. These bucks even occasionally made full-fledged scrapes during late spring and early summer.

My observations indicate that, on Northern range, where deer migrate seasonally, bucks intensively scent-mark their favored summer habitat as soon as they return in spring. Such marking likely helps bucks reclaim familiar range that has been devoid of deer for several months. Buck marking in spring might also intimidate does, causing them to seek other areas for fawn-rearing. This creates rather uniform use of available space during the fawn-rearing and antler-growing period.

Based on limb breakage or the presence of deer hair on limb tips, I found 94 percent of my test limbs were scent-marked by bucks. Further, 60 percent were marked before scraping started while bucks carried velvet antlers. In all, 83 percent of branches scent-marked in summer developed into scrapes in autumn.

Seasonal Factors

In my studies, bucks occupied and scent-marked tiny ranges in May and June, which is the period of maximum antler growth. Nutritious forage at that time of year is abundant, and new antlers are fragile. In late July, however, when antler growth was nearly complete and the antler core began to mineralize, some bucks wandered into adjacent doe-occupied ranges, where they also scent-marked overhead limbs.

So the intensity and distribution of scent-marking changed as the summer progressed. Even the secretions, messages and audience might have changed from one month to the next.

I detected no serious limb-tip mutilation until October, at which time bucks began to paw the sites. Instead, before scraping, bucks marked overhead limbs gently, giving heavily used tips an oily or greased appearance. This indicates that the manner in which bucks scent-mark limbs changes seasonally. It also suggests that substances deposited and messages conveyed while marking might differ throughout the year.

Clearly, adult bucks are the primary markers and readers of social messages attached to overhead limbs during summer. But I defy anyone to prove which marking ingredients are used, when they are used, and where they come from.

Sophisticated Codes?

When marking branches, most of which are about head high, a buck mouths the branch tips, and rubs them with his forehead, nose, antlers, chin and preorbital area. He also pauses periodically to sniff and lick the branches. It's as if the process involves some highly sophisticated signal code.

When marking branches, most of which are about head high, a buck "mouths" the branch tips, and rubs them with his forehead, nose, antlers, chin and preorbital area. He also pauses periodically to sniff and lick the branches. It's as if the process involves some highly sophisticated signal code.

Given our understanding of such things, Miller cautions: "Sources of scent deposited on the overhanging limb (during any time of year) are highly speculative."

I concur, but let's speculate a bit anyway. Where could these secretions come from? What messages might they carry? And what purpose could they possibly serve?

In summer, bucks place scent on limb tips with their heads, largely for the benefit of other bucks. But are the secretions actually produced on the head, or do bucks merely use their head to transfer secretions from other parts of their body to overhead limbs?

Two types of glands are most responsible for producing chemical signals: sebaceous glands and sudoriferous glands. Both are found over the skin surface, but are concentrated in certain areas and undergo seasonal changes in activation and function.

A buck's forehead glands are known to produce pheromones that express dominance. All deer possess these glands, but the most active glands are on dominant mature bucks during the rut. When bucks make rubs, they create signposts that are visually attractive and carry the maker's odor, signaling the presence of a dominant animal.

Because of their obvious behavioral importance, it's tempting to credit the forehead glands as the primary source of year-round secretions attached to limb tips — and many scientists do. However, histological examination of the forehead skin reveals that glands in this area are mostly inactive while bucks are in velvet. Increased secretion from the forehead glands doesn't occur until the antlers harden and velvet sheds. Also, the use of these secretions is normally associated with agonistic, threatening behavior, while scent communication between bucks in summer is more informative and less threatening.

It seems illogical that bucks would use the same secretions to present friendly information concerning identity and presence, as well as threatening information concerning dominance and social rank. If secretions from forehead glands are the primary source of odor used in limb-marking, then other changes in body chemistry, mixing of secretions and different behavior must be involved to produce messages that change with the seasons.

Other Scent Sources

Other potential sources of limb-tip marking substances

are the preorbital glands — also referred to as the antorbital or lachrymal glands — located in front of the eye, and nasal sebaceous glands, found inside the nostril.

In some species, such as the Thomson's gazelle, the preorbital gland produces a strong-smelling oily substance believed to carry pheromones used for marking territorial boundaries. In whitetails, this gland is a sac-like structure, generally filled with dead skin cells and foreign matter. Although white-tailed bucks seem to use this gland in limb-marking, researchers are uncertain if it produces socially important scent.

Nasal glands have been found in several deer species, but their function is unknown. Originally, investigators postulated that materials from these glands were atomized during snorting behavior. However, that idea has been abandoned because the glands were found to produce a lipid material of low volatility. Still, the fatty substance could serve as a carrier for other scents.

Velvet antlers are also well-endowed with sebaceous glands, which produce an oily substance called sebum. Sebum reportedly helps grease the antler's surface, making it slippery and resistant to abrasion or injury. According to the late Anthony Bubenik, bucks smear sebum produced by the velvet over their bodies, then onto vegetation at head-height, "leaving a strong scent track."

Bubenik proposed that hardened antlers also play a primary role in scent communication during the rut. He suggested that some species purposely "perfume" their antlers by urinating on them, rubbing them on certain glands, or thrashing them in urine-soaked wallows.

Even mature white-tailed bucks might occasionally rub their antlers in urine-marked scrapes or on their bodies. However, aside from the fact that subordinate deer occasionally sniff a dominant's antlers, I know of no firm data supporting the claim that deer antlers produce or are used to carry chemical signals.

The Most Crucial Gland?

The tarsal gland, located hock-high on the inside of the hind leg, is probably the whitetail's most important gland. Odors from the tarsal tuft allow deer to recognize each other and provide information on dominance status, physical condition and reproductive status. The bacterial action of urine trapped on tarsal hairs produces the buck's characteristic rutting odor.

All deer exhibit a behaviorism referred to as rub-urination, wherein they urinate over their tarsal glands while rubbing them together. Dominant bucks tend to rub-urinate into their scrapes. Some investigators propose that bucks also rub their urine-charged tarsals with their snout, then transfer the odors to overhead limbs. That's another plausible theory without supporting evidence.

Saliva is a potentially potent, but poorly understood, substance involved in chemical signaling among many species. In the boar, for example, some steroids (androstenol and androsterone) are produced by the salivary glands. They act as pheromones, which play an important role in courtship. There is also evidence of sex differences in the morphology of salivary glands in some species. Some observers suggest that saliva, when used directly or applied to the coat while self-grooming or grooming others, might function as a prime source of socially important odors among many mammals.

Even Charles Darwin recognized that scent communication among mammals — especially as it relates to reproduction and other matters of social significance — is highly dependent on the animal reaching adulthood.

White-tailed bucks salivate profusely during the rut. This habit, in addition to their behavior of licking overhead branches year-round, suggests they use saliva as a marking ingredient. Saliva might be a prime source of socially important odors when applied directly to overhead limbs, either alone or in combination with other glandular secretions. It might also be important when first applied to the coat and mixed with other substances while grooming. Unfortunately, researchers know little about such things.

Even Charles Darwin recognized that scent communication among mammals — especially as it relates to reproduction and other matters of social significance — is highly dependent on the animal reaching adulthood. The development of sebaceous glands depends on sex hormones produced by the testes, ovaries or adrenal glands, which are minimal before they reach puberty. Also, in most species, males tend to emit stronger body odors than females.

White-tailed bucks seem to have the capacity to emit a wide array of chemical signals, which presumably convey equally diverse messages, to satisfy their social needs. The ability to combine secretions, alter the proportions of certain ingredients, or hold and age the ingredients, provides deer with a complex set of odor signals. When combined with different methods of presenting odors, the chemical language of whitetails must be immense.

Conclusion

In our quest to understand chemical communication

in whitetails, it's tempting to search for simple answers and simple chemical compounds — as in the case of insect pheromones. It's important to recognize, however, that deer have a complex social system that depends on a complex communication system — something some scent-makers might consider before making exaggerated claims about certain products. So the simplistic

pheromonal concept might not apply to the whitetail's chemical communication in all cases.

Until we more fully understand white-tailed deer social organization, we will have difficulty determining how they "talk" to each other, which substances are used, and precisely what messages are conveyed. Deciphering the whitetail's chemical language will be no easy matter.

References

Bubenik, G.A., and A.B. Bubenik. 1990. Horns, Pronghorns, and Antlers: Evolution, Morphology, Physiology and Social Significance. *Springer-Verlag, N.Y.*

Gosling, L.M. 1985. The even-toed ungulates: order Artiodactyla. Sources, behavioral context, and function of chemical signals. Pages 551-617, in R.E. Brown and D.W. Macdonald (eds). Social Odors in Mammals. *Oxford University Press.*

Marchinton, R.L., K.L. Johansen, and K.V. Miller. 1990. Behavioral components of white-tailed scent marking: social and seasonal effects. Pages 295-310, in D.W. Macdonald, D. Muller-Schwarze, and S.E. Natynczuk *(eds.).* Chemical Signals in Vertebrates V. *Oxford University Press.*

Miller, K.V. and R.L. Marchinton. 1994. Skin glands. Pages 53-57, in D. Gerlach, S. Atwater, and J. Schnell (eds). Deer. *Stackpole Books, Mechanicsburg, Pa.*

Miller, K.V., R.L. Marchinton, and P.B. Bush. 1991. Signpost communication by white-tailed deer: research since Calgary. Applied Animal Behavior Science *29:195-204.*

Mark Raycroft

Chapter 3

PRIMING PHEROMONES:

What's Their Role in the Rut?

While photoperiod is the primary factor responsible for opening the whitetail's breeding window, it doesn't act alone. Sex pheromones produced by bucks and does probably help bring both sexes into peak breeding condition at about the same time.

White-tailed deer are short-day breeders, that is they breed in autumn when day length (photoperiod) is decreasing. It's the shortening daylight hours that trigger the production of certain hormones responsible for the doe's urge to mate.

But changing photoperiod is not the only factor involved. The whitetail's breeding season can be viewed as a window of opportunity that is opened by decreasing photoperiod. This window is narrow in the North, but widens southward until breeding takes place year-round near the equator. While photoperiod is the primary factor in opening the whitetail's breeding window, it doesn't act alone. Nutrition, genetics and certain poorly understood behavioral factors might also combine to determine when an individual doe breeds.

Scientists at the University of Georgia hypothesize that the glandular secretions and urinary deposits left by adult bucks at rubs and scrapes (signposts) also play a key role. These deposits could act as priming pheromones in stimulating breeding activity in does. In 1987, researchers Karl Miller, Larry Marchinton and Matt Knox presented their ideas at an international meeting of wildlife biologists in Krakow, Poland. They suggested buck rubs and scrapes carry estrus-inducing pheromones that assist in ending sexual dormancy while synchronizing estrus in whitetails.

Chemical Signals

Pheromones are chemical signals that relay information between animals. Priming pheromones cause a physiological response, releaser pheromones evoke an immediate behavioral response, and informer pheromones relay information but don't cause a response. In other words, priming pheromones cause physiological changes that might trigger the production of hormones responsible for breeding.

Chemical signals produced by adult males play an important, if not manipulating, role in breeding behavior. Such information is used routinely in controlled livestock breeding. For example, the presence of adult males or their odor — referred to as biostimulation — hastens and synchronizes the estrous cycles of sheep, goats and pigs. In these species, young females exposed to adult males generally show early puberty. But even mature females enter estrus sooner when interacting with males before their normal breeding period, as compared to does without such interaction. With sheep, a ewe's exposure to ram wax and wool induces ovulation almost as effectively as a ram's presence.

Controlled deer breeding studies that I helped conduct at the Cusino Wildlife Research Station in northern Michigan achieved similar results. Our research group reported that the presence of mature bucks affected the reproductive physiology of the does. Despite the relatively narrow breeding window in northern Michigan latitudes, confining adult bucks and does together in autumn advanced mean breeding dates by eight to nine days. In another study, 60 percent to 70 percent of doe fawns bred when penned with adult bucks. In contrast, less than 5 percent of doe fawns bred while living more naturally in a nearby enclosure.

The exact mechanisms involved here are unknown, but we believe the close, unnatural confinement of bucks with does had some type of biostimulating effect. It could have been caused by priming pheromones produced by males, which induced ovulation earlier than normal.

Close Associations

All male ungulates use some form of scent-marking to advertise their superior social status and breeding condition. Among whitetails, only mature bucks scent-mark frequently. Odors left by a dominant buck at his rubs and scrapes typically suppress the actions of subordinate bucks, but attract and stimulate does.

When discussing the whitetail's breeding behavior, remember that adult males and females live apart and have minimal contact except during the breeding season. As a result, they might not associate long enough or closely enough to prompt the biostimulation that results from frequent male-female contact. Such solitary behavior might be another reason that priming pheromones at rubs and scrapes are important in the whitetail's breeding behavior.

Adult bucks and does begin mingling in early autumn, about the time bucks shed antler velvet and start making rubs. On Northern range, mature bucks start antler rubbing nearly two months before breeding commences. Rubbing continues through the breeding season, and ends only when bucks shed their antlers. Although scraping starts later than rubbing, studies in the Cusino enclosure found that 50 percent to 80 percent of it occurs before the season's first mating. Therefore, rubs and scrapes seem to play the largest role before the primary breeding period.

A dominant buck's breeding range must literally fume with his identifying odors. These scent marks carry the maker's odors and serve as an extension of the animal. They also remain functional a long time, even in the maker's absence. Researchers speculate that a dominant buck's signposts are especially important. Does and subordinate bucks learn the dominant buck's odors and can identify them with scents on signposts.

Scent Identification

Do those odors stimulate females enough to induce mating? Field observations indicate that does respond to rubs by smelling and licking them. Miller suggests this might involve the vomeronasal organ, which opens on the roof of the deer's mouth and connects to the brain's hypothalamus, which controls the production of hormones responsible for reproduction. For this reason, researchers like Miller believe chemical signals on signposts strongly prime the doe's physiology and estrous cycle.

If so, mature bucks and their scent-marking could contribute to a timely, intense and brief rutting period, which benefits the herd in the long run. Conversely, such biostimulation would be minimal in herds where bucks are heavily harvested. That's because 1½- and 2½-year-old bucks show delayed and minimal scent-marking. In the Cusino enclosure, yearlings made only 15 percent as many scrapes as mature bucks, and none appeared until one week before the first doe was bred. Younger bucks also made only half as many rubs as older bucks. Miller reported similar findings in South Carolina, where mature bucks made nearly 5,000 rubs per square mile, as compared to 500 to 1,500 rubs per square mile in areas where bucks were heavily harvested and few reached maturity.

The priming pheromone hypothesis has some supporting field evidence. Studies in the Southeast have clearly demonstrated the value of mature bucks in populations to promote short, intense breeding seasons.

Dave Guynn and his co-workers established a long-term research project on South Carolina's Mount Holly Plantation to study the effects of quality management on deer populations that were nutritionally and socially out of balance. Using selective harvest, Guynn's group lowered deer densities, balanced the sex ratio, and increased the age structure of bucks. Within five years, the herd's breeding period was reduced from 96 days to 43 days. The researchers also observed earlier breeding, with the mean breeding date shifting from Nov. 11 in the first year to Oct. 15 in the fifth year. Professor Harry Jacobson reported similar results in a project on Davis Island in Mississippi.

There is no denying that lower deer densities improved nutrition for deer in these studies, but apparently, sociobiological factors were also involved. Increased biostimulation of females by mature bucks was likely an important factor, because the availability of males to breed females, by itself, could not account for advancing the breeding season.

Interestingly, we could not demonstrate the reverse effects in the Cusino enclosure, where we live-trapped the herd every winter and controlled the sex and age composition of the reintroduced population. We could not induce a delayed or protracted rut when we limited herd sires to yearling bucks. We saw no difference in the rut's timing or length, regardless of sire age, and does were equally productive whether bred by mature bucks or yearling bucks.

It's important to note, however, that the Cusino enclosure's herd was well-nourished. Had these young Northern bucks been poorly fed, they might not have achieved favorable physical and sexual development in such a timely fashion. If that had happened, they probably wouldn't have fulfilled the role of rut-experienced bucks so promptly, which could have contributed to a delayed, extended rut.

A sidelight in the Cusino study was the unexplainable difference in the breeding response of does depending on their age and the bucks' ages. Although data were not significant, yearling does tended to be bred earlier when courted by yearling bucks, and later when mature bucks were present. The reverse was generally true for adult does, which seemed to shun young bucks.

Mate Selection?

In a nutshell, it seemed that Cusino's estrous females preferred mates closer to their own age, or at least they were more responsive to the "mature" courtship style. Whatever the reason, it's tempting to think female whitetails exhibit some degree of mate selection.

Bucks, of course, also respond to priming pheromones produced in the doe's reproductive tract and deposited in her urine. The buck will not only sniff the doe's urine, but he will also taste it and perform a lip-curl, or Flehmen. In doing so, he holds his neck and chin up at about a 45-degree angle, opens his mouth slightly, curls his upper lip, and closes his nostrils. These actions pump some urine fumes into the vomeronasal organ for analysis.

It's likely that these priming pheromones from the doe's urine affect the buck's reproductive physiology, but they might not evoke an immediate behavioral response. Miller and Marchinton believe "a male's analysis of (a doe's) urine through this system likely primes that physiology and thereby ensures that he reaches peak reproductive condition at the same time as do the females." This means, essentially, that bucks use the Flehmen to determine if a doe is approaching estrus, not if she's already receptive.

The Role of Silent Estrus

The role of the so-called "silent estrus" is equally mysterious. It likely involves potent female-priming pheromones.

Detailed studies of blood chemistry indicate that some female whitetails undergo an infertile estrus 12 to 23 days before their first receptive estrus of the season. It's believed that this silent estrus-ovulation is caused by an insufficient secretion of estrogen by the ovaries, which would account for the doe's unreceptive behavior.

Some researchers speculate that silent estrus is accompanied by the secretion of female-priming pheromones that excite males, and possibly females, too. For example, in the Cusino studies, I think it was more than coincidence that scraping activity rose sharply and yearling bucks abruptly left their birth range each year in late October, one or two weeks before the first doe bred. Thus, it's my guess that the doe's priming pheromones in silent ovulation stimulate male reproductive behavior, regardless of their age.

Conclusions

Although poorly understood, it appears bucks and does use priming pheromones in conjunction with the vomeronasal system to ensure reproduction is synchronized. Females probably receive priming pheromones from glandular secretions and urine deposited by bucks at rubs and scrapes. Bucks, in turn, receive the critical messages by analyzing doe urine. In both cases, these signals trigger reproductive readiness and help bring bucks and does into peak breeding condition at about the same time.

Even so, photoperiod appears to be the most powerful force influencing the whitetail's breeding window in the North, where female-priming pheromones might be a safety valve to ensure a timely rut. In the South, however, where the breeding window is wider, adult male biostimulation and male-priming pheromones are probably far more important, if not mandatory, for an early, condensed rut.

Whatever the driving forces might be, delayed breeding generally leads to delayed physical and sexual maturity of the offspring. Also, according to Miller, such unfavorable circumstances tend to be self-perpetuating in the South. That's especially true when they're fueled by nutritional shortages and social unrest, which is often caused by the underharvest of antlerless deer and overharvest of bucks.

References

Miller, K.V., and R.L. Marchinton (Eds.) 1995. Quality Whitetails: The Why and How of Quality Deer Management. Stackpole Books, Mechanicsburg, Pa. 322 pages.

Miller, K.V., R.L. Marchinton and W.M. Knox. 1991. White-tailed deer signposts and their role as a source of priming pheromones: a hypothesis. Pages 455-458 in B. Bobek, K. Perzanowski and W. Regelin, eds. Global Trends in Wildlife Management. Vol. 1. Transactions 18th Congr. Inter. Union of Game Biologists 1987. Swait Press, Krawow-Warszawa.

Ozoga, J.J. 1989. Temporal pattern of scraping behavior in white-tailed deer. Journal of Mammalogy 70:633-636.

Ozoga, J.J. and L.J. Verme. 1982. Physical and reproductive characteristics of a supplementally fed white-tailed deer herd. Journal of Wildlife Management 46:281-301.

Ozoga, J.J. and L.J. Verme. 1985. Comparative breeding behavior and performance of yearling vs. prime-age white-tailed bucks. Journal of Wildlife Management 49:364-372.

Verme, L.J. and J.J. Ozoga. 1987. Relationship of photoperiod to puberty in doe fawn white-tailed deer. Journal of Mammalogy 68:107-110.

Verme, L.J., J.J. Ozoga, and J.T. Nellist. 1987. Induced early estrus in penned white-tailed deer. Journal of Wildlife Management 51:54-56.

Lance Krueger

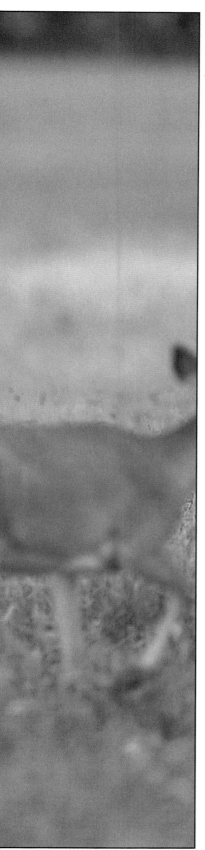

Chapter 4

SILENT ESTRUS:

Does it Trigger the Chase Phase?

It's tempting to think the first breedable doe causes bucks to suddenly go berserk. But I suspect the chase phase is mostly chasing and little breeding. The "quiet heat" produces the histological and physiological signs of estrus, including ovulation, but not the mating urge.

Fawn-rearing and antler growth dominate the whitetail's summer, but that behavior turns complex by early autumn as the herd ends several months of sexual segregation.

On Northern range, the whitetail's pre-rut starts with velvet stripping, generally in early September. Stripping lasts about six weeks, depending on latitude, before finally giving way to that brief, hectic period outdoor writer and photographer Charles Alsheimer calls the "chase phase." Soon after, serious seeking and breeding begin.

The pre-rut is characterized by increased activity, intense socialization, mixing of the sexes, sparring among bucks and early stages of signposting. These interactions involve ritualistic and stereotypical behaviors. Tolerance, social order and even predictability prevail. One senses the herd is following a strict social system molded by centuries of adaptation to environmental pressures.

Everything changes again by late October. Almost overnight, bucks seem to go berserk. Scraping activity explodes, and bucks won't tolerate each other as they wildly chase every doe in sight. All semblance of social order

vanishes — or so it seems — as belligerent bucks scurry in all directions day and night, testing every doe they find.

Why the sudden change? What mysterious force causes such wild behavior during the chase phase? Is it the first breedable doe? Or is it another signal that alerts bucks to impending breeding opportunities?

In the Upper Midwest, the whitetail's breeding window is relatively narrow, and it is tightly controlled by decreasing daylight, or photoperiod. Changes in reproductive behavior are abrupt and easily recognized, at least to trained eyes. If you plot the breeding dates of does in any Northern area, you find a truncated pattern, not a standard curve. The first does to breed generally become receptive during the last week of October or the first few days of November. Thereafter, breeding frequency escalates rapidly, peaks at midmonth, and tails off gradually. Some breeding will occur in December and even January where doe fawns breed.

On Northern range, the chase phase occurs after mid-October each year. Therefore, given that timing, it's tempting to think the first breedable doe causes bucks to suddenly become frenzied. To the contrary, I suspect the chase phase is just that: much chasing and testing of does by energetic bucks, but little or no breeding.

The Silent Estrus

What about the phenomenon called the "quiet heat" or "silent estrus"? In this case, the female shows the histological and physiological signs of estrus, including ovulation, but not the mating response, or psychological heat. This condition is common in cows and mares, but it has also been reported in elk and deer. Some researchers, including myself, believe silent estrus might mysteriously spur the whitetail's crazy behavior a couple of weeks before breeding begins. In other words, a doe's silent ovulation might emit pheromones that alert bucks to her status, but she won't be in the mood to mate and will flee the bucks' advances.

Professor Karl Miller at the University of Georgia says the term *estrus* denotes a period of heat and a willingness to mate. Therefore, technically speaking, there is no such thing as a silent estrus.

"More correctly, such a condition should be called a silent ovulation," Miller said.

Not all does exhibit a silent ovulation. For those that do, it generally occurs two or three weeks before breeding. Estrogen, the female sex hormone, causes the doe's receptive breeding behavior. Trace amounts of progesterone, another female hormone, are also necessary. It seems estrogen is needed more greatly in some does than in others, and silent ovulation might occur when ovaries don't secrete enough estrogen.

In some cases, however, stress might produce excessive progesterone from the adrenal glands, and block the stimulating effects of estrogen. Therefore, hormones must be properly balanced to prompt psychological estrus and the doe's mating response.

The Restless Doe

Studies at the Cusino Wildlife Research Station in Upper Michigan revealed that female deer become unusually active a day or two before they breed. Many species demonstrate such apparent restlessness, which is presumably caused by increased estrogen secretions. In particular, young does breeding the first time often become hyperactive 40 hours or more before they breed.

Our Cusino group used that knowledge to conduct breeding studies with penned deer by monitoring the does' pacing activity with mechanical counters. We also introduced the buck during periods of peak doe activity to pinpoint breeding time. This system also allowed us to calculate the does' estrus cycles and conduct detailed studies of blood chemistry around the time of estrus.

While monitoring autumnal hormonal changes in the does' reproductive systems, we found that some does had elevated progesterone in their blood 12 to 23 days before their first behavioral estrus. Generally, a slight increase in progesterone secretion is associated with ovulation, the

release of eggs from the ovaries, while high levels occur with pregnancy. Because the does would not mate, however, we believe that some does had a silent ovulation before successfully breeding in November.

Researchers studying a high-density herd in northern Ohio also concluded that most does silently ovulated in late October or early November. That was followed by a true estrus and successful breeding in less than 15 days.

Black-tailed deer have exhibited similar patterns. Based on histological exams of deer ovaries, researchers concluded that does ovulated at intervals of eight to nine days until they successfully bred. The researchers also said the season's first ovulation was silent or did not produce a lasting pregnancy. Failed pregnancies are sometimes caused by insufficient progesterone production.

Given the physiological conditions involved, the researchers speculated that a blacktail's first silent ovulation might stimulate one or both sexes, thereby helping to bring both into breeding condition about the same time.

While investigating the breeding behavior of Cusino's whitetails, we found that does usually bred eight to nine days earlier when confined with a mature buck than did does exposed to a buck only once daily. The exact mechanisms are unknown, but some type of biostimulation must be involved. Our group's hypothesis was that this unusually early breeding activity was induced by the buck's constant and unnatural presence in a relatively crowded pen.

We also theorized that the normally silent first ovulation, which typically occurs one to two weeks before breeding, was transformed by biostimulation into a fertile estrus. However, Georgia studies under Miller's guidance indicated that probably wasn't the case. Miller believes it's more likely that buck-doe interaction or excitation in the Cusino studies advanced the does' first behavioral estrus periods.

Social Stress

Be cautioned, however, not to conclude that breeding will be advanced in free-ranging high-density herds. Social stress caused by crowding might cause certain hormonal imbalances that delay estrus in young does by as much as two weeks. It could even prevent breeding altogether — especially when accompanied by overbrowsing and nutritional shortfalls that cause subpar physical conditions.

It's also important to note that not all does exhibit a silent ovulation. In the Cusino studies, four of 10 does we sampled around the time of estrus had blood hormone levels that indicated silent ovulation. (Unfortunately, we didn't identify the does' ages.) In fact, Georgia research suggests only young does nearing their first breeding season have a silent ovulation. In most regions, these would be 1½-year-old females, but could sometimes include doe fawns or older does.

Studies led by Matt Knox at Georgia showed that female hormone secretion a month before breeding varied greatly, depending on the doe's age. Four of five young does, which had never bred before, had blood hormone values that indicated silent ovulation occurred seven to 29 days before breeding. Older, sexually experienced does did not.

Knox and the other researchers concluded that silent ovulation in whitetails might play an important role when does reach puberty. Silent ovulation might not be so critical in adults as they shift from sexual dormancy to breeding condition in autumn.

Dramatic Changes

A compelling reason to associate the chase phase with silent estrus is the dramatic change in buck behavior. Some stimuli — presumably involving releaser and/or priming pheromones — trigger wild behavior in yearling bucks as they vacate their birth range and the sharp increase in new scrapes made by mature bucks. But even in the absence of older bucks, yearlings in the Cusino studies suddenly began making scrapes at this time.

The important pheromones that signal a doe's breeding condition are found in the mucus of her vaginal secretions. She carries these around, of course, but also deposits them in her urine. The exact chemical compounds aren't known. Studies led by Miller and Indiana University's Bozena Jemiolo indicate that certain volatile compounds in vaginal secretions and doe urine depend on ovarian hormones. Further, those compounds are present only during estrus.

For the first time in scientific literature, Jemiolo and her co-workers documented that the composition of volatile chemical compounds emitted by does changes with the stage of their reproductive condition.

The Indiana researchers wrote: "Estrous females discharged (vaginal) mucus that was richer in the characteristic volatiles than that of females (not in estrus). Nine of 14 (64 percent) characteristic compounds were produced only by estrous females, whereas only two (14 percent) were produced by females (not in estrus). Certain aromatic hydrocarbons, whose presence may or may not be significant, along with two alcohols and two ketones occurred only in estrous vaginal samples. Since estrous vaginal secretion, but not mid-cycle (non-estrus) secretion, has been shown to elicit courtship behavior in male white-tailed deer, these compounds may represent behaviorally important chemosignals."

Jemiolo and her co-workers emphasize, however, that the research is far from over. They wrote: "Further biological and behavior research is needed to determine which chemical compounds identified in this study (if any) are important in communicating sexual/reproductive status."

Chemical Signals

Therefore, it seems logical that certain chemical compounds function as pheromones that signal estrus to the buck. Also, because these compounds depend on ovarian activity, the same signaling agents could be present in silent ovulation, but more research is needed to clarify this.

To my knowledge, a buck's behavioral responses to does in silent ovulation haven't been studied. It's also not certain whether adult does exhibit silent ovulation. If such an estrous warning system is linked solely to young (pubertal) does, then nutritional range conditions and sexual maturity rates could also greatly affect the intensity and timing of bucks' pursuit behaviors during the rut's chase phase. Poor range and slowed maturity could contribute to decreased rutting activity, even in the presence of mature bucks.

While I'm not an advocate of the so-called second rut, some considerations might justify the theory. In my home region along the southern shore of Lake Superior, I see no second rut. In milder environments, however, patterns could be different. If important pheromones — whatever their source — accompany silent ovulation in pubertal does, additional late-season excitation signals possibly rekindle the bucks' pursuit responses. This could be especially true in Southern regions where many doe fawns breed, generally in December. If that's the case, hunters might see a resurgence of chasing behavior in late November or early December.

Further, given the season's lateness and potential for stress from unfavorable environmental and miscellaneous conditions, some doe fawns might exhibit silent ovulation in late November or early December, but never achieve behavioral estrus. If so, rutting bucks might become excited in the late season despite minimal breeding activity.

Conclusion

Currently, no concrete evidence supports my contention that important pheromones accompany silent ovulation in whitetails, but circumstantial evidence points that way. If some does consistently exhibit silent ovulation before the main breeding season, and important chemical signals accompany this physiological change, then it's my guess this condition triggers the rut's chase phase.

Selected References

Jemiolo, B., K.V. Miller, D. Wiesler, I. Jelinek, M. Novotny, and R.L. Marchinton. 1995. Putative chemical signals from white-tailed deer (Odocoileus virginianus). Urinary and vaginal mucus volatiles excreted by females during breeding season. Journal of Chemical Ecology 21:869-879.

Knox, W.M., K.V. Miller, D.C. Collins, P.B. Bush, T.E. Kiser, and R.L. Marchinton. 1992. Serum and urinary levels of reproductive hormones associated with the estrous cycle in white-tailed deer (Odocoileus virginianus). Zoo Biology 11:121-131.

Ozoga, J.J. 1989. Temporal pattern of scraping behavior in white-tailed deer. Journal of Mammalogy 70:633-636.

Ozoga, J.J., and L.J. Verme. 1985. Comparative breeding behavior and performance of yearling vs. prime-age white-tailed bucks. Journal of Wildlife Management. 49:364-372.

Plotka, E.D., U.S. Seal, L.J. Verme, and J.J. Ozoga. 1977. Reproductive steroids in the white-tailed deer (Odocoileus virginianus borealis). II. Progesterone and estrogen levels in peripheral plasma during pregnancy. Biology of Reproduction 17:78-83.

Chapter 5

FRIEND OR FOE?

Should You Doctor Scrapes?

Hunters must decide for themselves if doctoring a scrape with scent is worth it. The right urine lure — used in the right place at the right time for the right buck — might bring results. But, it might be asking too much for one lure to consistently attract rutting bucks.

Deer hunters today can choose from an amazing variety of paraphernalia to help bring down the big one. Estrous urines, often referred to as doe-in-heat lures or sex scents, rank high on my list of products that "sometimes will/sometimes will not" work.

Don't get me wrong. I'm not implying there aren't important biological messages in naturally deposited deer urine. There are, especially during breeding season.

Scents produced by a deer's various glands undoubtedly serve as important communication. Further, there's evidence deer can communicate individual identity, dominance rank, physical condition, breeding status, and many other bits of information through urine deposits.

Deer of both sexes and all ages are attracted to scrapes, and readily urinate in or near pawed sites. Some scientists speculate that the estrous doe, especially, urinates at the scrape to advertise her ready-to-breed condition, but that theory has not been proven. In fact, the exact messages exchanged via urine at the scrape

have not been deciphered by scientists.

Assuming important chemical signals are present in deer urine, the question becomes this: Can these critical messages be collected, preserved and locked in a bottle with original and lasting punch? I ask because pheromones produced by many species are known to be highly volatile. However, scientific literature won't help much in answering these questions.

A Secret Code

Work being conducted by professors Karl Miller, Larry Marchinton and their students at the University of Georgia involves intriguing investigations into the world of scent communication among white-tailed deer. For example, these researchers documented the existence of three deer glands — the forehead, nasal and preputial — so one wonders what they'll discover next. But even they confess that scientists are a long way from truly understanding how and what deer communicate through scent.

"For us just to get a clue about what types of information deer get out of each whiff of air, we must spend months, or years, in the laboratory working with highly sophisticated analytical equipment," Miller said. "Even after we identify a number of suspected compounds, we still only have a guess as to what these compounds tell the deer, if anything."

Hard to Outsmart

In one experiment, which was part of Dan Forster's master's degree program, Georgia researchers tested the attractiveness of bladder urine from bucks, does in heat, and does not in heat, as compared to a commercial doe-in-heat lure. In addition, they used saline solution as a control.

Researchers used automatic aerosol dispensers to release test materials about every 15 minutes into circular areas of lightly tilled soil. These sites measured about 3 feet in diameter, about the size of a dandy scrape. They then tallied the number of deer tracks at each site after 24, 48 and 72 hours to see if deer were more readily attracted to any of the test solutions. The tests were repeated six times on two sites in Georgia and Florida.

The study revealed that deer visited about a quarter of the test sites each day. However, the researchers detected no great preference by the deer for any of the solutions. Interestingly, however, buck urine scored highest in both study areas. One could theorize that commercial doe-in-heat urine used in the tests was of poor quality, or was just a bad batch. But why shouldn't doe-in-heat urine drawn carefully from the doe's bladder bring bucks running?

The answer seems obvious: Even urine collected directly from the bladder of an estrous doe lacks the magical sex pheromones that attract bucks.

In another investigation, student Mark Whitney and the Georgia professors conducted an involved series of trials with penned deer in which bucks were introduced to does artificially treated with water, estrous urine, non-estrous urine or estrous vaginal secretions. Although individual responses varied, bucks devoted significantly more attention to does treated with estrous vaginal secretions.

These experiments provide evidence that the female reproductive tract and associated vaginal secretions, and not the excretory tract itself, are the primary sources of pheromones during estrous that serve as sexual attractants. Follow-up studies by Brian Murphy, under the guidance of Miller and Marchinton, confirmed these findings. Using seven captive does and three adult bucks, they again anointed the does with test substances and monitored the bucks' behavior. In this series of investigations, however, they used naturally excreted urines, not urine drawn from the bladder.

Once again, all three bucks devoted significantly more attention to females treated with the estrous vaginal secretions, but didn't respond positively to does anointed with non-estrous urine. Interestingly, one of the three bucks was more readily attracted to does treated with estrous urine than he was to those treated with non-estrous urine or water. The investigators emphasize that this buck (2½ years

old) had lived with does in a large outdoor enclosure. The other two bucks (2½ and 3½ years old) had been housed primarily in a barn. Consequently, experience and learning might have affected the buck's ability to discriminate estrous and non-estrous urine.

On the other hand, one of the test bucks performed more courtship approaches on does treated with water than on those treated with non-estrous urine. This exemplifies the unpredictable nature of the white-tailed deer. It might also suggest that deer show individual preferences and demonstrate mate selection.

The Georgia investigators emphasize that deer urine used in commercial lures is collected after it has been excreted naturally. Therefore, it likely contains materials not found in the unattractive bladder urine used in their studies. Whether those scents include pheromones presumably found in estrous vaginal secretions — and whether those pheromones are preserved in the bottle — remains unknown.

The Visual Approach

These and other studies should make us realize that visual cues play an important role in deer scent communication. Using does to test the bucks' responses to scents in the pen studies provided an initial strong visual attraction. Likewise, in Whitney's study, the bare soil apparently drew the attention of deer, even without urine attractants. The direction of the wind and the deer's approach might also play a role.

The scrapes commonly seen during the whitetail's breeding season are highly complex signposts. The average scrape involves much more than urine and glandular secretions that emit complex olfactory signals. The typical scrape also presents distinct visual cues that even humans can recognize.

Humans can't identify buck scrapes by smell at a long distance, but experienced hunters can spy one from far off if they know what to look for. Even if you can't see the pawed turf, the ever-present overhanging branch in the proper setting hints that a scrape is likely.

After observing hundreds, if not thousands, of natural buck scrapes, I was convinced that bucks could hardly resist scent-marking a bowed limb that hung at about head height over a frequently traveled deer trail. I suspected these limbs served as strong visual attractants, and that many of the limbs scent-marked during the summer months represented full-fledged scrapes during the rut.

A Little Trickery

In 1989, I published an article in *The Journal of Wildlife Management,* which explained that mature bucks, under proper habitat conditions, could be induced to scrape at a given location with reasonable regularity. Only a properly positioned bowed overhead limb was necessary. In fact, 24 of 40 such sites that I created in Upper Michigan's square-mile Cusino enclosure on Oct. 8, 1987, became full-fledged scrapes during the following five-week period.

My observations also suggested that preferred scrape sites were those with concentrated deer activity, open understory vegetation, relatively level ground, and moderately dry, easily exposed soil. Many such places exist. The only missing ingredient is the right kind of overhead limb. I conducted a companion study that same year to test whether adding a commercial doe-in-heat urine lure to artificially created scrape sites enhanced buck use. In other words, would lure-treated sites be scraped more frequently than non-treated sites?

Similar to my earlier tests, I selected 20 areas along deer trails that met my criteria for favored scrape sites. Then, at each site, I set up a pair of sugar maple limbs about 30 feet apart overhanging the same trail and trimmed off the leaves and lateral branches. Each limb was 5 to 6 feet long, and bowed slightly downward when suspended horizontally. I positioned the small diameter terminal tips so they were centered about 5 feet above the ground. I then cleared away the leaf litter beneath each limb to expose a circular area of soil about 12 inches in diameter.

Beginning Oct. 8, I applied doe-in-heat lure beneath one randomly selected limb of each pair every Monday, Wednesday and Friday during a three-week period. I compared weekly pawing rates beneath the treated and untreated limbs through Nov. 12, which covered the most active scraping period in northern Michigan.

During the test, bucks pawed 14 treated sites and 14 untreated sites. Six treated sites and seven untreated sites were repawed one or more times. I couldn't prove that treating the scrapes made them more or less attractive.

In 1988, I conducted another study using 25 paired limb sites. This setup gave bucks the chance to paw a 20-by-30-inch oval of freshly exposed soil, which closely resembled an authentic large scrape, or to paw beneath a nearby limb in unexposed soil. I applied no urines or scents to any of the sites.

Before the study, all 50 limbs were kept upright to prevent bucks from scent-marking them. Then, on Oct. 8, I lowered the limbs into position, tilled the soil beneath one of each pair, and monitored scraping activity beneath each limb until Nov. 14. For whatever reason, deer pawing at the test sites was unusually high in 1988, possibly because most of the artificially established sites had also been available, and many were pawed by bucks, in 1987. In 1988, 22 of 25 sites with a large area of exposed soil turned into real scrapes, but so did 23 of 25 sites without exposed soil. Further, many of the 50 sites — including 20 with only the limb and 16 with a limb and exposed soil — were repawed one or more times.

The results agreed with earlier findings, which suggested the overhead limb is more important than exposed soil in scrape site selection by bucks. Also, evidence suggests bucks are just as likely to develop their own scrapes than take over those made by other bucks.

These studies do not represent the last word on the subject. But, they emphasize that buck scrapes involve some important visual attractions to deer, in addition to strong the olfactory stimuli that soon occurs at sites which are reworked and repeatedly rescented.

To Each His Own

Research into the reproductive behavior of white-tailed deer has revealed considerable variations in rutting behavior among bucks, dependent upon their age and breeding experience. Although much of what bucks do is instinctive, many aspects of their behavior change with experience and learning. The elaborate courtship finesse demonstrated by rut-experienced mature bucks, for example, differs greatly from the seek-and-chase courtship style of yearlings.

Even among older rut-experienced bucks, however, there are considerable differences in behavior among individuals. The reasons for this are unknown. One buck might make many times more rubs or scrapes than the next. And now it appears that bucks might even differ in their ability to detect estrous does based on the chemical signals involved in urination.

A Message in the Bottle

Highly active scrapes, no doubt, emit a great deal of aromatic attractiveness. But the identity of those potent olfactory elements — called pheromones — still eludes scientists.

Logically, any deer urine should interest some deer sometimes, but so might Chanel No. 5. If your lure somehow contains those elusive magical sex pheromones, it should do an even better job attracting the big one. But don't be surprised if your lure attracts one deer and repels the next.

Is doctoring the scrape with doe-in-heat lures worth it? I think it's iffy, but this is something each hunter should decide for himself. The right urine lure — used in the right place at the right time for the right buck — might bring results. But I think it's asking a bit much for one lure to consistently attract rutting bucks.

Maybe the neutral results I reported from my studies were caused by low-grade lures or the inevitable bad batch. Maybe a different lure would have produced better results. I can't prove it either way.

But frankly, I see no substitute for developing and applying a good understanding of deer biology and behavior. If you're looking for an easy way to success, I'm afraid your search won't end any time soon.

Charles J. Alsheimer

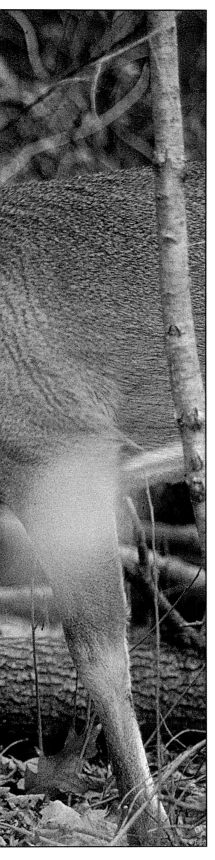

Chapter 6

BUCK-RUB TRAITS:

How to Induce Rubbing

Even the seemingly complex structural components of a deer rub can be reduced to certain basics. Once those basic features are identified, the information can be used to induce rubbing.

Buck rubs are signposts. They're eye-catching, they carry the maker's distinctive odor, and they convey a message to other deer. Therefore, buck rubs are an extension of the maker and function as a sign of his presence, even though he might temporarily be absent from the scene.

It's probably been only a couple of decades since researchers determined that antler-scarred tree trunks possess certain olfactory and visual communicative traits. Now we believe those traits play an important role in white-tailed deer reproductive behavior.

The role of antler rubbing in olfactory communication became more evident when University of Georgia researchers Thomas Atkeson and Larry Marchinton (1982) reported that the forehead skin of whitetails contains glands that become especially active during the breeding season. Further, they found a buck will use secretions from these glands, in conjunction with antler rubbing, to mark his breeding range. Research findings also suggest older, dominant bucks rub more than younger subordinates, and that rubbing activity helps establish

dominance and dominance areas in preparation for the breeding seasons.

Marchinton and Karl Miller, a fellow Georgia researcher, (Marchinton et al. 1990, Miller et al. 1991) propose that signposting by dominant bucks, in the form of antler rubs and ground scrapes, plays a critical role in maintaining social harmony in white-tailed deer populations. These investigators suggest that primer pheromones deposited by dominant bucks at rubs and scrapes help synchronize reproductive cycles, bring adult does into estrus early, and suppress the aggressiveness and sex drive among young bucks — conditions that improve the health and vitality of the herd.

If so, a better understanding of signpost behavior in whitetails could lead to changes in harvest management practices that allow — and sometimes even encourage — exceptionally heavy and untimely cropping of mature bucks. Therefore, knowing which deer make and which deer read buck-rub sign is of more than just academic interest.

Leaving a Mark

At this time in buck-rub research, more

is probably known about message senders than message readers. That is, scientific evidence shows dominant bucks 3½ years and older do most of the rubbing. On the other hand, there isn't much data that shows younger, subordinate bucks and does are the primary inspectors of buck rubs.

As early as 1985, in an article titled, "Marks of Excellence," in *Michigan Sportsman*, I reported observations of deer inspecting fake antler rubs:

"One October evening while my wife, Janice, was assisting me in behavioral observations of the enclosed Cusino herd (in Michigan's Upper Peninsula), we tested the response of deer to artificial rubs. I had cut several nice-sized (1- to 2-inch diameter) aspen saplings from outside the area, scraped them to resemble buck rubs, and literally "planted" them within view of our (separate) blinds.

"The artificial rubs were, of necessity, for show only, as they lacked the most essential ingredient — deer forehead scent. During the evening watch, two bucks approached my blind, but neither paid attention to the fake rub. Surprisingly, nearly all of the dozen or so does and fawns that came near stopped to investigate. One doe seemed particularly puzzled, making three repeat visits, each time carefully sniffing the dummy rub, apparently searching to identify the odor of the mysterious maker.

"Meanwhile, Jan's observations went much the same way, that is until the area's "No. 2" buck came by. He went directly to the fake rub, sniffed it briefly, and then lowered his head and converted the fake into an authentic rub. Unfortunately, I had not planted the stem deep enough. After a few vigorous strokes, the buck toppled the sapling to the ground."

Jan reported: "He just stood there awhile, then calmly walked away as if nothing had happened."

That was my first experience with fake rubs. And to my knowledge, no one else has employed artificial buck rubs in their studies of the whitetail's rut behavior.

Inducing Scrapes

Not until 1991 did I begin to experiment with remote sensing cameras to record deer responses to fake and natural buck rubs. Deer response to the fake rubs was excellent. However, finding a "hot" natural rub to conveniently monitor proved frustrating. As I've mentioned previously, even the seemingly complex structural components of a deer scrape can be reduced to certain basics. Once those basic features

All that was required was to identify the primary components of the ideal rub, and then try to duplicate them. Presto! The result was down-to-earth buck rubs where none had existed before.

are identified, the information can be used to induce scraping without elaborate soil preparation and application of high-tech scent concoctions as some hunters propose. I believe if you put an overhanging limb in the right place and let the bucks do the rest, you'll induce scraping — simple as that.

It seemed to me that the same logic could be applied to buck rubs. All that was required was to identify the primary components of the ideal rub, and then try to duplicate them. Presto! The result was down-to-earth buck rubs where none existed before. Think about what was said earlier: The buck rub is a signpost. It serves for "show and smell." Scientific literature provides considerable insight into the tree and shrub preferences of white-tailed bucks when establishing rubbed signposts. Location, however, is also important.

Duplicating Preferences

The work of Marchinton and Gerald Moore (1974) in southern Georgia produced some of the first solid findings about the communicative role buck rubs play in the whitetail's social organization during the breeding season. They found that Eastern red cedar, winged sumac, sourwood, sassafras, short-leaf pine and longleaf pine were rubbed most often. Stems selected for rubbing ranged from a half-inch to 4 inches in diameter, with the average being about 1 inch.

Follow-up work by Marchinton and Terry Kile (1977) showed bucks preferred to rub trees and shrubs with smooth bark and no lower limbs. They also found aromatic tree species, such as black cherry and sweet gum, were rubbed more frequently than expected. As a result, they suggested the aromatic qualities of a rubbed tree increase its effectiveness as a visual and olfactory signpost. In both of the above studies, researchers reported a clumped distribution of rubs. That is, a newly formed rub was commonly nearby one made earlier, suggesting some locations were preferred for rubbing.

Work conducted by David Nielson and co-workers (1982) on a tree farm in Ohio confirmed much of the Georgia findings. The Ohio study revealed the clumping nature of rubs might be related more to location and size classes of preferred tree species than other factors. Under plantation conditions, bucks commonly struck several small trees in a row or a neighboring row in a single rubbing episode, which led to clumping of rubs. Also, non-preferred trees like hawthorn were sometimes rubbed when found near preferred species, but seldom when growing with other hawthorns in a block. Miller and his associates (1987) found that bucks rubbed 47 of 58 tree species available on study areas in northern Georgia.

Preferred tree species for rubbing included alders, cherries, Virginia pine, Eastern juniper, white pine, common witch hazel and striped maple. Other trees with low branches or warty bark were avoided. The researchers recorded buck-rub densities ranging from 474 to 1,502 rubs per square mile, and they found rub density closely related to the number of bucks older than 2½ years old in the population. That is, older bucks produced far more rubs than younger bucks.

Rub density and distribution also changed each year depending on the abundance of acorns. More rubs were recorded during years of good acorn production when rubs were more concentrated in oak habitat types. Therefore, these researchers concluded that buck-rub counts are not a useful index to buck abundance.

Aside from preferring trees with certain physical characteristics, the above studies generally found rubs concentrated at trail junctions, along old roadbeds and in woods adjacent to open areas, especially where small, aromatic saplings were abundant. Somewhat different results were reported in Maine, where Merlin Benner and Terry Bowyer (1988) documented abundant deer rubs along forested edges of open fields. Twelve species of trees and shrubs were rubbed by deer, among them, staghorn sumac, trembling aspen, and willows; while choke cherry, black cherry, paper birch and sugar maple were avoided. It's interesting to note that sumacs were rubbed often by deer in Maine and Georgia. In contrast, Georgia deer preferred cherry trees while Maine deer avoided them.

Deer in all of the above studies seemed to prefer smooth-barked trees with small trunks devoid of lower branches, but deer in Maine did not show preference for aromatic species as in the Georgia and Ohio studies. Benner and Bowyer concluded: "Some variation in selection by deer of tree species for scent marking on different areas may be explained by the relative abundance of these trees and how likely other deer are to locate scent marks on them."

The Test

Given the above evidence, I decided to use an artificial approach when attempting to induce buck rubs. My general observations agreed with Benner and Bowyer, namely that most attractive buck rubs were found along

More rubs were recorded during years of good acorn production when rubs were more concentrated in oak habitat types. Therefore, these researchers concluded that buck-rub counts are not a useful index to buck abundance.

forest-opening edges where deer could see them from a fair distance. Stems about 2 inches in diameter with no lower limbs were preferred. Also, the stem should be of a type that is easily debarked, not especially hard or warty barked, as most other study evidence has shown.

And when rubbed, the inner cambium of the stem should show a light color with reasonably long-lasting brilliance. Although some researchers suggest bucks prefer aromatic tree species for rubbing, I disagree. Further, I couldn't see why the right kind of stem had to be more than 5 or 6 feet tall. In fact, there seemed no reason why a potentially attractive rubbing stem even had to mimic a real live tree or shrub, as long as it possessed certain properties that made it an effective and attractive signpost.

I tested my theory in the Cusino square-mile enclosure by using trembling aspen, a common and frequently rubbed species in the upper Great Lakes region. On Sept. 24, 1993, I cut 25 aspen saplings, each about 2 inches in diameter, from outside the enclosure. I then cut off their tops and trimmed away all of their branches, leaving poles about 8 feet long. I set them along opening edges after coring out 18-inch-deep holes using a 2-foot length of 2-inch diameter thin-walled pipe. I simply stuck the poles in the holes and tamped the soil firmly to hold them in place.

The Results

Given what other studies had shown and my earlier experience with fake rubs, I was confident at least some poles would be rubbed. As it turned-out, buck response to the poles bordered on the unbelievable. Twelve of the 25 poles were rubbed by bucks during the first week. Within two weeks, 23 poles had been rubbed and many showed signs of repeated rubbing. Within four weeks all 25 had been rubbed, and within five weeks all stems had been rubbed multiple times.

The high frequency of rubbing was certainly a surprise, but the repeated rubbing of the stems was even more mystifying. Generally, except in the case of traditional rubs — rubs that appear at least three years on the same tree that is 3½ inches in diameter or larger as defined by Clemson University researcher Grant Woods — bucks only rerub about 5 percent to 10 percent of their established rubs during the same season.

Having 15 antlered bucks in the enclosure, five of which were 3½ years of age or older, certainly contributed to the high incidence of rubbing. However, these bucks were also terribly deprived of choice rubbing stems. The area had no timber harvesting for more than 20 years. Therefore, preferred rubbing stems in the small size classes were scarce along opening edges, which likely made the artificially placed stems even more attractive.

Two weeks into the study, I set a second unrubbed pole beside each of the 23 poles that had already been rubbed. My question was: Which stem would bucks prefer to rub, one that had already been marked or a new stem? Considering previous research findings, one would expect a revisiting buck to rub the unrubbed stem, thereby leading to rub clumping. That's exactly what happened.

Given the opportunity to rerub or make a new rub, bucks rubbed the new stem. However, in some cases both stems were rubbed during the same 24-hour period. Within three weeks, all of the new poles were rubbed, and 21 of 23 showed signs of being rerubbed. In other words, not only did all 48 aspen poles I placed turn into buck rubs, but 46 of 48 were rerubbed one or more times.

After seeing bucks respond so favorably to aspen stems, I conducted a short experiment using hand-placed poles to determine if bucks had a species preference for rubbing. I chose four species that differed in bark toughness and aromatic quality: aspen, which was easily stripped and non-aromatic; black cherry, which was only slightly more difficult to strip and somewhat aromatic; balsam fir, which stripped quite easily and was highly resinous and aromatic; and sugar maple, which was difficult to strip and non-aromatic. All were cut into pole lengths (2-inch diameter and 8 feet tall) and trimmed of branches.

I again set my test rub poles along small openings, four species randomly positioned about 25 feet apart in a line to assure all four species were offered in the same area at the same time, and that a given stem's position relative to others was not important. I chose 25 locations, and established five lines each week for five weeks, starting Sept. 28. I checked each stem weekly for signs of rubbing, and my last examination occurred Dec. 2.

Of the four species tested, trembling aspen stems scored the highest. They were most frequently rubbed (100 percent) and rerubbed (96 percent), and showed the greatest average rub length (21 inches). Black cherry rated a respectable second place in all three categories

It was also obvious a buck rub didn't have to be aromatic to draw the attention of other deer; it just had to look like one. Deer couldn't really tell a fake was a fake until they just about stuck their nose on it, and even then they didn't seem sure.

(88 percent rubbed, 77 percent rerubbed and average rub lengths of 15 inches). Balsam fir and sugar maple were less frequently rubbed (60 percent and 44 percent, respectively) and seldom rerubbed (20 percent and 9 percent, respectively). Average rub lengths on balsam fir (11 inches) and sugar maple (6½ inches) were also less.

This experiment supported some previous study findings, challenged others and demonstrated that bucks can be induced to make antler rubs when provided with the right kind of stem in the right location. Although I did not test for location, the exceptionally high rate of rubbing success I achieved in these experiments — when poles were placed in forest openings — strongly suggests that openness and good visibility are important factors in determining buck rub signposts. First and foremost, a buck rub should be highly visible to draw the attention of other deer from a fair distance.

What it Takes to Fool a Buck

It was also obvious that a buck rub didn't have to be aromatic to draw the attention of other deer; it just had to look like one. Deer couldn't really tell a fake was a fake until they just about stuck their nose on it, and even then they didn't seem sure. Stem diameter is probably important, but I did not test for size preference. Once again, the high success rate of 2-inch diameter stems indicates bucks like them in that size range, which agrees with results from most other investigations.

Certainly, the fact that I used poles with good success indicates the rub stem's upper structure, or lack thereof, has little to do with determining desirable buck-rub traits. Once again, the stems I used were limbless. Whether bucks would have hit limbed stems as readily is unknown. However, given the experience of other researchers, as well as my own, I believe a lack of limbs on the lower 3 or 4 feet of the stem makes it more preferred for rubbing.

In my study, bucks showed a strong preference for trembling aspen stems, which are smooth barked, easily debarked and non-aromatic, even though this species in the smaller size classes is seldom found in the Cusino enclosure. The enclosure contains small stands of 6- to 12-inch diameter aspen, but aspens of that size tend to have thick, tough bark and normally are not rubbed. This, too, suggests bucks select stems for high visibility, not for aromatic traits.

The use of poles in these relatively simple experiments offers a unique and untapped opportunity to investigate other aspects of buck-rub signposting behavior via rather artificial but highly controlled means. I have used hand-placed stems in conjunction with remote sensing cameras to record some unusual competitive behavior at buck rubs, and I've also used these poles to document buck-rub visitations.

Meanwhile, the imaginative deer hunter might use my system of inducing buck rubs to good advantage, particularly in areas where preferred stems are not readily available.

References

Atkeson, T.D., and R.L. Marchinton. 1982. *Forehead glands in white-tailed deer.* Journal of Mammalogy 63:613-617.

Benner, J.M., and R.T. Bowyer. 1988. *Selection of trees for rubs by white-tailed deer in Maine.* Journal of Mammalogy 69:624-627.

Kile, T.L., and R.L. Marchinton. 1977. *White-tailed deer rubs and scrapes: spatial, temporal and physical characteristics and social role.* The American Midland Naturalist 97:257-266.

Marchinton, R.L., K.V. Miller, R.J. Hamilton, and D.C. Guynn. 1990. *Quality deer management: biological and social impacts on the herd.* Pages 7-15 in Proceedings of the Tall Timbers Game Bird Seminar (C. Kyser, D.C. Season, and J.L. Landers, eds.). Tallahassee, Fla.

Miller, K.V., K.E. Kammermeyer, R.L. Marchinton, and E. Moser. 1987. *Population and habitat influences on antler rubbing by white-tailed deer.* Journal of Mammalogy 51:62-66. * Miller, K.V., R.L. Marchinton, and W.M. Knox. 1991. *White-tailed deer signposts and their role as a source of priming pheromones: a hypothesis.* Transactions of the International Union of Game Biologists Congress 18:455-458.

Moore, W.G., and R.L. Marchinton. 1974. *Marking behavior and its social function in white-tailed deer.* Pages 447-456, in The behavior of ungulates and its relation to management (V. Geist and F. Walthers, eds.). International Union for Conservation of Nature Publication 24:I-511.

Nielson, D.G., M.J. Dunlap, and K.V. Miller. 1982. *Pre-rut rubbing by white-tailed bucks: nursery damage, social role, and management options.* Wildlife Society Bulletin 10:341-348.

Ozoga, J.J. 1985. *Marks of excellence.* Michigan Sportsman. 10:44-46.

Ozoga, J.J. 1994. *"Competitive Signposting."* Deer & Deer Hunting (June 1994).

Bill Lea

Chapter 7

SCRAPE TERMINOLOGY:

Confusing a Complex Topic

In discussing scrape behavior, some folks take tidbits from scientific literature and blow them clear beyond firm, scientific turf. I doubt any other subject about whitetail behavior has been more elaborately abused and fictitiously presented.

A review of popular deer hunting books and magazines reveals an amazing array of jargon about whitetail scraping behavior. There are mentions of many types of scrapes, including boundary, territorial, pause, communal, hub, primary, secondary and more. In fact, it appears we might have "scrapeologists" in our midst.

The implication of such terms is that white-tailed bucks — and sometimes does — purposely use many types of scrapes to convey different messages. Of course, these writers seldom agree on the terms.

Quite frankly, all that terminology is a bit overwhelming — and possibly intimidating — to any serious hunter. I'm the first to acknowledge that scraping behavior — best described as one type of signposting — represents a complex form of scent communication. Unfortunately, some writers have taken tidbits from scientific literature and blown them clear beyond firm, scientific turf. In fact, I doubt any other subject about white-tailed deer behavior has been more elaborately abused and fictitiously presented.

For instance, I was amazed to read an article by a well-known outdoor writer who described in great detail how most primary scrapes are made where a doe leaves estrous urine. The writer failed to state, however, that a mature buck makes 50 percent to 80 percent of his scrapes before the first doe enters estrus. Sometimes mature bucks even scrape in spring, when neither bucks or does are in breeding condition.

Myth and Mysteries

Professors Karl Miller and Larry Marchinton, and their students at the University of Georgia, have probably contributed more to our understanding of whitetail signposting than any other researchers. I asked Miller what he thought of the many types of scrapes identified in deer hunting articles.

"You want my honest opinion?" he asked. "I think it's a bunch of bull ..."

A terse reply, no doubt, but in my view, highly accurate.

Miller warns, "The more we learn about scrape behavior, the more we realize how little we really understand it."

To help unravel some of the mysteries of scrape behavior, Miller suggests we stick to the basics: Carefully consider a scrape's anatomy and physiological reasons before trying to psychoanalyze every bit of pawed turf you find. Recognize that the full scrape sequence involves three behavior patterns: scent-marking overhead limbs, pawing the ground and urinating into the pawed area. Further, these patterns might occur independently of each other year-round.

Also, remember that a buck's scraping ability is determined by his physical, physiological and behavioral maturity. It's also affected by his reproductive condition, dominance status and probably many other factors we don't know much about. Highly dominant, mature bucks invariably do the best job of scraping. Regardless of age, subordinates exhibit minimal scraping.

You might occasionally find 2½-year-old bucks that avidly make scrapes, but only if they're physically and sexually advanced, as well as highly motivated in the absence of older bucks. Even when older bucks are absent, my research shows 1½-year-old bucks make only 15 percent as many scrapes as mature bucks. Some studies suggest these young bucks make no scrapes at all.

Therefore, you'll find little serious scraping activity in deer populations where sires are younger than 3½ years old. These young males become sexually active later in the season, and they exhibit delayed and less intense scraping behavior. They use more of a seek-and-chase style instead.

Overhead Limbs

In the September 1996 issue of *Deer & Deer Hunting*, I discussed the importance of scent-marking by bucks in spring and summer (See "Scent-Talk: Why Deer Think with their Noses" on Page 58). To review, scent-marking overhead limbs probably serves as the primary means of communication among bucks throughout the year. Although some mature bucks demonstrate the full scrape sequence in spring and early summer, most scent-marking of overhead limbs doesn't include pawing except in autumn.

The Georgia researchers found that bucks of all social ranks — from subordinate to dominant — commonly marked branches and inspected those marked by other bucks. Marchinton and his co-workers concluded:

"The temporal distribution of overhead branch marking and the communal use of marking sites suggest that it communicates a buck's identity. In fall, scrapes were usually associated with branches that had been marked during summer, but not all marked branches became scrape sites."

The overhead limb is a critical part of a full-fledged scrape. Take it away, and you'll virtually destroy an active scrape. Conversely, add low-hanging limbs at the right location and new scrapes will form.

What Isn't a Scrape?

That every pawed site is a scrape is no more true than the idea that every scent-marked limb inspires a scrape beneath it. Deer of both sexes occasionally paw the ground for many reasons, sometimes even urinating into the exposed soil. However, I believe pawed sites shouldn't be labeled as scrapes unless an overhead scent-marked limb is present.

The communicative significance of pawing is unknown. However, the Georgia researchers found that bucks commonly pawed the ground before or after aggressive interaction. Bucks sometimes even pawed when approached by dogs or humans. The researchers concluded that pawing was primarily a threat display and sign of dominance.

As part of the full scrape sequence, pawing is closely related to a buck's testosterone level, which determines his dominance and aggression. Subordinate bucks — those with low testosterone levels and/or those psychologically suppressed by dominant bucks — seldom paw. Young bucks might visit and scent-mark limbs above active scrapes, but they rarely paw or urinate into the scrape.

Even the scientific community sometimes falsely labels scrape behavior. References to doe scrapes, for example, probably aren't justified. While does might paw the ground and even urinate at the site, they haven't been observed scent-marking limbs. Because they don't exhibit full scraping sequence, such behavior shouldn't be termed scraping.

Urination combined with squatting and rubbing the tarsal glands together — referred to as rub-urination — is also an important part of a full-fledged scrape. Dominant bucks commonly rub-urinate into their scrapes, leaving a distinctive musky odor. Miller notes that buck urine is much darker in color than doe urine, at least during the rut. This suggests it has a special composition that might relay information about the buck's dominance, health status and reproductive condition.

What the Sequence Means

The complete scraping sequence probably serves two primary purposes: It's an expression of dominance directed at other males, and it allows a dominant buck to advertise his presence, status and breeding condition to females.

Therefore, any given scrape might have a suppressing effect on other bucks, but an attractive and stimulating effect on does. However, there is no evidence that bucks purposely use different scrapes for contrasting messages.

Scrapes are not randomly distributed. They're generally made along deer travel ways or clustered in areas of high activity where they attract the most deer. The area must have an open understory, the duff should be easily removed by pawing, and a suitable overhead limb must be present.

Some hunters have success hunting scrapes along deer trails or travel lanes, which have been tagged by some writers as secondary scrapes and by others as primary scrapes. Most writers, of course, suggest ignoring scrapes they refer to as peripheral, boundary, territorial or perimeter scrapes.

But because bucks are not truly territorial, no scrape is made strictly to mark territory. In fact, all scrapes can be termed communal in nature because all deer are attracted to them. Quite likely, scrapes that draw little or no attention from other deer aren't reworked. Although bucks sometimes defend scrapes from other bucks, subordinates can generally visit and scent-mark overhead limbs, as long as they don't paw or urinate at the sites.

We still have much to learn about adult buck sociability. However, socially compatible bucks probably can travel freely in a dominant buck's breeding range if they behave. In a high-density herd, it's not unusual for six or more bucks to visit and scent-mark limbs at an attractive scrape.

On the other hand, an outsider — especially a young dispersing buck — might not enjoy such freedom. He might even be intimidated by such scent-marks, and be driven off if the dominant buck discovers him at a scrape.

For whatever reason, scrape re-use patterns vary greatly. Some researchers have found that fewer than 15 percent of scrapes were reopened during the same season. But in my studies, 50 percent to 60 percent were reopened. Therefore, it's not surprising some hunters place great importance on locating the so-called primary scrape.

OK, What's a Primary Scrape?

Outdoor writers seldom agree on the definition of a primary scrape. Some consider it to be any full-fledged scrape with frequent repawing. Others reserve the term for highly reworked scrapes visited primarily by estrous does — also referred to as breeding scrapes. Still others claim trails to these scrapes form after the scrapes are made.

The most active scrapes, whatever you call them, are likely to be around the greatest deer activity — provided the habitat is suitable for scraping. Evidence indicates adult does and fawns show interest in scrapes, and are attracted to them, but actual courtship between bucks and does at a particular scrape tends to be exaggerated. For instance, while following tame deer, Timothy Sawyer, a University of Georgia researcher, found that does encountered scrapes by chance. Upon finding a scrape, does frequently stopped to sniff it, walked through it, or occasionally urinated near it.

Related does tend to concentrate their activity in fairly small areas during the breeding season. Does also tend to become active during the rut, but generally in small areas. Bucks, in turn, concentrate their scraping activity in such areas, not only to attract prospective mates, but also to warn competitive bucks. Also, remember that the most intensive scraping activity precedes peak breeding, while peak scrape visitation coincides with peak breeding.

Moore and Marchinton reported that does commonly approached scrapes and urinated into them, leaving a strong scent trail. Upon returning to check his scrape, the buck was then observed making grunting sounds as he encountered the doe's scent trail. With his nose to the ground, the buck generally found the doe within 200 yards of the scrape. In most cases, they associated only briefly.

Does and Scrapes

Pheromones signaling a doe's estrous condition are found in her vaginal secretions; not her urine per se. When deposited with urine, these signals probably remain effective only briefly. In contrast, the doe carries the strongest attractive odors with her. These odors might be detectable 12 or more hours before she will stand for breeding, which gives the dominant buck plenty of time to locate the doe, even if it means chasing off a more alert subordinate. So, in most cases, a buck is courting the doe before she visits a scrape.

In some cases, however, if a buck isn't nearby when the doe approaches estrus, she might wander in search of a mate. Conceivably, she will be attracted to any buck's scrapes she encounters. This might explain an observation by Moore and Marchinton, where a buck and doe bred more than a mile from the scrape where the doe's trail began.

Considering the personal nature of scrapes and the fact bucks tend to cluster scrapes where does concentrate, the question arises: Do female whitetails demonstrate mate selection by selectively visiting scrapes? In theory, the doe that chooses a large-bodied, large-antlered buck is selecting a buck with superior hereditary traits, thus assuring thrifty progeny and perpetuating the herd's genetic fitness.

Conclusion

To date, the above question remains essentially unanswered. Obviously, for such a selective process to work, the sexes must communicate their identity, reproductive state and other critical information. The female must relate specific male odors at the buck's signposts to the individual buck. If does demonstrate a form of mate selection, the scrape might be a good place for the transfer of such information. But, the dominant buck's scrapes also carry a strong message to all other bucks.

Given our current understanding of buck scraping behavior, it seems any hot scrape addresses both needs, no matter what name someone gives it.

References

Kile, T.L., and R.L. Marchinton. 1977. *White-tailed deer rubs and scrapes: spatial, temporal and physical characteristics and social role.* American Midland Naturalist 97:257-266.

Marchinton, R.L., K.L. Johansen and K.V. Miller. 1990. *Behavioral components of white-tailed deer scent marking: social and seasonal effects. Pages 295-301 in D. W. MacDonald, D. Mullar-Schwarze and S. E. Natynczuk, eds.* Chemical signals in Vertebrates 5. *Oxford Univ. Press.*

Miller, K.V., R.L. Marchinton, K.J. Forand and K.L. Johansen. 1987. *Dominance, testosterone levels, and scraping activity in a captive herd of white-tailed deer.* Journal of Mammalogy 68:812-817.

Miller, K.V., R.L. Marchinton and P.B. Bush. 1991. *Signpost communication by white-tailed deer: research since Calgary.* Applied Animal Behaviour Science 29:195-204.

Moore, W.G., and R.L. Marchinton. 1974. *Marking behavior and its social function in white-tailed deer. Pp. 447-456, in V. Geist and F. Walters, eds.* The behavior of ungulates and its relation to management. *Intern. Union of Cons. of Nature Publ. 24:1-511.*

Ozoga, J.J., and L.J. Verme. 1985. *Comparative breeding behavior and performance of yearling vs. prime-age white-tailed bucks.* Journal of Wildlife Management 49:364-372.

Ozoga, J.J. 1989. *Temporal pattern of scraping behavior in white-tailed deer.* Journal of Mammalogy 70:633-636.

Ozoga, J.J. 1989. *Induced scraping activity in white-tailed deer.* Journal of Wildlife Management 53:877-880.

Sawyer, T.G., R.L. Marchinton and K.V. Miller. 1989. *Response of female white-tailed deer to scrapes and antler rubs.* Journal of Mammalogy 70:431-433.

DIRT & INTRIGUE:

How Mock Scrapes Affect the Rut

The author believes the mock scrapes he made, complete with the odor of a foreign buck, were at least partly, if not totally, responsible for social disruptions — namely buck fighting — in the herd.

Scrapes are of great interest to deer hunters, especially big-buck fanatics. One reason for this high interest is that scrapes tend to be made by big, dominant bucks that sometimes return to check and rework their scrapes. In addition, fresh scrapes are highly attractive to passing deer, including subordinate bucks. As a result, well-maintained scrapes can become deer social centers during the rut.

It's no wonder some hunters try diligently to duplicate these deer magnets with artificial, or mock, scrapes in huntable locations. How effective are mock scrapes? When are they most effective? How are they made? Where are they made? Will a dominant buck readily take over a mock scrape? Are they really worth the effort?

Few deer researchers have pondered these questions. However, I've found the man-made scrape to be a useful research tool and a fascinating source of information when studying scent communication.

Bob McGuire:
Father of the Mock Scrape

I've admittedly not scoured popular literature for every possible article on mock scrapes. But as far as I can determine, Bob McGuire is credited with developing the mock scrape concept. If nothing else, he was one of the first to detail the idea in print.

I can appreciate McGuire's feeling of self-satisfaction as he watched the first buck approach one of his mock scrapes. He said it was "a big 10-point Ohio whitetail, with his head low, grunting with every step." That's the potential reward behind employing mock scrapes: making big bucks show up where you want them.

Even if there aren't big bucks in the vicinity, a well-made fake scrape might attract young, subordinate bucks. Yearling and 2½-year-old bucks, as well as does and fawns, seem drawn to inspect anything resembling an authentic scrape.

McGuire's original mock scrape technique was a complex affair. The essential items included a 4-foot-square plastic ground cover; rubber gloves; rubber boots (sprayed with fox urine); a forked 2-foot hardwood stick; bottled swabs taken from the gums, eyes or forehead of freshly killed deer; an assortment of other scents and urines; and a pack basket.

McGuire explained his technique: "After locating a likely looking spot, I spread the plastic sheet and set down my basket pack. Hard swats at the overhanging limb tips with my scraping stick prepare them for whichever odor I apply for marking (normally saliva swabs). To scrape the ground, I pull the stick toward me (as I stand where the buck likely would). I throw the debris a foot or so to both sides of me as I switch hands. Care must be taken not to touch the overhanging limbs. Finally, after depositing buck lure at the nearest edge of the scrape, I back away and pack out."

Testimonials

It seems as though every outdoor writer in the country jumped on the mock-scrape bandwagon during the late 1980s and early 1990s. Dozens of articles expounded the wondrous results of mock scrapes. Each writer seemed to add a few wrinkles to make each scrape even more attractive.

Unfortunately, mock-scrape techniques discussed in popular literature are generally a glowing recount of one person's reported success, and are often based on a test sample of one. Such embellished accounts seldom provide supporting data, and rarely give readers sufficient information to fairly judge the technique's merits. It's also unlikely you'll read much about mock scrape failures.

Changing Views

The scientific method requires an investigator to have controls with which to compare test results. As McGuire's work with mock scrapes continued, he compared buck scraping rates at sites with and without overhead branches, with and without artificial pawing, and with and without scents.

Although his initial mock-scrape efforts involved heavy use of commercial and natural scents and urines, his views changed with experience.

He later wrote: "It is ironic that our own research conclusions now refute much of my past personal experience, and many of my earlier writings. As often happens, this hunter misunderstood much of what he thought he saw."

McGuire eventually concluded: "The most important part of a scrape (to the bucks) is the overhanging marking branch."

That is, if test sites were located in good travel corridors beneath low, drooping branches, "squirting gallons of urine scent made little difference ... in buck take-over rate." In other words, good sites became active scrapes while others did not, regardless of the artificial treatment.

A Complex Structure

A scrape is no simple structure. It represents a complexity of visual and olfactory signals, many of which remain poorly understood. The full-fledged scrape sequence involves mutilation and scent-marking of overhead branches, as well as ground-pawing and urination.

Human duplication of the scrape's visual signals — mutilating the overhead branch and pawing the earth — is relatively simple. However, reproducing the mysterious odor signals that relay significant social information is another matter that might be impossible to imitate given our current lack of understanding.

The Overhead Limb

Based on tests in Upper Michigan's square-mile Cusino enclosure, I discovered preferred scrape sites had important similarities: concentrated deer activity, open understory vegetation, relatively level ground, and moderately dry and easily exposed soil.

Further, when mature bucks were present, it didn't take much to induce them to establish scrapes at such sites. All that was required was a slender, bowed, properly positioned limb of 5 or 6 feet. All I did was center the limb tip about 5 feet above a well-traveled trail.

In my first tests, 24 of 40 such artificially positioned limbs turned into buck scrapes within five weeks — without additional treatment.

Later, I established 100 such limbs, in pairs, throughout the enclosure. That allowed me to test different treatments, using one limb from each pair as the test, and the other as the unaltered control. In subsequent tests, about 80 percent of the artificially positioned limbs became active scrapes each autumn. However, exposing the soil beneath the limbs or applying commercial doe-in-estrus urine did not increase the rate at which bucks made them active.

In other words, my findings generally agreed with McGuire's. Namely, the overhead marking branch is the most important part of the scrape. If you have mature bucks and a proper site, adding an overhanging limb will likely induce a scrape to appear where none existed before. Or, conversely, remove the limb above a scrape and it will soon become inactive.

Pawed Earth

I'm not implying that pawed earth under an overhanging limb is unattractive to deer. For whatever reason, subordinate deer (males and females) seem attracted to exposed soil, even in the absence of urine odors.

As part of his master's degree program at the University of Georgia, Dan Forster tested the attractiveness of bladder-collected urine from bucks, does in heat, does not in heat, and commercial doe-in-heat lure. He used salt water as a control substance. The test materials were automatically sprayed into areas of lightly tilled soil measuring about 3 feet in diameter. The study revealed that deer visited about 25 percent of the test sites each day. However, based on the presence of tracks, deer showed no preference for any of the solutions. Because deer responded just as readily to water, one might assume they were attracted to the sites primarily because of the freshly tilled soil, rather than the solutions sprayed into them.

The Missouri Experience

Grant Woods and Lynn Robbins also studied deer responses to mock scrapes in Missouri. Their technique included the following: "After finding a flat, open area that had some sign of deer use, we would locate a suitable overhanging limb 4 to 5 feet off the ground and less than ¾-inch in diameter. We would rub the limb with our 'scrape-making stick' (any hard wooden stick with a small fork at one end), to remove some of the bark and rough it up fairly well. Then we would scrape all the leaves off the soil in a 2- to 3-foot circle below the limb. We had more success if we removed the top ½-inch of soil along with the leaves. We let this scrape age for two or three days, and then placed scent in the scrape. We applied scent by pouring it over the overhanging limb we had roughed up."

Woods and Robbins also used several commercial scents and human urine to build their mock scrapes. They reportedly "had good responses with all of them, provided we built the scrape as described above." The researchers observed bucks and does using their mock scrapes. They also reported that "deer not only would smell the scrape, but would perform maintenance on it, just as they would a natural scrape."

Todd M. Katke

Although mock scrapes seem to trigger early scraping behavior in bucks, they don't alter breeding activity in does. An overhanging limb is the most critical component of a properly located scrape. Without the branch, a scrape will no longer appeal to whitetails.

Cusino Tests

In 1988, I began a four-year study to evaluate the effect of mock scrapes on the behavior and breeding performance of deer in the Cusino enclosure. I wanted to know how deer responded to artificial scrapes. More importantly, I wanted to see if I could advance the rutting behavior of enclosure bucks and, in turn, trigger earlier-than-normal breeding in enclosure does.

I alternated years of treatment to compare deer response. That is, in 1989 and 1991 I made mock scrapes, while in 1988 and 1990 I applied no special treatment.

For my testing, I used the 100 artificially positioned limbs I established previously. Beneath one limb of each pair I made a mock scrape, while the companion limb served as the control and received no treatment. As a result, during treatment years, I made and maintained 50 mock scrapes.

In addition to having an overhead limb, I scraped away the leaves to imitate pawing and added about 2 ounces of urine collected from a prime-age buck during the rut. During treatment years, I serviced the 50 mock scrapes daily from Sept. 5 to Oct. 6, but only freshly pawed the mock scrapes twice a week from then until Nov. 7.

I tallied all scraping activity in and around the 100

BUCK DROPS ANTLERS ONE MONTH APART

In white-tailed bucks, the timing of antler casting depends largely on a decline in blood levels of testosterone, the male hormone.

Physically weakened and malnourished bucks generally drop their antlers first. It tends to happen suddenly. One day a buck can literally be dragged by his antlers, but a day or two later the antlers can fall under their own weight.

Because antler casting is controlled by hormones, both antlers usually drop off about the same time, sometimes only minutes apart, but seldom more than a few days apart. In fact, on a few occasions I've found shed antlers lying side by side in the Cusino enclosure, as if they fell simultaneously while the buck gazed about.

During Winter 1989-90, however, I was mystified when the enclosure's most dominant buck (then 8 years old) dropped one antler Dec. 23 and the second on Jan. 22, nearly a month apart.

For whatever reason, 1989 was a time of serious social turmoil in the Cusino enclosure. Two bucks died from fighting injuries, one Nov. 4, the other Nov. 14, only a few hours after serious combat. I believe the most dominant buck — which later demonstrated the asynchronous antler casting — was involved.

A search of scientific literature revealed few clues as to why a buck would retain one antler much longer than the other. However, Czechoslovakian researcher Dr. Ludek Bartos observed that older and highly dominant male red deer are most likely to drop antlers several weeks apart.

According to another antler authority, Dr. George Bubenik of Ontario, frequent fighting contributes to hyperactive adrenal glands, increased secretion of certain steroids, and prolonged elevated blood levels of testosterone. Such stress occurs most often among highly dominant animals when frequently challenged by other prime-aged bucks. Super high testosterone levels result, causing unusually deep mineralization of the antler pedicle, which can cause prolonged and uneven antler retention.

Bubenik has also observed that damage to blood vessels around the pedicle can result from fighting, or rubbing trees or fencing. Such damage can disrupt nutrient flow to the antler base and influence antler retention, sometimes causing earlier casting of one or both antlers.

Therefore, Bubenik believes, and I agree, that "asynchronous antler casting is a sign of psychological stress and social disruption within the population."

— *John J. Ozoga*

sites weekly from September through November. I also periodically set remote sensing cameras to monitor activity at the mock scrapes. I determined individual doe reproductive performance by capturing and X-raying each doe in March. Fetuses observed on X-rays were aged, and back-dated to determine breeding dates.

Mock Scrapes Attract Deer

Deer visited about one-third of the mock scrapes daily during September, as evidenced by tracks in the tilled soil. More than 90 percent of the sites were visited during the first week after their construction. The daily visitation rate in September was nearly double that of earlier studies when I only tilled the soil beneath limbs. Therefore, it appears buck urine odor enhanced the attractiveness of the mock scrape sites.

The response of deer to mock scrapes varied highly, but did not seem selective. That is, based on photographs of 67 deer at mock scrapes, bucks, does and fawns visited the sites in about the same proportions as they existed in the population. Some deer were photographed as they smelled and examined the mock sites, while others simply walked by with no interest.

Intensity and Patterns

Scraping intensity varied during my study. I recorded 183 scrapes in 1988, 218 in 1989, 140 in 1990 and 140 in 1991. In other words, scraping intensity was highest during the first year of mock scraping, but was not higher than normal the second year.

Annual differences in scraping intensity were probably caused by differences in the behavior of individual bucks. Bucks in 1988 and 1989 not only made more scrapes, but were also more responsive to mock scrapes than bucks in the 1990 and 1991 populations.

Seasonal scraping patterns during the nontreatment years (1988 and 1990) were similar to patterns recorded previously when mature bucks were present. In 1988 the first scrape appeared Sept. 26, and in 1990 the first scrape was made Oct. 2. Less than 2 percent of the scraping occurred before Oct. 3. As expected, peak scraping during the control years occurred the last week of October and the first week of November, when more than 50 percent of the season's total scraping took place.

I had little doubt, however, that early mock scraping stimulated the enclosure bucks, which led to earlier-than-normal scraping. In 1989, the first scrape was made Sept. 6, less than 24 hours after mock scraping started, and scraping escalated rapidly thereafter. I recorded 32 scrapes by Sept. 26, 1989, compared to only one during the same period in 1988.

Although the effects of mock scraping were not so dramatic and were overall less intense, in 1991 a similar advanced seasonal pattern of scraping prevailed. The first scrape was made Sept. 9. Nine scrapes, or 7 percent of the season's total, were tallied by Sept. 26. As in normal years, peak seasonal patterns of scraping occurred the last week of October and the first week of November, even with early September mock scraping.

Repawing Rates

Bucks readily pawed my mock scrapes, but were twice as likely to repaw scrapes they initiated. In 1989, for example, bucks pawed 39 of 50 mock scrapes, but only six were pawed three or more times. By comparison, bucks converted 40 of 50 paired (untreated) limbs into scrapes, 14 of which they reopened three or more times.

While bucks commonly pawed my mock scrapes, they often pawed and maintained their own circle of exposed soil beside the scrape I made. In other cases, they enlarged my area by pawing the mock scrape edge, sometimes exposing an unusually large area, but they only maintained their portion.

This suggests bucks will take over mock scrapes, but are more inclined to form and maintain their own scrapes, albeit, nearby and occasionally under the same limb.

Does Unaffected

While mock scraping in early September induced earlier-than-normal scraping activity among enclosure bucks, the breeding dates of does weren't affected. Regardless of treatment, or lack thereof, the first enclosure does bred each year during the first week of November. Although a few bred in December, most bred during November. During the four-year study, mean breeding dates ranged from Nov. 16 to 18, the normal pattern in this Northern environment. In other words, earlier-than-normal scraping behavior by bucks did not

trigger earlier-than-normal estrus in does.

Unexpected Consequences

Granted, small sample sizes can cause erroneous conclusions. Nonetheless, the fighting mortality of four mature bucks during this study, plus one a year later, seems more than coincidental.

Two bucks (3½ years old and 7½ years old) died from fighting injuries in 1989 (a mock scrape year); two (3½ years old and 4½ years old) died in 1991 (a mock scrape year); and one (5½ years old) died in 1992 (one year after the study).

To my knowledge, no enclosure bucks died from fighting injuries during the previous 24 years, not even in 1977 when 47 antlered bucks were in the herd. This leads me to believe that my mock scrapes (complete with the odor of a foreign buck) were at least partly, if not totally, to blame for the social disruption that resulted.

Conclusion

Mock scrapes, complete with overhead limbs, pawed earth, and rutting buck urine can attract deer and influence their behavior, provided the scrapes are properly built and located in areas of high deer activity.

In my studies, intense mock scraping in September induced earlier-than-normal scraping in bucks. However, advanced buck-rutting activity did not trigger earlier-than-normal estrus in does.

If a mock scrape looks good and is in the right place, it will likely draw the attention of subordinate bucks, does and fawns. The mere presence of a good overhanging branch in a travel corridor will likely encourage bucks to open a scrape, and tilling the soil beneath the limb might improve the site's attractiveness.

Applying scents and urines to a mock scrape, however, does not seem critical. In fact, applying rutting buck urine to a mock scrape might sometimes discourage bucks from converting a mock scrape into a real one, and could even produce some unpleasant consequences.

In my view, this is a fascinating subject deserving further study.

References

Forster, D.L. 1988. *Attractiveness of conspecific bladder urine in white tailed deer.* M.S. Dissertation. University of Georgia. 62 pages.

McGuire, B. 1983. *Advanced Whitetail Hunting Techniques.* B.H.P. Books, Johnson City, Tenn. 37602. 124 pages.

McGuire, B. 1988. *"Scrape Secrets."* American Hunter. June, pages 38, 39, 62, 64.

Ozoga, J.J. 1989. *Induced scraping activity in white-*tailed deer. Journal of Wildlife Management. 53:877-890.

Ozoga, J.J. 1989. *Temporal pattern of scraping behavior in white-tailed deer.* Journal of Mammalogy. 70:633-636.

Weiss, J. 1987. *Advanced Deer Hunting: New Strategies Based on the Latest Studies of Whitetail Biology and Behavior. Outdoor Life Books. 334 pages.*

Woods, G. and L. Robbins. 1987. *"The Biology of Scrape Hunting, Part 3."* North American Whitetail. *November, pages 8-11, 68-69.*

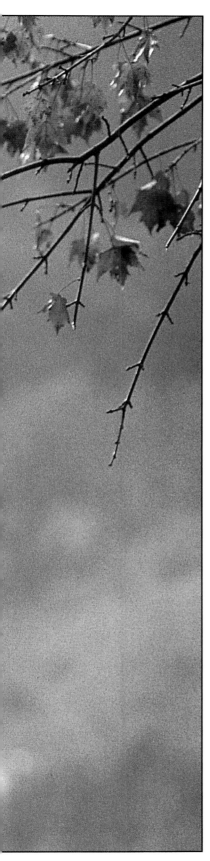

Chapter 9

THE OVERHEAD LIMB:

Is it a Sign Only Bucks Understand?

Without the overhead limb there is no full-fledged scrape. Period! I found that does and fawns paid more attention to olfactory messages deposited through urine in pawed soil than to glandular secretions left on overhead limbs. Bucks, however, were highly attracted to limbs above active scrapes.

The limb above a well-pawed scrape is intriguing. Sometimes it's a large, elaborate branch with many tips. Frequently, however, that special limb above the scrape consists only of one slender arching stem — similar to a bent fishing pole — with a mutilated, pencil-thin tip. And yet when that fragile twig is carefully manipulated and anointed by bucks, it takes on magical powers that draw passing bucks like an electro-magnet sweeping up pins. Without the overhead limb there is no "full-fledged" scrape. Period! Think about that.

Take away the limb and the most traditional, diligently pawed scrape disappears. Add a limb in the right location, however, and bucks paw the turf with dedication, forming a new scrape where none had ever existed.

How can these frail, frayed twigs, marked with some mysterious substance (or substances), command so much attention? When are they made? Why are they made? Who marks them? With what? Who reads them? What messages do they convey? Researchers have pondered these questions for several decades, because the scrape is a much more complex puzzle than most hunters realize. It has many pieces, and each new bit of information helps make the overall picture a little clearer.

Remember, whitetails are social creatures that normally live in dense cover. Individual recognition and communication are essential for them to live together harmoniously and, in fact, are critical for the species' survival. With a forest-dwelling animal like the whitetail, scent-marking might play a more important role in communication than visual signals or vocalizations.

Karl Miller, a University of Georgia researcher who is one of North America's leading authorities on scent communication in whitetails, states: "Deer have evolved a system of scent communication that involves placing signposts throughout their range. These signposts relay information on the identity of deer in an area, along with their sex, dominance status and reproductive condition."

Researchers at the University of Georgia have focused their attention on determining the role scent-marking plays in the whitetail's reproductive behavior. In the process, they've solved many mysteries that once surrounded antler rubbing and scraping behavior. Only recently, however, have these investigators attempted to describe the types and frequencies of scent-marking done by both sexes throughout the year.

What Does it Say?

In August 1988 at the "Chemical Signals in Vertebrates V Conference," held in Oxford, England, U-Georgia's Larry Marchinton presented a paper titled, "Behavioral Components of White-tailed Deer Scent Marking: Social And Seasonal Effects." Marchinton summarized the results of many studies at the university, emphasizing that, "much remains to be learned about year-round marking and its function in this species."

The Georgia work indicates scraping, in particular, represents a highly complex combination of various behaviors. The full scrape sequence combines overhead branch-marking, ground-pawing and urination. These actions suggest that scraping carries several messages and serves multiple functions. Although most scraping occurs in the autumnal rut period, deer also scrape at other times of the year. This is another reason to suspect that scrapes serve different purposes in different seasons.

Bucks, in particular, might paw the ground independently of the full scrape sequence. Marchinton noted that this occurred most often before or after competitive interactions, but even sometimes when bucks were approached by dogs or humans. The communicative significance of pawing is unclear, but Marchinton believes that pawing, as a separate behavior, is an unlikely source of olfactory cues, and is primarily a visual threat or dominance display.

Does also occasionally paw the ground, sometimes even urinating in the site they paw. But seldom, if ever, do they mark overhead branches in association with their pawed areas.

Part of the Puzzle

Overhead branch-marking can be performed as an important part of the full scrape sequence, or it can be done separately. The Georgia research, conducted in small pens, revealed that unlike antler rubbing and ground-pawing, white-tailed bucks readily marked over-

Although most scraping occurs in the autumnal rut period, deer also sometimes scrape at other times of the year. This is another reason to suspect that the scrape serves different purposes in different seasons.

head branches year-round. Bucks of all social ranks commonly marked branches and inspected those marked by other bucks.

Marchinton suggested that overhead branch-marking during the non-reproductive period communicates a buck's identity. He also reported that some, but not all, branches scent-marked by bucks during summer become scrape sites in autumn.

Observing a Herd

I had a special opportunity to investigate branch-marking by whitetails in the square-mile Cusino Enclosure in Upper Michigan. Why was this opportunity special? For two reasons: One, I had developed a convenient technique for determining the frequency of limb-marking; and two, I dealt with a fairly wide-ranging captive herd of known sex and age composition that displayed normal social behavior patterns.

I had earlier shown that bucks could easily be induced to scent-mark limbs and scrapes where I wanted. All that was necessary was to have the proper type of overhead limb in the right place. Based on my observations, I concluded that preferred scrape sites were those with concentrated deer activity, open understory vegetation, relatively level ground, and moderately dry, easily exposed soil. The ground could definitely not be brush-covered or sod-bound.

Given the presence of rut-experienced mature bucks, an artificially positioned limb at such a site attracted bucks, encouraged them to scent-mark, and resulted in regular scrape-making. In the above-mentioned study, 24 of 40 such test sites turned into scrapes within a five-week period. An even higher success rate was achieved in subsequent years.

In 1988, I arbitrarily divided the Cusino Enclosure into 15 compartments that averaged about 42 acres in size. Within each compartment, I selected one to four favorable scrape sites that lacked overhead limbs. In all, I selected 50 sites. I then set up two sugar maple saplings (trimmed of leaves and lateral branches) about 30 feet apart along a deer trail at each site to serve as scent-marking limbs. The stems varied from about 4 to 8 feet in length, but each was relatively slender and bowed slightly downward when suspended over the trail. These 100 limbs, distributed throughout the enclosure, served as my experimental sites the next five years.

In April 1988, I positioned one limb from each pair so its tip was centered about 5 feet over the trail, making it available to deer for marking. The companion limb at each site was left in an upright position so deer could not scent-mark it. My objective here was twofold: One, I wanted to determine if the enclosure's deer scent-marked during summer; and two, I wanted to determine if prior scent-marking played a major role in establishing scrapes in autumn.

The advantage of my scheme, of course, was that I not only had established areas to inspect for pawing, but I also had a large number of specific limb tips to examine for evidence of scent-marking.

From May 2 through Nov. 21, 1988, I examined the 50 limb tips weekly for deer hair and/or evidence of mutilation by deer, and the ground beneath them for evidence of pawing. When I found the first test site pawed by deer on Oct. 3, I lowered the 50 companion limbs in the same manner and inspected them weekly for the rest of the study.

In 1990, I again monitored deer scent-marking and pawing rates at the test sites from May through late November. This time, though, I positioned all 100 limbs for use by deer throughout the observation period. Because there was little difference in study results between years, I pooled the data from both years to illustrate the seasonal pattern of scent-marking, limb breakage and ground-pawing at the test sites.

Reaction to Introduced Limbs

Based on limb breakage or the presence of deer hair on the limb tips, I found 94 percent of the test limbs were scent-marked by deer. Further, 60 percent were scent-marked before scraping started. I detected especially frequent limb-marking in May and June when the only evidence was deer hair stuck to the limb tips. Intense limb-marking from late October through November often included damage to the limb or its tip, which was commonly accompanied by pawing of the soil beneath the limb. Obviously, however, some subtle marking of the limb tips could have gone undetected.

It's interesting that I detected no serious limb-tip mutilation until October, at the same time bucks began to paw the sites. Deer marked overhead limbs gently during summer (non-reproductive months), giving heavily used limb tips an oily or greased appearance. They treated the limbs more roughly during autumn (reproductive period). This suggests the manner in which deer scent-mark limb tips changes seasonally. It also hints that substances deposited and messages conveyed might differ throughout the year.

Keep in mind that the deer in my study were offered a simple limb for scent-marking, which likely minimized the amount of certain "pre-conditioning" behaviors reported by other researchers. That is, deer did not have to pull off leaves or nip buds from the stem before depositing scent.

In the 1988 tests, deer tended to scrape more beneath limbs that were available for scent-marking all summer. Forty of 50 (80 percent) limbs that were in a down posi-

tion all summer developed into scrapes, and 17 were repawed during three or more weeks of study. By comparison, although deer formed scrapes beneath 31 of 50 (62 percent) limbs that were not set up until October, only seven sites were repawed with such intensity.

Most (25 of 30, or 83 percent), but not all, overhead limbs scent-marked during Summer 1988 developed into scrapes in autumn. On the other hand, 15 of 20 overhead limbs (75 percent) that did not show obvious scent-marking during summer also became scrapes in autumn.

Although active scrapes were distributed evenly among the 15 compartments, most summer scent-marking occurred at sites in the enclosure's northern one-third, where adult bucks were known to concentrate.

Further Monitoring

From May 1991 through February 1992, I used the TrailMaster infrared triggering system in conjunction with remote sensing cameras to photograph deer using overhead limbs. I employed various protocol, including a random sampling of the 100 test sites, but I also monitored other natural sites that seemed to exhibit abnormally high deer use.

The TrailMaster system served ideally for this study. The infrared beam could be directed just beneath the limb tip, or at ground level, to compare markers and readers of the overhead branches with those at the pawed scrape. Results of these photographic studies confirmed my suspicions and supported Marchinton's findings. Namely, that the primary markers and readers involved in limb-marking are bucks. Of 76 deer photographed marking or inspecting overhead limbs, 65 (85.5 percent) were bucks, five (6.6 percent) were adult does, and six (7.9 percent) were fawns, despite a herd comprised of roughly 30 percent bucks, 30 percent does, and 40 percent fawns.

Bucks were detected marking or inspecting limb tips during each month of study except for September. However, peak periods of limb-tip activity, as determined by photography, were May, October and November, which agreed with my gross examination of limb tips during 1988 and 1990. Even then, however, only two to three deer were seen at the limb tips for every 1,000 hours of monitoring.

While that might seem a low marking rate, just think of the thousands of limbs available to deer for marking. Bucks, in particular, must scent-mark dozens of times, or possibly even hundreds of times, during their daily travels. Certainly, the deer's world must literally fume with chemical signals at every turn.

None of my 100 test-limb sites was pawed by deer in May or June. However, deer pawed several other sites each spring and summer, indicating the full scrape sequence played a subtle but potentially important role in buck behavior even during the nonreproductive period. Typically, bucks exhibit a slight rise in testosterone production in spring, which might contribute to such behavior, particularly among mature bucks.

For example, camera monitoring at one site on April 30 revealed a large 4½-year-old buck standing on his hind legs to mark limbs more than 6 feet above the ground. Also, fresh urine could be seen in the pawed site. About three hours later, a 2½-year-old buck inspected the site.

Seasonal Differences

Because of deep snow and cold weather, bucks in the enclosure leave much of the uplands in winter and congregate in protective lowland conifers. In spring, soon after snow-melt, bucks seem anxious to return to their traditional summering grounds. These are uplands at the enclosure's north end, which are dominated by sugar maples. Although this habitat provides limited browse after the leaves fall, it typically supports lush and highly nutritious herbaceous growth in the form of flowering plants in spring and early summer, the critical antler-growing period.

My observations indicate that, at least on Northern range, bucks intensively scent-mark their favored summer habitat as soon as they return in spring, probably as a means of reclaiming range that was vacant for about four months.

Such marking, which is done primarily on overhead limbs, could serve to intimidate other deer, including pregnant females that require solitude for fawn-rearing. This could thereby help distribute the herd more evenly and segregate the sexes during the non-breeding period.

If you're fortunate enough to find an active scrape in spring or early summer, you can be assured at least one resident buck survived the previous autumn and winter. Generally, this will be a site that was actively worked the previous autumn.

During the pre-rut and rut in October and November, I found that limbs overhanging certain active scrapes attracted considerably more attention than normal. In November 1992, for example, deer inspected or marked limbs above choice scrape sites at an average of 15 deer per 1,000 hours of monitoring vs. only three deer per 1,000 hours at randomly selected scrapes.

Community Signposts

Of 16 adult bucks in the enclosure during 1992, all

Watching a buck marking an overhead branch is somewhat like watching a baseball coach using coded sign language to signal a batter or base runner — the many signals tend to include numerous meaningless gyrations that confuse all but the well-informed viewer.

but two (one of which was injured) were identified in photographs at limb tips overhanging active scrapes. Seven different bucks were photographed at one limb between Nov. 6 and Nov. 12, while five were recorded at another between Oct. 23 and Oct. 28.

It was rarely possible, however, to determine beforehand which limbs would attract the most attention. That is, limbs overhanging the largest scrapes did not always attract the most attention. Of the two most active limbs I found, one was a limb I had placed and the other was a large aspen branch that had broken loose and lodged so its tip hung head-high over a two-track woods road. Most bucks were photographed smelling the limb tip, some had their antlers or forehead up to the limb, and others were obviously mouthing the tip or moving it along their snout. Most of the scent-marking seemed to be by bucks 3½ years or older, especially during the breeding period. But even younger bucks marked limbs during summer.

Watching a buck marking an overhead branch is somewhat like watching a baseball coach using coded sign language to signal a batter or base runner — the many signals tend to include numerous meaningless gyrations that confuse all but the well-informed viewer. When marking overhead limbs, a buck might mouth the limb gently; chew it vigorously; thrash it with his antlers; or rub it with his nose, chin, cheek, forehead or preorbital area. Even when in velvet, it's difficult to determine if the buck uses his antlers or only his forehead area.

These same mysteries are evident in my photographic documentation of buck limbing behavior. Secretions of likely importance in limb-marking might come from the forehead glands, preorbital glands, nasal glands or saliva. It might well be that a number of glandular secretions are used in concert, and that the use of any given secretion varies seasonally. (Some members of the deer family reportedly use their velvet antlers to transfer body secretions to signpost limbs.) At this point I just don't know. And I defy anyone to give me a sound, scientifically based answer.

Nonetheless, given the seasonal differences we see in limb use, the signal ingredients and messages conveyed must change. I speculate that secretions from nasal glands or preorbital glands (or possibly from some yet unidentified source), in conjunction with saliva, play an important communal role among bucks year-round.

Meanwhile forehead glandular secretions, associated with antler thrashing of the limbs, become more important in conveying dominance status during the breeding season.

Mark of the Maker

Remember, the individual deer's signposts serve as extensions of the animal. That is, the rub, scrape and scent-marked limbs serve as visual and olfactory reminders to other deer that the maker is not here now, but was earlier and will be later.

During the nonbreeding period, such sign might carry a rather congenial message: "If you'd like, leave a message and I'll get back to you as soon as possible."

On the other hand, during the rut, that message might convey a totally different meaning, indicating the "No. 1" buck is still alive, healthy and ever-present. "So beware! Heed my warning, or be prepared to suffer the consequences."

It might be more than coincidence that two of my most photogenic bucks (at limb tips) later died from injuries sustained in fighting. Their physical strength obviously did not match their egos. On Nov. 25, 1991, I found a 4½-year-old buck dead in the stream that bisects the enclosure. His front shoulder was shattered and he had suffered severe gashes on one hind quarter. He had been an avid limb-marker all autumn, even when his gouged hip showed clearly on the film.

On Oct. 17, 1992, I found a 5½-year-old buck dead near one of the enclosure's feeders. He had no external gashes, but a necropsy revealed his back and sides were pulverized, apparently from repeated pounding after he was down and unable to rise. He had been photographed limb-marking less than 24 hours earlier. Of the five adult does photographed, two were tallied in November, and one each during June, July and August. Two fawns (animals less than 1 year old) were tallied in November, two in January and one each in December and February.

Given that the artificially placed limbs were positioned so the tips were about 5 feet off the ground — considered to be about normal height — four of the six fawns photographed raised one or both front hoofs off the ground to reach the limb tip.

Unfortunately, I could not determine the sex of those fawns. I'd be willing to bet, however, that male fawns were more involved than females in such signal testing. Also, such behavior by male fawns could be associated with puberty, wherein those that achieve sexual maturity (probably by late November or early December) respond most readily to adult male scent-marking.

In addition, I photographed 68 deer at ground level in or near active scrapes between Oct. 21 and Nov. 22 in 1991. Included in the photographs were 23 bucks, 12 does and 54 fawns. Compared to the known herd composition, these observations were not significantly different than expected. In other words, all deer were attracted to scrape sites, but does and fawns paid more attention to olfactory messages deposited through urine in pawed soil than to glandular secretions left on overhead limbs. Bucks, however, were highly attracted to limbs above active scrapes.

Conclusion

My observations are in general agreement with those of Marchinton, indicating that does and fawns do little scent-marking on overhead limbs. However, I did not expect to see such a strong sex difference. If a doe visited an active scrape, and smelled the urine-marked soil, I would have expected her to also smell the overhead limbs, which was not always the case.

Until I see strong evidence to the contrary, I'm inclined to believe that messages attached to overhead limbs by white-tailed bucks are primarily for the benefit of other bucks. More importantly, although limb-marking serves as a mode of communication among bucks year-round, the precise messages being exchanged probably differ with the seasons.

Charles J. Alsheimer

Survival of the Herd

A COMBAT WITH NATURE

D eep December snows, genetic mutations, overbrowsed habitat and dwindling food sources are just a few of the many disruptions that complicate the whitetail's world.

Despite constant individual setbacks and deaths, the species continues to thrive because of the whitetail's incredible ability to adapt, improvise and overcome when encountering nature's many obstacles. These challenges range from imminent mortal danger they encounter almost daily to long-term stress factors that wear on them from season to season or even year to year.

Deer must also cope at times with freakish biological occurrences that afflict individuals within the herd. So far, though, no matter what the battle, whitetails have exhibited an unwavering will to survive.

Chapter 1

WEATHERING WINTER:

The Deeryards of Old

The whitetail's environment is not static. It has always been in constant change, even in the absence of European settlers. Furthermore, whitetails have always demonstrated some degree of shelter-seeking behavior when faced with severe winter weather.

Many believe that before 1850, whitetails were scarce, or even absent, from much of the nation's Northern Forest, which includes northern Minnesota to Michigan and northern New York state to northern Maine. Some believe deer did not exhibit yarding behavior before the advent of settlement and extensive logging.

Others, however, including myself, contend that white-tailed deer lived throughout this Northern region before the white man arrived, albeit usually in low numbers. I also believe whitetails have always demonstrated some degree of shelter-seeking, or yarding, behavior when faced with severe winter weather.

Whitetails typically yard up on Northern range during winter for two main reasons: energy conservation and as a defense against predators. The selective pressures for this adaptation likely existed since the Ice Age, when the adaptable whitetail first advanced northward. This probably occurred about 10,000 to 15,000 years ago behind the receding ice sheets that once covered most of the whitetail's current Northern range.

Forests Always Had Openings

There is also considerable debate about the region's forest cover before the white man's arrival. Many historians present a picture of towering virgin pines blanketing the North before the logging era — which would have provided inhospitable habitat for whitetails throughout the year. Other evidence, however, suggests the region's forest cover was broken by windfalls, wildfires and insect infestations, creating varied habitat that supplied favorable food and cover for whitetails year-round.

In their 1959 review of forest-cover conditions and deer population densities in early northern Wisconsin, (published in the *Wisconsin Academy of Sciences, Arts and Letters*, Volume 48), J.R. Habeck and J.T. Curtis provided evidence that many areas in northern Wisconsin and Michigan's Upper Peninsula offered good summer range for whitetails before 1850. Apparently, all the land was not covered by towering pines.

In their words: "There seems little doubt that the early northern Wisconsin landscape was actually a mosaic of forest types, with mature, secondary and pioneer communities (of trees) interspersed. The intervention of natural catastrophes, particularly fire, prevented the (growth) of a vast, unbroken virgin forest."

As early as 1736, Jesuit missionary J.P. Aulnean observed that American Indians were responsible for some fires in the Lake Superior region. He wrote: "I journeyed nearly all the way through fire and a thick stifling smoke which prevented us from even catching a glimpse of the sun. It was the savages who in hunting had set fire to the woods, without imagining, however, that it would result in such a terrible conflagration."

While on a government assignment to survey the Wisconsin and Michigan border in the early 1840s, Capt. T.J. Cram described the following:

"All the timber which was once pine has been consumed by fire, as far as the eye can reach, all round on every side. The prospect is one of a broken landscape of barren hills, studded here and there with charred pine stubs with scarcely a living tree except the second growth of white birch and poplar."

Dr. J.G. Norwood, a professional geologist, traveled through northwestern and northcentral Wisconsin from 1847 to 1848. He gave this account of conditions 25 miles south of what is now Superior, Wis.:

"A good deal of it is prairie, covered with wortleberry (*Vaccinium*) and strawberry vines; while in the low grounds, hazel abounds. Small pines, birch and scrubby oak succeeded, with strips of sugar maple. From this point to Kettle River, the country presents a succession of small lakes, swamps, meadows and ridges covered with birch and small pines."

These and similar accounts led Habeck and Curtis to conclude — given what is now known about the whitetail's habitat requirements — that "deer could not have been scarce in northern Wisconsin prior to 1850. It is more likely that deer were rare only in a relative sense, compared with the abnormally high densities that build up after extensive cutting, man-made fires and predator control."

Based on their analysis of historical records, Habeck and Curtis also wrote: "There was apparently a sufficient number of lowland swamp communities in early northern Wisconsin to meet the winter range requirements of the deer, which were present at that time. Prior to 1850, the deer population density in northern Wisconsin could not have been limited by the winter range."

Habeck and Curtis acknowledge: "More recently, however, the winter range in northern Wisconsin has played a very important role in limiting deer density. The area of white cedar communities has decreased greatly. The present acreage of white cedar swamps is approximately 182,000 acres if it's considered that white cedar occupied but one-third of the lowland areas in northern Wisconsin in 1850 (about 747,000 acres), which may be taken as a minimum, the decrease of cedar swamps amounts to more than 75 percent."

Habitat in Flux

The whitetail's environment is not static. It has always been in constant change, even before European settlers arrived. Differing weather patterns, the impact of American Indians and other predators — or lack thereof — and the changing characteristics of vegetation must have presented good and bad times for deer in Northern forests, which are at the extremity of the whitetail's geographic range.

Records regarding the relative abundance of whitetails in the Upper Great Lakes before settlement are sketchy and often contradictory. However, in 1953, A.W. Schorger published numerous notes about whitetails in this region. His notes appeared in the *Wisconsin Academy of Sciences, Arts and Letters* (Volume 42). While citing 104 references, he generally concluded that, while whitetails were generally scarce in northern Wisconsin and Upper Michigan before 1850, they might have periodically been more abundant than some sources lead us to believe.

As early as 1850, J.W. Foster and J.D. Whitney, while reporting on Upper Michigan's geology, wrote: "Within this township (Iron County) the Mackigamig (river) receives from the right its two principal tributaries, the Mitchikau or Fence River and the Nebegomiwini or Night-Watching River. The origin of these terms as explained by our voyageurs was this: At one time the deer were observed to be very numerous about the mouth of the former, and the Indians, to secure them, built a fence from one stream to the other. They (deer) would follow rather than leap over this barrier, until they were entrapped by their concealed foe. This method of capturing the deer is also practised on the Menomonee."

I might add, the Indians' use of drift fencing to capture deer might also lend some credence to naturalist George Shiras' notion that many deer from Upper Michigan, as well as from northern Wisconsin, migrated southward during winter.

A similar report from northeastern Wisconsin (Vilas County), says that three Indians, employing a 15-mile long fence, killed 150 deer, "for their hides only," in a few days.

If American Indians were that successful in capturing deer with fencing, deer must have been abundant. Either that or they moved through the area in great numbers at certain intervals, most likely early winter and spring, to make such laborious fence-building worthwhile.

Even early reports from Wisconsin indicate deer in northern parts of the state sometimes migrated southward in winter in the 1840s. T.J. Cram states that American Indians of the Lac Vieux Desert region moved southward, "following the deer for the winter hunt." And when Richard Dart came to Green Lake County, Wis., in 1840, he observed that "deer were plentiful, except when they went south in winter to escape the cold."

Foster and Whitney also mention deer remains discovered in the ancient Indian copper mine pits along the Upper Peninsula's Ontonagon River, where deer bones and antler fragments were discovered under 19 feet of debris.

This suggests the presence of whitetails in this region long before the arrival of settlers.

In his 1832 journal regarding an expedition into "Indian Country," Lt. J. Allen reported that Indians of Grand Island lived on fish and some game, principally the "common red deer," which were killed between the island and Lake Michigan. Other documentation indicates Indian women on Grand Island "embroidered beautiful leggins, and coats too, of deerskin." Another account in Summer 1855 by J.G. Kohl, read: "I recently saw a hunter who had returned from the hunting grounds in the Upper Peninsula with an extraordinary quantity of game. In six weeks he had killed to his own gun no less than 55 deer."

Although Shiras said there were "only a few" deer along the southern shore of Lake Superior in 1870, he reports that 80,000 deer were killed annually (most within 10 miles of Lake Superior) in 1879, 1880 and 1881. If so, something here doesn't jibe. Either whitetails were abundant along Lake Superior by 1870 or the harvest figures were inflated.

Shelter Requirements Vary

Generally speaking, annual snowfall is greater, winter travel conditions tougher, and the need for quality shelter more critical for whitetails living near Lake Superior than it is near Lake Michigan. That is, certain swamp areas that afford only mediocre protection do not normally support wintering deer herds in the deep snow belt along Lake Superior. But cover of comparable quality usually supports deer in winter along Lake Michigan's shoreline where annual snowfall is less.

Food availability can be an important factor in determining where deer yard during winter. Important trade-offs exist between the amount of energy (calories) consumed in food in relation to the amount spent in travel, body-heat loss and the avoidance of predators, including humans. For a whitetail, burning fat and losing weight over winter is normal. But, a total depletion of fat reserves before winter's end could seriously weaken the animal, thus making it easy prey for coyotes, wolves or bobcats. This loss of fat reserves could also cause the deer to die from malnutrition.

Deer that subsist solely on natural browse in winter are generally on a negative-energy balance. Therefore, they must have decent protective cover to survive. Such protective areas must offer good travel conditions for deer, thus reducing body-heat loss, and safe cover, where they can stay inactive for long periods without danger from predators.

A blowdown or modern-day logging operation near protective cover, however, could improve the deer's energy balance. It could greatly increase a relatively poor site's capacity to support wintering whitetails by providing easy access to a temporarily abundant supply of nutritious browse. In addition, regrowth on heavily burned uplands near yarding cover could provide sufficient browse for a limited number of deer.

If highly nutritious food is available, as is the case today where many wintering whitetails feed on agricultural crops or are supplementally fed high-energy grains or pelletized rations, whitetails can survive winter even in poor-quality cover. In such cases, the animals can sacrifice some shelter quality when they have access to abundant high-energy food, even with a fairly high risk of predation.

Although the whitetail's habit of feeding on farm crops is a recently exaggerated phenomenon, the trait is not totally limited to modern times. While recounting his boyhood years (in the 1850s) in Marquette County, Wis., John Muir noted that whitetails were fond of winter wheat after it had grown for about a month. According to Muir, deer were easily killed by hunters lying in wait at night. Muir said one man killed 30 to 40 deer in one small field.

After scouring the archives, Habeck and Curtis concluded: "White-tailed deer have used lowland swamp communities, particularly those dominated by white cedar, from the earliest times for which historical records are available. There is no evidence that the winter yarding behavior of the deer is a recently acquired characteristic; it is very probable that the deer have always possessed this behavior." And I concur.

Deer researcher William Severinghaus found that whitetails have used some of the same yarding areas in northern New York for more than a century. Severinghaus wrote: "There are some wintering areas in the Adirondacks in which it is known that deer have used since 1890 or earlier. We know of two locations that were deeryards during the early 1800s and still are used today."

Conclusion

The whitetail's environment, and the behavior of the whitetail itself, has changed immensely in recent times. Remember, this animal is noted for its opportunistic nature. Certainly, the white man's alteration of natural habitats has permitted the species to extend its range northward in the past 100 years. And, sometimes these manipulations, in conjunction with reduced predation, have resulted in concentrations of hundreds, if not thousands, of animals in certain deeryards.

I suspect, however, that even though they were not so abundant before 1850, whitetails have lived throughout much of the Upper Great Lakes region and the Northeast for centuries. Also, it's likely that whitetails have always employed a form of winter yarding behavior, sometimes migrating 50 or more miles, if necessary, to survive winter in deep-snow country.

Judd Cooney

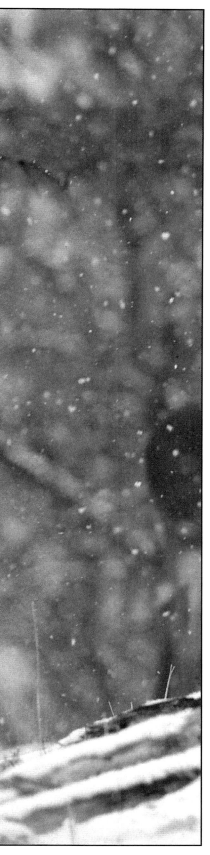

THE WINTER OF 1995-96:

A Tough Time for Northern Whitetails

After many mild winters and a big 1995 fawn crop, bulging Northern deer herds entered the winter primed for disaster. In the Northeast, rain and a freak warm spell broke winter's back in mid-January, but in the Great Lakes region, hundreds of thousands of deer curled up and died.

After a May 1, 1996, snowstorm, headlines in the *Marquette Mining Journal* in Michigan read: "Snowed Under! Superiorland weathers record snowfall."

Earlier headlines from Michigan's Upper Peninsula were: "Whitetail death tally expected to be severe," "Die-off — Harsh winter could claim as many as 200,000 U.P. deer, DNR official says," and "DNR: Deer are dying all over."

The Marquette, Mich., area received more than 21 feet of snow that winter. The Keweenaw Peninsula and other areas along Lake Superior recorded even more. In fact, some areas had continuous snow cover for seven months!

As snow and cold temperatures hit Michigan in early November 1995, I began forecasting serious problems for whitetails in parts of the U. P.

Some accused me of crying wolf, but the stage was already set for severe problems. Anytime a large population of young Northern deer is cut short in its growth and development and then forced into browsed-out winter habitat earlier than normal, you can expect a heavy winter-kill — even during a winter with moderate conditions.

Influential Factors

The welfare of wintering whitetails on Northern range is influenced by many factors, some of which occur long before winter. The importance of an early, or timely, birth, combined with excellent nutrition for proper growth, cannot be over-emphasized for Northern whitetails.

All deer in winter are on a negative energy balance while eating woody browse, meaning they burn more calories for basic bodily needs than they obtain from their food. Small-bodied deer are especially handicapped because physical laws work against them. Deer weighing less than about 80 pounds lose body heat quickly in cold weather. They're metabolically less efficient than large-bodied deer, and don't last long on a browse diet during bitter cold weather.

The availability of energy-rich foods in autumn — such as acorns, beechnuts, fruits, farm crops and green herbaceous growth —

will also directly affect how well deer prepare and survive winter.

Once winter sets in, the availability of food provided by farm crops, supplemental feeding or abundant natural browse at logging operations might mean the difference between life and death for many whitetails. During a prolonged winter, deer forced to forage solely on woody browse might find tough pickings in crowded, browsed-out deeryards.

Setting the Stage

During the 1980s and early 1990s, the stage was set for widespread winter die-offs. A string of consecutive mild winters, conservative deer harvests, increased timber cutting, supplemental feeding — and, no doubt, other factors — led to a deer population buildup across the North. As a result, overly abundant herds in northern Minnesota, Wisconsin, Michigan and Ontario now occupy every conceivable winter habitat niche. Much the same can be said of herds in the Northeast. Further, many of these herds have established patterns that won't help them survive the limitations of severe winters.

After a string of mild winters and a bountiful 1995 fawn crop, deer herds entering the 1995-96 winter in some parts of the Upper Great Lakes region were bulging — and primed for disaster.

In 1995, winter struck early, bringing regular snow beginning in November from Minnesota to Maine. Heavy snowfall and cold temperatures followed. From December through mid-January, conditions were severe in the Northern tier of states and southern Canada. On Jan. 15 and 16, however, warm, heavy rains swept across the Northeast from Pennsylvania to Maine, washing away the snows. After that, the Northeast enjoyed an average winter. But in the Great Lakes region, winter never let up. In the region's Northern Forests, it lasted until late April and early May, longer than anyone could remember. The sustained cold and snow hit whitetails with devastating consequences.

In areas where summer and winter ranges were depleted by too many foraging deer, winter losses of young deer were staggering. Where populations were in balance with the range, biologists contend that adult deer fared well, considering the prolonged sub-zero conditions that prevailed.

Just how severe was Winter 1995-96 across the North? How heavy were winter deer losses? I called many of the states' experts to find out. My report follows:

Michigan

In the words of Ed Langenau, Michigan's big-game specialist: "What a winter! It started early and ended late, which was a deadly combination for the white-tailed deer herd."

The 1995-96 winter ranked as the seventh most severe winter in Upper Michigan since 1969, when Michigan initiated its winter severity index, or WSI. However, when April is included in the total, the combined WSI for 1995-

96 was the highest ever recorded. In fact, northern Michigan's winter was the longest on record, with weather in December, April and May more severe than normal.

The Michigan WSI combines the effects of air chill (temperature plus wind), total snow depth and the weight support of snow. The air chill is measured by recording the amount of electricity (KWH) required to keep water temperature at 39 degrees inside a standard pot or *chillometer*. The snow hazard rating is derived by adding the snow depth and support factor, the latter determined by dropping a weighted copper tube onto the snow. Measurements are recorded weekly at check stations from Dec. 1 through April.

Langenau said the WSI of 120.4 in Michigan's U.P. was the seventh highest. It was less than the all-time record of 147.7 set in 1978-79, but far above the 87.6 average for the past 10 years. The WSI in the northern Lower Peninsula was the ninth highest on record at 77.2. The record for that region is 99.1, set in 1978-79, and the average is 60.1.

Had it not been for a thick crust that formed on the snow in late winter, the WSIs for northern parts of Michigan would have been much higher in 1995-96.

"The crust was like concrete, and allowed deer to move around and feed until the next layer of snow arrived," Langenau said. Widespread supplemental feeding also probably kept deer alive in some local situations.

Many parts of northern Michigan had snow cover beginning the first week of November. In fact, deer along some Lake Superior shorelines started migrating toward winter yards before the firearms season opened Nov. 15. On opening day, snow covered the ground statewide. The deer completed their move to winter cover in late November in most of the U.P., and in early December in most of the Lower Peninsula.

December was hard on deer across northern Michigan and it got worse in January. Sault Ste. Marie, for example, received 55 inches of snow during a 72-hour period. Fawns that died from starvation began showing up across the North Woods during late January and early February, which is unusually early. Further, deer in northern parts of the U.P. didn't leave winter cover until early May.

Michigan DNR completed a dead deer survey in the U.P. after the snow melted in May. Working in pairs, biologists searched 442 randomly selected plots that covered 12.8 to 16 acres. The findings confirmed earlier predictions of high winter losses: an estimated 198,785 deer had died in the U.P. That's an average of more than 12 deer per square mile, nearly twice the legal hunting harvest in 1995.

Deer losses were greatest in the western U.P., which is District 1, with an estimated toll of 62,495. The central U.P., or District 3, lost 61,764 deer; the southern U.P., District 2, lost 36,473; and the eastern U.P., District 4, lost 38,053 deer.

Although no systematic dead-deer survey was conducted for northern Lower Michigan, biologists estimated 50,000 deer died. Some put the figure closer to 100,000. (However, a special dead-deer search was held in northeastern Lower

Michigan, where tuberculosis was detected in deer in 1994. Based on samples from 138 searched plots, Harry Hill — a Michigan DNR biometrician — estimated 5,667 deer died within the 572 square-mile area.)

Langenau said the worst factor was that the state entered winter with too many deer.

"At high deer densities, deer tend to distribute themselves more in marginal habitat, which is deficient in food and cover," Langenau said. "Deer are vulnerable to nutritional stress and predation when living in marginal habitat."

Based on previous studies at the Cusino Wildlife Research Station, I calculated that 55 percent of fawns born in the U.P. in Spring 1996 died because their mothers were malnourished. Additional losses from predation, accidents and other factors pushed the losses even further.

Despite a respectable deer harvest by hunters in Fall 1995 and high death rates in winter and spring, the U.P.'s herd was still far above the population goal and the forest's carrying capacity in 1996.

Wisconsin

Keith McCaffery, Wisconsin's DNR wildlife research biologist, reported that the North's 1995-96 WSI was the highest on record. Further, it followed Wisconsin's second mildest winter on record and a decade of mild and moderate winters.

Wisconsin's WSI is derived by tallying the number of days with 18 or more inches of snow cover, plus the number of days below zero. Such data are collected at 30 Northern Forest stations. Using that formula, an average WSI above 80 is considered severe in Wisconsin. The WSI for 1995-96 was 130, and several locations exceeded 160.

"Some observers claim it was the longest winter since 1935-36," McCaffery said.

McCaffery noted that winter started early with snow cover arriving the first week of November in parts of the North. Freezing rain in mid-December created a crust of 7 to 12 inches above ground. That created difficulty for some deer, particularly those in certain farm-fringe units. Snow continued to accumulate and reached the 18-inch mark at some stations by late-December. It exceeded 18 inches at most stations by Jan. 18. Freezing rain on Jan. 18-19 provided a walking crust about 18 inches above ground in some parts of the North. Snow accumulated to the high 20-inch mark over much of the North, and sometimes exceeded 40 inches.

Leonard Lee Rue III

Many regions entered Winter 1995-96 with too many deer. Under such crowded conditions, deer tend to distribute themselves in marginal habitat, which is deficient in food and cover. That leaves deer vulnerable to nutritional stress and predation.

"It's noteworthy that the Wisconsin method for gauging winter severity doesn't take into account the support quality of snow crust," McCaffery said. Depending on its density, a crust could be harmful or beneficial to deer.

Orrin Rongstad, a retired professor from the University of Wisconsin, has done extensive radio-tracking research of whitetails in Northern Wisconsin's Clam Lake area. Rongstad tracked 11 adult does in Winter 1995-96, and those deer did not leave their yarding cover until April 27, the latest exit Rongstad recorded during a decade of study.

Despite the severe weather, only one of Rongstad's study animals died during winter, falling sometime around April 24. He found six dead deer in the area, most of them fawns, when he went to examine the dead radio-tagged animal.

The Wisconsin DNR didn't conduct systematic dead-deer searches. But based on historical data, and given a worst-case scenario, McCaffery estimated about 150,000 deer died in northern Wisconsin. Given that estimate, about 30 percent of the North Woods' herd, which numbered about 500,000 deer, died in Winter 1995-96.

With heavy winter losses in the North, and an increased herd in agricultural areas to the south — caused by inadequate antlerless harvests and a highly successful fawn crop — the Wisconsin herd numbered about 1.5 million deer in 1996, about the same as in 1995. With such high numbers, huge harvests continued statewide, reaching a record 494,116 kills in 1999 for bow- and gun-hunting combined.

Minnesota

Winter 1995-96 was especially harsh in the forests of northeastern Minnesota. In fact, Mark Lenarz — Minnesota DNR wildlife research biologist — said it was probably the most severe winter since the late 1930s. Some authorities claimed northern Minnesota endured the snowiest and coldest winter of the past 100 years.

Minnesota computes its WSI by tallying the number of days with 15 or more inches of snow on the ground, plus the number of days below zero. A total score higher than 100 is considered severe. Jay McAninch, then a wildlife research biologist with the Minnesota DNR, said several northern stations had WSIs exceeding 200.

Biologists reported that average November temperatures were consistently 7 to 10 degrees colder than normal across northern Minnesota. In addition, heavy snowfall began after Thanksgiving. Conditions moderated during late December, but worsened in mid-January. By the end of January, Lenarz said, the combination of deep snow and arctic temperatures put the WSI as much as 65 percent higher than the same time during Winter 1989, a severe winter for northern Minnesota.

In an effort to curb deer losses from 1995-96, Minnesota's Legislature ordered the DNR to conduct a massive state-funded deer feeding program that cost more than $1 million. Because deer feeding in forested areas was ineffective during the 1988-89 winter, emergency feeding efforts in 1996 were concentrated in the more accessible farmland of northwestern Minnesota.

McAninch estimates 30 percent to 50 percent of the fawns died in the forested one-third of northern Minnesota, with the worst losses in the northeastern corner. Deer wintering in the farm-dominated northwestern corner and southern sections fared better, where 10 percent losses were expected. Many of those deaths, McAninch believes, were caused by the previous mild winter. Given ideal nutrition into early winter, more doe fawns than normal (30 percent to 50 percent) bred in 1994. Because most of them probably bred in December, many small, late-born fawns — extremely vulnerable to winter stress — entered the winter.

On the other hand, McAninch suggested good nutrition for deer during the spring and summer of 1995 allowed adult deer to enter winter in good condition. As a result, most deer that died were fawns, and few adults were lost.

Although deer populations in parts of northern Minnesota declined because of severe winter, the herds remained at or close to goals throughout most of the state.

The biggest change in Fall 1996 was that in the northeastern part, Zone 1, antlerless permits were 93 percent lower. Further, all hunters — including archers and muzzleloaders — were limited to bucks. In transitional areas from east-central to northwestern Minnesota, Zone 2, antlerless permits were cut 28 percent. In agricultural areas, zones 3 and 4, permits remained similar or higher.

Ontario

Northern Ontario was also affected by the 1995-96 winter. Dennis Voigt, a ministry research scientist, said the winter was the most severe since 1958-59.

"It created a huge panic," he said.

The Ontario DNR also computes its WSI by combining air chill and snow hazard measurements. The only difference is that Ontario uses a spring-loaded device to estimate how deep deer will sink in the snow. Voigt said WSI readings approached 200 at most northern Ontario stations.

As in Michigan's U.P., deer migrations to yards in Ontario started during early to mid-November. Normally, such movement does not occur until December. Midwinter saw more cold and snow, and deer did not leave yards until late April or early May.

"In northern Ontario, deer normally spend about 110 days in yards," Voigt said. "We expect 10 percent to 20 percent mortality during a normal winter. (In Winter 1995-96) deer were confined to winter yards for 150 to 160 days."

Deer populations in northern Ontario peaked around 1990. Since then, most yarding populations either stabilized or declined. Mild weather had also resulted in greater deer distribution, thereby relieving browsing pressure and allowing for browse recovery in some traditional yards. As a result, deer in traditional yards might have fared better than expected during such a harsh winter.

In contrast, because they established new yarding habits during previous mild winters, some deer didn't go to traditional yards. Voigt suggests those in poor shelter became easy prey for wolves.

The Ontario DNR does not financially support artificial feeding of deer, but biologists provide technical advice. In Ontario, feeding is generally conducted on an emergency basis, not beginning until late March. This is designed primarily to save adult deer. Biologists recommend feeding a ration of 50 percent cereal grains (such as oats) and 50 percent corn.

Winter 1995-96 was especially harsh in the forests of northeastern Minnesota. In fact, Mark Lenarz — Minnesota DNR wildlife research biologist — said it was probably the most severe winter since the late 1930s. Some authorities claimed northern Minnesota endured the snowiest and coldest winter of the past 100 years.

Deer in southern Ontario's farmlands came through the winter with minimal mortality, caused largely by a January thaw that also swept through the Northeast's states. In northern parts of the province, however, Voigt said more than 50 percent of the fawns might have died, and high numbers of newborn fawn losses were expected.

Voigt emphasizes that, unlike the U.P. of Michigan, where deer were overly abundant, Ontario deer were close to goal.

The Northeast

Contrary to some premature reports, the 1995-96 winter was of only average severity for deer from Pennsylvania to Maine. Things did look bleak from December through mid-January, with all indications pointed to a very severe winter. But, on Jan. 15, a freak warm spell and rainstorms moved through the region, breaking winter's back by melting almost all of the region's snow.

"(Winter 1995-96) was average or milder in 16 of 18 districts in Maine," said Gerry Levigne, Maine's chief deer biologist. "The other two districts — which are in the western mountains — were slightly above average in severity."

Levigne termed December and the first half of January as "very severe."

"Things looked real bad in early January, but the conditions didn't last," Levigne said. "A series of 'interglacial periods' moved through Maine last winter, warming the air and bringing rain instead of snow. After one mid-January thaw and rain, about two-thirds of the state was cleared of snow. That caused excellent deer mobility and survival."

Levigne said the quick turnaround should remind everyone not to panic too soon.

"I've learned not to make predictions during winter about winter conditions and deer," he said. "It's impossible to know what will take place until winter is over and you have time to analyze all the data. Each winter pattern is different, and each has a different impact on survival."

Much the same story held up across Vermont and New Hampshire.

"It was an odd winter," said Steve Weber, New Hampshire's deer biologist. "We had two rainstorms in mid-January that were a godsend for deer. We got 3 inches of rain and the temperature was 65 degrees. We lost 30 inches of snow overnight."

Weber said the winter rated average for severity.

John Buck, chairman of Vermont's deer management program, said deer that survived winter's first six weeks roamed their entire winter range because all the snow melted and washed away Jan. 15.

"The late-born fawns didn't survive early winter, but everything else did," Buck said. "Many people were concerned in early winter, but the rains washed away all the fears."

Dave Riehlman, a senior wildlife biologist in New York, agreed that winter ended abruptly. "As it shook out, the deer fared pretty well," Riehlman said. "The January thaw came in the nick of time."

Riehlman said spring field surveys found a few starved fawns, but nothing out of the ordinary.

"Deer went into winter thinner than desired because our summer was dry and we didn't have much of a mast crop," Riehlman said. "Then, winter got off to an early start. If it had kept going in that style, the deer would have had a tough time of it. That thaw turned the tide."

In Pennsylvania, the winter-kill was minimal, with isolated problem pockets in the northcentral and southcentral regions. For the most part, however, the state's herd was unaffected by the winter, despite some of the heaviest snowfalls since 1993-94.

Conclusion

Whitetails have endured tough winters for thousands of years. They live at the Northern extremes of their geographic range, and have evolved certain physiological and behavioral adaptations to cope with winter. When healthy, and behaviorally wise, they are hardy creatures. So equipped, they can survive cold temperatures, deep snow and nutritional hardship, even under the eye of wolves, coyotes and wildcats.

But the winter of 1995-96 was not a routine tough winter in the Great Lakes region. In some sectors, it was one of those real killers that come only once every 50 to 100 years. Such times remind us that winter remains the grim reaper and the major selective force operating against whitetails in the North Woods.

We'll continue to have ups and downs in deer populations as the adaptable and opportunistic whitetail capitalizes on good times. Ultimately, however, the availability of favorable food and cover year-round, combined with winter's lethal forces, will control the Northern herds' welfare and abundance. Keeping deer populations in balance with their range by harvesting adequate numbers of antlerless deer is essential in preventing deer from destroying their range.

So, my compliments to Northern hunters who bypass young bucks and fill their antlerless tag — especially if you purposely shoot a fawn. Despite the ridicule you might endure, you are playing your role as a predator by selectively harvesting from the greatest, most vulnerable surplus.

Conversely, hunters who extol intensive buck cropping but deplore killing antlerless deer, especially fawns — which prompts "boom and bust" deer populations — I implore you to re-evaluate your thinking.

Charles J. Alsheimer

Chapter 3
PART III

SEASONAL PATTERNS:

The Science of Fall Migrations

Although deer usually settle into winter range during late December, weather patterns in October and November might induce exciting deer activity. Prolonged snowfall and cold weather can trigger strong migratory deer movements toward winter habitat.

Historically, according to naturalist George Shiras III (1935), white-tailed deer living along the southern shore of Lake Superior migrated southward en masse each autumn to escape harsh winter weather. Migrating whitetails were reported to be so abundant and their routes so well-established that they cut deep paths in the soft, swampy soil — "like the caribou trails found in Newfoundland."

These ancient migration trails referred to by Shiras, which supposedly led to deer wintering grounds along Lake Michigan and even into Wisconsin, are no longer evident. Some even doubt they ever existed.

Nowadays, deer in the Upper Great Lakes region seem to travel in all directions from their summering grounds to reach favored wintering grounds. Even so, most migrating whitetails still leave areas with deep snow to travel southward to winter in areas with less snowfall. Every autumn, thousands of whitetails trek southward along historic routes, many crossing more than 50 miles to escape bitter conditions that prevail closer to Lake Superior.

For wildlife managers, knowing the deer's seasonal movement patterns and winter habitat requirements is critical to deer management. Also, because hunting in the Upper Great Lakes region — especially late muzzleloading and archery seasons — coincides with deer migrations, it's equally important that deer hunters understand this phenomenon.

Changing Landscape

Today, not all Northern deer migrate. During the past 200 years, European settlers changed the landscape with ax, plow and fire to create a mosaic of vegetative conditions vastly different from pristine times, and whitetails have changed accordingly.

In many parts of the North today, deer are seldom far from winter food and protective cover. And whereas deer once meandered about browsing on choice shrubs, many are now attracted to abundant felled browse at logging operations. They also eat standing corn, or are hand-fed highly nutritious artificial rations. For these deer, there is no need to migrate far — as long as winter weather is not too severe and their food supply holds out. However, they sometimes suffer dire consequences during tough winters (as in 1995-96), when shelter is poor and nutritious food becomes scarce.

Scientists have studied the whitetail's migratory habits since at least the 1930s. Initially, many Northern states conducted winter trapping to tag and release wild deer. They then relied primarily on hunter recovery of tagged deer to determine herd movements from winter to summer range.

Winter Habitat

Those early studies revealed a small portion (about 10 percent) of the total deer range in the Upper Great Lakes region supported deer during severe winters. Lowland areas of mature hemlock, white cedar, balsam fir, and white and black spruce — when available in fairly large and uniform stands with dense canopies — provided the best winter cover for whitetails. Such cover still attracts densities of several hundred deer per square mile in winter. However, upland hemlock/hardwood, jack pine, white pine and even red pine provide adequate shelter where weather isn't too severe.

The size of deeryards and deer densities also varies greatly by region. Generally, smaller areas of shelter — possibly 50 to 100 acres — might be enough for small deer herds where snowfall is light. Deer tend to require larger areas of conifer protection in heavy snow country. In central Upper Michigan, for example, the 360-square-mile deeryard in northern Menominee County provides winter habitat for deer that occupy summer ranges scattered over 1,400 square miles. The number of deer using the yard varies by year, but an estimated 43,000 wintered there in 1987.

The distance deer migrate to suitable winter shelter also varies greatly, depending on many related factors. These include the availability of dense conifer cover, its distribution relative to food sources, the quantity and quality of food available, the winter's severity and a host of other lesser factors. In Upper Michigan, for example, researcher Louis Verme (1973) found that deer living in the peninsula's eastern half, where the terrain gently rolls, travel significantly farther to winter yards than those in the peninsula's rugged western half (9.3 vs. 7.5

It's only been since the early 1960s that researchers have used sophisticated telemetry gear to research deer behavior. Readily locating and following radio-equipped deer has provided insights into many mysteries surrounding the Northern whitetail's migratory habits and shelter needs.

miles, respectively).

In Minnesota, A.B. Erickson and his co-workers (1961) observed that deer in the state's prairie-deciduous western region traveled farther (males, 14 miles; females, 9.7 miles) to reach winter range than those in the conifer-dominated northern region (males, 6.7 miles; females, 3.7 miles). One yearling buck tagged in central Minnesota was shot 165 miles from its winter tagging site, whereas the longest movement distance for an adult doe was 85 miles.

B.L. Dalberg and R.C. Guettinger (1956) reported shorter movements for Wisconsin deer. There, deer traveled an average of only 3½ miles from winter to summer range. The researchers concluded that six miles was about the average annual cruising radius for deer in a given yard.

New Age of Research

It's only been since the early 1960s that researchers have used sophisticated telemetry gear to research deer behavior. Readily locating and following radio-equipped deer has provided insights into many mysteries surrounding the Northern whitetail's migratory habits and shelter needs.

Although scientists debate the issue, Northern whitetails presumably evolved migratory habits and shelter-seeking tendencies that minimize the energy they expend. The energy-robbing factors include exposure to cold, deep snow and evading predators.

During winter, the Northern whitetail must become a master at energy conservation. To survive severe winters, the whitetail must greatly reduce its movements. It must find a comfortable and safe location, and lie in its bed for hours on end. Social grouping and trail formation also play important roles during stressful and dangerous winters.

The Temperature Trigger

Most studies reveal that cold temperatures are the primary stimulus prompting deer to seek heavy cover. Mounting snow depths might later restrict deer movement to core areas of the best shelter, but, in itself, snowfall seldom causes migrations. A major blizzard, combining appreciable snowfall, low temperatures and high winds, certainly can cause massive deer migrations. However, during most years, deer migrate to winter yards long before the snow is deep enough to seriously obstruct travel.

Nonetheless, the migratory response of deer tends to

vary each year between areas and even within the same areas. Sometimes neighboring family groups of deer demonstrate markedly different migration dates, even though they're presumably exposed to the same climatic conditions.

While radio-tracking deer in northern Minnesota, M.E. Nelson and L.D. Mech (1981) found a high percentage of deer migrated to winter ranges as temperatures rapidly decreased in November. The first temperatures below 19 degrees initiated migrations for about 52 percent of the deer. However, some deer didn't migrate until immediately after a major cold period, when temperatures were actually increasing. In other cases, deer showed no response during initial cold weather and didn't migrate until December and January as snow depths increased.

One doe monitored by R.L. Hoskinson and L.D. Mech (1976) left her summer range when the temperature dropped below freezing and traveled six miles toward her wintering grounds. When the temperature rose, the doe returned to her summer range within a few days, having traveled about 14½ miles round-trip. These observations revealed that although a temperature drop might trigger migration, some deer immediately return to their summer ranges if temperatures rise again.

Nutrition might also be an important variable influencing migration dates. According to Nelson and Mech, "Nutrition may also affect the physiological threshold to thermal changes that induce migration." As with bears, wherein a good food supply tends to delay dormancy, improved nutrition, especially a diet high in energy, might also delay deer migrations from summer to winter range.

Studies conducted by Orrin Rongstad and Tim Lewis (Lewis 1990) on the effects of supplemental feeding on whitetails in northern Wisconsin support the theory that a deer's autumnal diet can influence its migration date. In this study, Rongstad and Lewis reported that deer eating highly nutritious pellet feed in autumn migrated to winter cover about two weeks later than deer subsisting solely on natural browse. However, even the supplementally fed deer eventually migrated.

As in the Minnesota studies, Rongstad and Lewis found that fall migration was not always a direct movement from summer to winter range. Most deer took 24 to 31 days to complete the migration. Many deer made several trips from summer range toward winter range. They returned to their summer range as temperatures rose, and never reached their wintering grounds. Some deer migrated to a nearby deeryard, where they remained if the winter was mild, but then moved onto the main yard if the winter became more severe.

During many years of radio-tracking deer in northern Wisconsin, Rongstad found that some deer migrated to winter habitat only during severe winters. Some deer he studied failed to migrate for several years

when winters were mild, but promptly migrated to traditional yards during tough winters. About 22 percent of the deer he studied were not migrants. However, many years of supplemental feeding appeared to alter the ratio of migratory deer. In one area where deer had been fed for more than 40 years, 57 percent of the deer were year-round residents.

Even in Illinois, Charles Nixon and his co-workers (1991) found that about 20 percent of whitetails living on intensively farmed land migrated from summer to winter range. Deer frequently remained on their summer ranges all year during winters with little snow. But low temperatures and snowfall seemed to cause deer to move to more secure wintering habitat. Also, winter severity determined if, how soon, and how long deer remained on traditional wintering areas. The investigators reported that fall migrants "appeared reluctant to return to their winter ranges." Most deer did not migrate until crops were harvested, leaf-fall had occurred, and archery hunting was well under way.

How Many Migrate?

Group size probably varies greatly, but members of deer family groups tend to migrate to winter yards together. Related does and fawns normally band together and migrate in groups, but migratory habits of adult bucks have been poorly documented.

Rongstad and Lewis found some neighboring doe-fawn family groups migrating at different times. In some cases, different migration dates could be attributed to contrasting nutritional conditions. In other instances, however, researchers speculated that the migration timing was caused by traditional habits, because several deer families consistently migrated early each autumn, even in mild weather.

Nelson and Mech found some yearling bucks reunited with their mothers and migrated with the family group. In other cases, however, observations suggested yearling bucks joined buck groups in autumn and migrated together. Such differences in young-buck behavior might be attributable to differences in a deer herd's sex-age composition and herd density.

In 1988, I unknowingly established a comfortable deer blind along a migration route leading to the Whitefish deeryard in central Upper Michigan. That was a year when bitter cold weather and heavy snow set in early. As a result, many northern Michigan deer migrated to winter quarters in mid- to late November, which is rifle season in Michigan. After a few days of seeing several deer pass by, it finally dawned on me that they were headed toward the core of winter cover about eight miles away. During the course of our 16-day season, my wife and I tallied 74 deer — all of them does and fawns.

In 1978, when the weather was more severe, I saw the opposite phenomenon. Temperatures plummeted to below zero, and deer started migrating in early November, before rifle season. I had built a blind along a well-established migration trail leading to the Petrel Grade Deeryard. Despite considerable blind time, we saw only two deer in a week of hunting. Both were bucks.

Reluctant Bucks

Despite scant research evidence, I'm inclined to believe a buck in rut is reluctant to leave his breeding range. Further, I believe he seldom migrates until most deer have left the area. In some cases, however, bucks might routinely shift to occupy certain areas of heavy cover nearer yards where does and fawns concentrate before moving to the main yard.

In one of the most recent publications regarding deer migratory behavior, Nelson (1995) examined the behavior of 194 adult female deer captured and radio-collared in northeastern Minnesota from 1975 to 1993. Of 149 does he tracked during autumn, two (1 percent) migrated in September and October, weeks before other deer migrated in response to cold weather and snowfall. For four consecutive years, one of these does migrated to a site midway between her summer and winter ranges. She lived there several weeks before migrating to winter cover with other deer after cold weather and snowfall had set in. The other female migrated directly to winter cover during October every year, generally a month before other deer migrated.

In Nelson's study, fall migration consistently started after temperatures dropped below 19 degrees the first time, which occurred in late October in three years and during November in 14 years. Snowfall usually accompanied or preceded such cold.

During three autumns, six of 43 does migrated toward winter cover after two- to seven-day periods of cold weather, even without snow. All but one of the does returned to her summer range, however, once temperatures moderated.

In the other 14 autumns, 58 of 113 does (44 percent) first migrated toward winter range when the temperature dropped below 19 degrees, coincident with snowfall. With permanent snow cover, 91 percent of migrants stayed on winter range.

Nelson found a combination of prolonged cold weather and snowfall was most effective in stimulating migrations. The duration of cold weather was particu-

larly important. Even with snowfall, migrations didn't start during each of the five years when temperatures were below 19 degrees less than five days. In contrast, migrations started in each of the 14 years when temperatures below 19 degrees lasted at least five days.

In summary, Nelson reports: "During years with no early November snow, a small percentage (14 percent) of females migrated to their winter ranges, clearly in response to temperatures below 19 degrees Fahrenheit. Furthermore, they migrated primarily in response to longer periods (five days or more) of decreasing temperatures, an effect also evident during migration onsets with snowfalls."

Nelson notes, however, that "decreasing temperature alone was a weak stimulus for keeping deer on their winter ranges (only 2 percent stayed). Snowfall prior to or concurrent with declining temperatures tripled the percentage of females initially migrating (44 percent), and nearly all migrated permanently."

Unfortunately, despite detailed study, Nelson could not accurately predict the timing of fall migration in November and December based on snow depth and temperature measurements. Individual deer just simply varied too much in their migratory habits.

Conclusion

Because there is no magical formula to predict deer migration, it's essential that Northern hunters study deer habits in their own areas. Differences in food, snow, temperature, nutrition, traditional habits, cover distribution and many other factors might explain why some deer migrate to distant yarding areas and others don't.

Although deer usually settle down in winter range during late December, changing weather patterns in October and November might induce some exciting deer activity for hunters. Prolonged snowfall and cold weather can trigger strong migratory deer movements toward winter habitat sooner than expected. On the other hand, moderating weather and snow melt can cause deer to return to summer range. So, depending on where you hunt during the seasonal change, you could face feast or famine hunting.

Hunting areas with low deer densities far from winter range during bluebird weather early in the season can be rewarding, especially if you like solitude. But when temperatures hover in the teens or lower for more than

Because there is no magical formula to predict deer migration, it's essential that Northern hunters study deer habits in their own areas. Differences in food, snow, temperature, nutrition, traditional habits, cover distribution and many other factors might explain why some deer migrate to distant yarding areas and others don't.

five days, especially with persistent snow, hunt dense conifer cover near traditional wintering habitat.

During some years, hunting the middle ground —

somewhere between summer deer concentration areas and winter habitat — might produce phenomenal deer viewing for late-season hunting.

References

Dalberg, B.L., and R.C. Guettinger. 1956. The white-tailed deer in Wisconsin. Technical Wildlife Bulletin No. 14, *Wisconsin Conservation Department, Madison. 281 pages.*

Erickson, A.B., V.E. Gunvalson, M.H. Stenlund, D.W. Burcalow, and L.H. Blankenship. 1961. The white-tailed deer of Minnesota. Technical Bulletin No. 5., *Minnesota Department of Conservation. 64 pages.*

Lewis, T.L. 1990. The effects of supplemental feeding on white-tailed in northwestern Wisconsin. Ph.D. Thesis, University of Wisconsin-Madison. 79 pages.

Nelson, M.E. 1995. Winter range arrival and departure of white-tailed deer in northeastern Minnesota. Canadian Journal of Zoology *73:1069-1076.*

Nelson, M.E., and L.D. Mech. 1981. Deer social organization and wolf predation in northeastern Minnesota. Wildlife Monograph 77. 53 pages.

Nixon, C.M., L.P. Hansen, P.A. Brewer, and J.E. Chelsvig. Ecology of white-tailed deer in an intensively farmed region of Illinois. Wildlife Monograph 118. 77 pages.

Shiras, C. III. 1921. The wildlife of Lake Superior, past and present. National Geographic 40:*113-204.*

Verme, L.J. 1973. Movements of white-tailed deer in Upper Michigan. Journal of Wildlife Management 37:*545-552.*

Richard P. Smith

Chapter 4

WINTER HABITS:

Why do Northern Deer Yard?

When provided with good shelter, healthy whitetails are well-equipped — physiologically and behaviorally — to withstand severe weather in midwinter. It is the prolonged winter that starts early and ends late which can devastate deer.

My introduction to the whitetail's bitter life along Lake Superior was the winter of 1964-65. That winter was relentlessly severe in the northern reaches of Upper Michigan. Its harshness bordered on unbelievable. But as I learned, so did the deer's hardiness.

A fierce blizzard swept inland off Lake Superior during late November in 1964, driving deer into my study area in the Petrel Grade Deeryard earlier than normal. And there was no let up. Mounting snows and sub-zero temperatures prevailed, confining deer to the best sheltered sites in the dense cedar swamp, trapping them until late April.

Malnutrition started to kill fawns in February. Old deer began dropping in March, and even prime-age deer died in April. By spring, bones and deer hide lay strewn along manure-packed deer trails, mute evidence of the lengthy hardship. More than 140 deer perished in my square-mile study area. Almost miraculously, however, the superior stock survived the five grueling months of frigid weather, deep snow and scarce food, while trying to evade roving coyotes, bobcats, and an occasional wolf.

Scientific evidence indicates whitetails originated in the Southeast, under a relatively mild climate. In such environments, adult deer live out their lives within a relatively small range, without migrating great distances in winter for protective cover.

Whitetails probably did not develop yarding behavior — which sometimes requires long migrations — until they extended their range northward. Therefore, yarding and other seasonal adjustments to winter stress are probably not deep-seated genetic traits. Yarding behavior is more likely a recent adaptation, or learned behavior, in response to cold weather, snow cover and increased predator risks.

Although scientists debate the evolutionary basis for migration and yarding, natural selection must have been involved. Yarding behavior normally occurs with little regard to food availability (at least in natural situations), and it probably evolved as an energy-conserving and predator-defense adaptation. Historically, deer that exhibited yarding behavior survived to perpetuate the trait, while those that didn't adapt died.

Migration

Various nutritional, social and climatic factors interact to trigger Northern deer migrations from summer to winter range. Also, some deer migrate and some don't, and some migrate during severe winters but not in mild winters.

Most studies show cold temperatures are the primary factor prompting deer to seek protective cover. Mounting snow depths might later restrict deer movement to core areas of prime cover, but, in itself, snowfall seldom triggers migration. During most years, deer migrate to yards long before snows are deep enough to seriously hinder travel.

Even so, researcher Mike Nelson in Minnesota contends that snow and its effect on deer mobility is the ultimate cause of migrating to yards as a predator defense. Once in heavy cover, the deer's trail system and social habits allow greater movement from cover to food, and also improve chances for escaping predators. In northern Minnesota, Nelson found higher survival rates for yarded vs. nonyarded deer when threatened by wolves.

It's also obvious that tradition, nutrition and social relationships are important factors influencing the timing of migration. For unknown reasons, neighboring deer family groups sometimes migrate at different times, even when presumably exposed to similar environmental conditions.

Because well-fed deer tend to migrate later than underfed animals, however, I suspect the animal's energy balance and the nutritional quality of the autumnal range affect when some deer migrate. Deer on a browse diet experience a negative energy balance after temperatures drop below 19 degrees. This change forces deer to seek shelter to maintain a more favorable energy balance. Deer eating acorns or other high-energy foods can maintain a positive energy balance at lower temperatures, and thus need not migrate as soon.

Research by Nelson also suggests migratory patterns are learned, not inherited, because some migratory deer become nonmigratory and vice versa. In Nelson's studies, even translocated deer continued their established migration patterns despite being moved to new areas. Therefore, Nelson believes migratory deer remember compass bearings and migration distances, Also, he believes deer are born with this capacity to learn migratory patterns.

Deer Yard Ecology
When winter begins, deer have not yet adjusted for severe weather, so they respond to climatic stress by eating more, becoming more active and seeking protective cover. Low temperatures and cold winds cause higher rates of body heat loss, while mounting snows increase energy expenditures and make deer more vulnerable.

My studies in the Petrel Grade Deeryard revealed wide differences in microclimate within the yard. No single niche provided maximum protection while still providing adequate browse. Of the habitat I sampled, dense, mature cedars offered the most comfortable microclimate and best travel conditions during the coldest weather.

I found the average temperature differed by only a few degrees from one forest cover type to the next, but dense swamp conifers had the narrowest temperature ranges.

In contrast, the amount of wind, air chill (convective heat-loss from cold and wind) and snow accumulations varied greatly. When compared with dense stands of mature cedar, wind flow averaged five to 30 times greater in younger browse-producing stands, but 60 to 200 times greater in nearby uplands. Also, as would be expected, the closed canopy of mature cedars was most efficient in intercepting and storing snow. Snow that sifted through the thick canopy also packed more firmly, greatly improving travel conditions, as compared to other habitat types. The better footing then allowed for a good trail system from bedding sites to food sources, and enhanced escape from predators.

Adjusting to Winter Weather
During their initial adjustment to winter, deer undergo physiological changes, including reduced thyroid function and decreased metabolism. By midwinter, deer gear down to an almost semi-hibernating state, decrease their food intake by about 30 percent and their activity by at least 50 percent. These adaptive tactics allow them to waste little energy when food is scarce and environmental stresses are high, and to coexist in a crowded, hostile environment. To accomplish this, however, deer must occupy safe, comfortable habitat.

Once acclimated to their winter environment, deer can become unbelievably stubborn. They're reluctant to explore new habitat or deviate from a daily routine. When severely stressed, they might restrict their activity to less than 80 acres, feed mainly during warmer daytime hours, and refuse to travel more than a few hundred feet from shelter to food.

Even mature bucks might abandon their preferred peripheral yarding cover (where better food sources prevail) to retreat to core areas of the yard if conditions become too severe. But it is generally the depth and supporting character of the snow pack that determines deer mobility and the areas used. Plowing through deep snow wastes energy and increases risk from predators, which might not be offset by the energy obtained in the food they're seeking.

Energy Balance
Despite an ultraconservative lifestyle, the whitetail's basic energy requirements in winter exceed energy gained from eating woody browse. In fact, Northern white cedar (3 to 6 pounds per deer daily) is the only browse that will sustain deer through 100 days of yarding. Hemlock, maple, ash, birch, aspen and various shrubs — which offer comparatively low nutrition — suffice only when available in great variety and abundance, or when consumed with more nourishing foods. The availability of high-energy crops or supplemental feed, however, is another matter.

The amount of digestible energy in a deer's winter diet can greatly determine shelter requirements. For example, researcher Aaron Moen found deer in western Minnesota readily bedded in open fields even when exposed to brisk winds and nighttime temperatures between zero and minus 34 degrees, as long as they had access to corn and soybeans. Even small amounts of high-energy food, when combined with a mixed browse diet, allow a deer's metabolic furnace to compensate for cold-stress in poor shelter.

During early winter, deer tend to move and feed most heavily at sunrise, midday, sunset and twice nightly. This pattern for healthy deer holds throughout winter, and probably in all other seasons. By midwinter, however, malnourished deer become most active in the warmest part of the day and greatly decrease nighttime travel. This, undoubtedly, is an energy-conserving adjustment to reduce exposure and body heat-loss, thus enhancing survival.

On Northern range, small-bodied deer are at a serious disadvantage. Moen found, for example, that more body heat is lost during cold, windy weather from the surface of a small deer than from a large one. According to Moen, deer weighing less than about 80 pounds are metabolically inefficient in conserving energy during cold weather. It is little wonder, therefore, that high deer densities, poor nutrition, slow growth rates and heavy winter-kill often go together.

The Effect of Prolonged Winters

When provided with good shelter, healthy whitetails are well-equipped to withstand severe weather in midwinter. It is the prolonged winter that starts early and ends late that can devastate deer.

Because of impending nutritional constraints (negative energy balance), browse-nourished deer lose considerable body weight over winter, regardless of the quality or quantity of browse available. Does and fawns that enter winter with maximum fat reserves can withstand a 30 percent weight loss without dying, but adult bucks commonly lose about 25 percent of their peak body weight during the autumnal rut, leaving them vulnerable if winter food is scarce. As might be expected, fawns regularly comprise about 70 percent or more of winter's mortality.

The whitetail's otherwise impressive strategy for winter survival weakens around mid-March, when its metabolism shifts back to a higher level. The response to increasing daylight accelerates energy, or food demands. Fawns from the previous year resume their growth, and the fetuses of pregnant does advance in their development. These changes rapidly sap the animal's remaining energy reserves. Depending on temperature, snow depth and the rate of snow melt, deer sometimes experience hazardous and exhausting travel at spring break-up, making a bad situation worse.

Dangerous Yarding Habits

Despite their remarkably adaptive nature, whitetails are not always ecologically wise. Food-stressed animals, in particular, might sacrifice shelter quality for superior but sporadic nutrition at feeding stations or winter logging sites. These trade-offs can result in dangerous yarding habits.

The whitetail's shelter requirements in Northern regions tend to vary, depending largely on the degree and duration of cold-stress and snow cover, which might vary greatly by year, even within the same area. Therefore, not all conifer forests provide adequate shelter every winter. A series of mild winters, like those that occurred throughout the Upper Great Lakes region in the 1980s and early 1990s, can allow deer to occupy scattered, poorly sheltered winter habitat.

While deer dispersals in winter might be considered a better alternative than large concentrations of deer in core areas, these satellite herds suffer high mortality or elimination when faced with tough winters. In Upper Michigan, for example, about 200,000 whitetails died during the harsh winter of 1995-96, and another 110,000 died in 1996-97. As a result, many small yarding groups that developed in previous mild winters disappeared.

Conclusion

To the uninformed, yarding might seem suicidal as hordes of deer rush to dense conifer stands stripped of browse by previous generations of wintering whitetails. However, many trade-offs — such as nutrition, shelter and predator risk — influence this behavior.

As I've said: "It's as though the Northern whitetail possesses a sophisticated computer to calculate energy cost-benefit ratios, predict potential predator risks, and make the best judgments in order to survive perilous winters."

It's this uncanny ability to adjust to prevailing and constantly changing circumstances that allows Northern whitetails to survive even when confronting extreme winter adversity. But remember, whitetails are expert opportunists.

Because of fluctuations in habitat quality and winter weather, Northern white-tailed deer populations have undergone boom and bust population trends ever since the white man altered natural habitats and reduced or eliminated natural predators.

I see no reason why such trends won't continue.

References

Moen, A.N. 1973. *Wildlife ecology.* San Francisco: W.H. Freeman and Co., 458 pages.

Nelson, M.E. 1994. *Migration bearing and distance memory by translocated white-tailed deer, Odocoileus virginianus.* Canadian Field Naturalist *108:74-76.*

Nelson, M.E. 1995. *Winter range arrival and departure of white-tailed deer in northeastern Minnesota.* Canadian Journal of Zoology *73:1069-1076.*

Ozoga, J.J. 1968 *Variations in microclimate in a conifer swamp deeryard in northern Michigan.* Journal of Wildlife Management. *32:574-585.*

Ozoga, J.J. 1995. *Whitetail Winter. Willow Creek Press.* Minocqua, Wis. 160 pages.

Ozoga, J.J., and L.W. Gysel. 1972. *Response of white-tailed deer to winter weather.* Journal of Wildlife Management. *36:892-896.*

Verme, L.J., and J.J. Ozoga. 1971. *Influence of winter weather on white-tailed deer in Upper Michigan. Pages 16-28 in A. O. Haugen, ed. Proceedings of the Snow and Ice Symposium, Iowa State Univ.*

John Ozoga

Chapter 5

CAPTIVE-RAISED BUCKS:

Do They Survive in the Wild?

Remarkably little effort has been made to document the survival of semi-domesticated deer after they are forced to fend for themselves. However, studies have found that many wild deer which are live-trapped and moved to a new area die during the first four months after relocation.

Each year, many injured or orphaned white-tailed deer are raised by private citizens and wildlife rehabilitators. Because it is illegal to raise such wild animals in most states without proper permits, many of these captive-raised deer are eventually released into the wild.

In states like Texas, many ranchers even release pen-raised deer in an attempt to improve the quality of bucks on their property. In fact, some wildlife agencies occasionally release surplus experimental deer as an alternative to "sacrificing" them.

Despite the fact that these practices are not uncommon, remarkably little effort has been made to document the survival of semi-domesticated deer after they are forced to fend for themselves. However, studies have found that many wild deer which are live-trapped and moved to a new area die during the first four months after relocation. The relative importance of mortality factors differ among studies, but malnutrition, predation, vehicle acci-dents, hunting, and capture-related stress and injuries have been blamed for high mortality.

Study Results

Deer relocation studies summarized by J.M. Jones and J.H. Witham (1990) showed that between 25 percent and 85 percent of wild deer live-captured and released in new areas died during the first year. In one of the few published research papers dealing with this topic, Thomas McCall and co-workers (1988) compared the mortality of pen-raised white-tailed bucks with that of wild bucks on two Texas ranches. They used 10 bottle-raised bucks and three bucks raised by their mothers — collectively referred to as pen-raised — that were released onto the Welder-Dobie Ranch in January 1987. The average age of the bucks at release was 1.7 years.

They also captured nine wild deer on the Camaron Ranch in September 1986, averaging 1.9 years old, and supple-mented the sample with 11 radio-collared wild bucks 3½ years and older. Four of these 11 wild bucks were captured on the Welder-Dobie Ranch in 1984 and 1985, and seven were captured on the Camaron Ranch in 1986. All deer were fitted with mortality-sensing radio collars and colored plastic ear tags. These bucks were then located from airplanes on an average of every 25 days. Bucks whose transmitters indicated they had died were located and examined to determine the cause of death.

During the one-year study, eight of 13 pen-raised bucks died, whereas none of the 20 wild deer died. Six of 10 bottle-raised bucks and two of three bucks raised in captivity by their mothers died. Five of the eight deaths occurred within three months of release. The only death within the first 20 days after release came through hunting, ruling out capture-related stress. In addition, another buck was later shot, one was killed by a bobcat or mountain lion, and five died from undetermined causes.

The authors suggest the unusually low mortality of wild bucks in their study was a result of their exceptionally good physical condition. Apparently, above-average rainfall produced excellent range conditions during the normally stressful summer and winter periods, which contributed to the high survival of wild deer during the study period.

The distance traveled by pen-raised bucks from their release site to death site or last location averaged 3½ miles, but varied from 0.3 to 12 miles. Four bucks made long-distance movements of seven miles or greater. Two of these bucks died and two survived. The average travel distance for bucks that died was similar to that of the survivors, and there was no difference in distances traveled between age classes of pen-raised bucks.

In discussing their data, the authors emphasized that they could find no published reports concerning mortality of pen-raised deer that were released into the wild. They concluded, however, that based on their study and previous reports concerning translocated wild deer, "wildlife agencies and breeders can expect high first-year mortality of pen-raised deer released into the wild. Most losses will occur within the first four months."

Work at Cusino

The lack of data on captive-raised deer released into the wild prompted me and a couple of cohorts to summarize the data we had collected for deer released from the Cusino Wildlife Research Station in Upper Michigan. Our study (Ozoga et al. 1992) was conducted in the cold, deep snow belt along the south shore of Lake Superior. In that area, losses from malnutrition and predation of weakened deer commonly occur in severe winters. Through the years, we had routinely released surplus experimental deer that we didn't need for our studies. This made them available for legal harvest by

hunters. Our captive deer were raised in small (50-by-100 feet) pens, where we conducted nutritional and breeding trials; or in the square-mile Cusino enclosure, where we studied various aspects of behavioral ecology. All deer received excellent nutrition in captivity. With the exception of some orphans, most of the deer were not tame, but neither were they truly wild.

In this study, we compared the hunter-harvest rates of captive-raised male deer with those for locally tagged wild bucks. Although nearly equal numbers of female deer were also tagged and released, infrequent antlerless deer harvesting in the immediate area prevented us from examining survival rates for both sexes. Wild deer for the study were captured in box traps during the winter in the nearby Petrel Grade Deeryard. They were ear-tagged, sexed, sometimes weighed, classified as fawns (less than 1 year old) or adults (more than 1 year old) and released on the spot. In all, 195 wild male deer, including 145 fawns and 50 bucks, were marked and released from 1955 to 1988.

During this time, we released 73 male deer (62 fawns, 11 adults) that were born and raised in the small research pens. Eight of these deer were orphaned at a young age and bottle-fed; the others were raised by their mothers. Forty-one of the pen-raised fawns (including all orphans) were released in September or October, while 32 were released in March or April.

As part of our enclosure studies, a complete trap-out census of resident deer was conducted each March. Therefore, each deer was ear-tagged, and we knew the age of every animal. This also meant handling every deer at least once annually. Those that survived the handling, but were not returned to the enclosure, were transported five to 10 miles and released in or near the Petrel Grade Deeryard.

Recovery Rates

During our study, we released 97 male fawns and 84 adult bucks. We could only categorize subsequent deer mortality in our study as hunting or nonhunting related. Only a few deer wore radio-transmitters, so we seldom knew when they died or what caused their death when natural causes were involved. Because most deer were released during winter, however, premature death of any tagged deer (captive-raised or wild), for whatever reason, reduced the numbers available to hunters in autumn. Therefore, we assumed that a high hunter-harvest of a given test group would reflect a low mortality rate from natural causes.

In all, 75 of the 304 male deer tagged as fawns (24.3 percent) and 62 of 145 (42.8 percent) tagged as adults were eventually recovered, with hunters accounting for 120 of the 136 recoveries (91 percent). Of the remaining 16 recoveries, 10 were road-kills, two were poached, one was killed by domestic dogs, and three died from unknown causes.

AN EXCEPTIONAL BUCK

Deer raised in captivity at the Cusino Wildlife Research Station and then released into the wild apparently had difficulty coping with the hostile environment along the Lake Superior shore. Of 254 bucks released, 188 vanished, suggesting that many succumbed to natural causes within a few months after being set free.

Although most of those recovered were shot by hunters within one year of their release, one buck was an outstanding exception — M70. Despite having been born in the Cusino square-mile deer enclosure, he lived 10 years, 9 months in the wild. The ear-tagged buck was finally shot about two miles from the release site by Jim Burton during the muzzle-loading season.

M70 was born in June 1977. He was a single fawn reared by a 4-year-old doe, and thus had a good start in life. When we released him Feb. 28, 1978, he was 9 months old and weighed 106 pounds. That might sound impossibly large to some readers, but that is no printing error. In fact, although M70 was the largest of 24 buck fawns raised inside the enclosure in 1977, other buck fawns raised there have weighed more than 120 pounds by the time they were 7 months old. Don't forget, this is the large *borealis* subspecies.

The next time we got our hands on M70 was March 29, 1982, when we live-trapped, examined and released him in the winter deeryard about one mile from his release site. It's interesting to note that among several hundred deer in the vicinity, we were fortunate enough to retrap this particular animal while using only one live trap. The secret was that we baited the trap with the same type of pelletized ration that is fed to the enclosure herd, which is a strange food to wild deer. (It's my guess that once a deer samples a new food it immediately makes a quality determination, and then locks that message into its mental computer. The experienced deer never seems to forget, even years later, making further sampling unnecessary when encountering a choice food again.)

Burton, a professional taxidermist who lived in the area and hunted "behind the house" for many years, never saw M70 until about 3:30 p.m. on Dec. 2, 1988, the first day of the muzzle-loading season. Whether the buck lived in the marshes and dense white cedar swamps nearby, or summered elsewhere and merely wintered near Burton's, is unknown. Burton said the buck dressed out at a lean 172 pounds, and said he could count every rib. Despite the buck's old age, however, he still carried a respectable 8-point rack with an inside spread of 19 inches, and one broken brow tine. The unusual light color of the antlers suggested the 11½-year-old buck had done minimal antler rubbing during his final rut.

If anyone is aware of a captive-raised white-tailed buck that lived longer in a wild, hunted area, I would like to hear about it. You can write to me in care of *Deer & Deer Hunting* magazine at 700 E. State St., Iola, WI 54990-0001.

— *John J. Ozoga*

Among the deer raised in small pens, 8.1 percent were killed by hunters, while 54.6 percent of pen-raised adult bucks were eventually shot. We saw a similar relationship among the enclosure-raised deer, where 17.5 percent of those released as fawns and 31 percent released as adults were reported harvested. Among wild deer, however, 30.3 percent of the fawns and 44 percent of the adult bucks were reported taken by hunters.

Hunter recovery rates for pen-raised and enclosure-raised fawns released in spring were similar (19.1 percent and 17.5 percent, respectively), but considerably lower than recover rates for wild fawns (30.3 percent). In contrast, most pen-raised fawns released in autumn disappeared, and likely failed to survive their first winter in the wild, as only one of 41 (2.4 percent) was known to have been recovered by hunters. None of the eight orphans was ever recovered. The captive-raised fawns we released in autumn were probably especially ill-prepared, physiologically and behaviorally, to endure the severe winters of this region. They had not attained full skeletal growth, and likely had the minimal fat reserves necessary for winter survival. We can only speculate that their lack of close social bonds with other deer further decreased their chances for survival.

Experimental Factors

The captive-raised male fawns we released in spring were presumably in excellent physical condition, at least initially, averaging 18 percent heavier in body weight than their wild counterparts. Further, spring-released deer were subjected to limited browse availability for only a few weeks before snow-melt, which should have enhanced their prospects for winter survival. Nonetheless, compared to wild fawns, we suspect that even the spring-released captive-raised fawns suffered higher than normal mortality their first winter.

We found considerable variation in the elapsed time from release to recovery for tagged deer. In general, hunters recovered most captive-raised deer the first autumn they were available for harvest, while more wild bucks were recovered in later years. There was one exception to this generalization, however. An enclosure-raised buck identified as M70 was released Feb. 28, 1978, when about 9 months old, and shot the first day of the muzzle-loading deer season in 1988. In other words, 10 years, 9 months passed before he was killed two miles from the release site. Of the captive-raised deer recovered, all seven pen-raised fawns, four of six pen-raised adults, 16 of 20 enclosure-raised fawns, and 29 of 33 enclosure-raised adults were recovered within one year of their release. By comparison, more of the wild fawns (50 percent) and wild adult bucks (52.2 percent) were recovered in subsequent years.

The captive-raised adult deer were of known age, ranging from about 22 months old to about 9 years old when released. Of the 56 bucks that were 22 months old when released, 25 (44.6 percent) were harvested, while 11 of 20 (55 percent) released at 34 months old were shot. It's interesting to note, however, that only three of 19 (15.8 percent) released at an older age were ever recovered. Some mortality of tagged deer was likely caused by stress or undetected injuries sustained in handling. Given our experience with enclosure animals, we expect about a 5 percent loss among adult bucks and 12 percent loss among fawns from handling. Because wild deer are more hyperactive, one might expect greater handling losses with them. Further, because of the added risk of coyote predation, even greater capture-related mortality likely occurred in our study than we were able to pinpoint.

Traveling Away from the Enclosure

In another study, seven of eight (87 percent) bucks equipped with radio transmitters were recovered after they were released or escaped from the Cusino enclosure. These deer ranged in age from 1 to 3 years old. During the first year after release, five were shot by hunters, and one was killed by an automobile. The seventh buck was shot 19 months after release. Those results reflect the extreme vulnerability of captive-raised male deer to humans, even in Upper Michigan, which has a relatively sparse human population.

As expected for migratory Northern deer that might travel long distances from summer to winter range, tagged deer in our study traveled much farther between the points of release and recovery than those in the Texas study. On average, wild fawns traveled farther (13.5 miles) than those raised in small pens (8.4 miles)

Another possible explanation for the disappearance of most older captive-raised bucks is that they could not maintain their high dominance status when competing in the wild, and died either directly or indirectly from fighting.

or the enclosure (10.1 miles). Wild adult bucks also exhibited a tendency to travel farther (11.7 miles), as compared to pen-raised (4.8 miles) or enclosure-raised (6.6 miles) adult bucks. The longest travel distances recorded were 32 miles for a wild deer tagged as an adult, and 29 miles for an enclosure-raised animal released as a fawn.

Adult Males

Considering the comparatively high (47.4 percent) hunter recovery of captive-raised male deer released when 22 and 34 months old, the disappearance of most (74.2 percent) captive-raised bucks released at older age is somewhat of an enigma. However, because all three of those recovered returned to and were shot within a half-mile from the enclosure fence, I suspect mature males had an especially difficult time coping with relocation.

As an interesting sidelight, in April 1987, I released the most dominant buck in the enclosure after transporting him 12 miles from the facility. This buck, A69, was 9 years old at the time. He was radio-equipped so we could follow his movements. A69 settled down during midsummer, but began to wander extensively in late August. We lost track of him in early September at about the time he should have shed his antler velvet. A few weeks later, however, we picked up his signal north of the enclosure's fence. Some hunters had seen him and his impressive antlers, and were plotting how to get him once the rifle season opened Nov. 15.

On Oct. 28, just about when the first enclosure doe was expected to breed, A69 and one of the enclosure's bucks engaged in a vicious fight — with the enclosure's fence between them! In the process, the bucks tore a large hole in the fence. This allowed A69 and another mature wild buck to enter the enclosure, and a yearling buck to escape.

Typically, mature bucks dominate younger subordinates and do most of the breeding in a given area. Because of fasting and strenuous rut-related activity, even mature enclosure bucks that receive unlimited nutritious supplemental feed regularly lose 20 percent to 25 percent of their weight during the rut, while younger bucks normally only lose 10 percent to 15 percent. As a result, captive-raised mature bucks might have been at a distinct physiological disadvantage when released.

Another possible explanation for the disappearance of most older captive-raised bucks is that they could not maintain their high dominance status when competing in the wild, and died either directly or indirectly from fighting. Therefore, it might be more than coincidence that A42, a pen-raised castrated buck, survived longer in the wild — more than 4½ years — than any other captive male released at adult age. His lack of sex drive and associated rut-related activity — which involves enormous energy expenditure and sometimes vicious fighting — probably enhanced his longevity.

Conclusion

Wild deer in our study occupied a fairly remote area of conifer swamp in winter, from which they normally dispersed northeast to occupy summer range even farther away from major highways and human habitation. This dispersal pattern had also been identified in earlier studies using automatic collaring devices. However, captive-raised deer were more frequently recovered to the southwest, closer to a major highway and somewhat greater human population.

One hunter harvested three enclosure-born bucks, all of yearling age, on his property. Another hunter shot two enclosure animals beneath the same apple tree during consecutive seasons. Given our experience in Upper Michigan, we expect considerable variation in survivability of captive-raised male deer released in Northern environments, with much depending on the time of year and the age of the deer when released. On average, the lowest nonhunting related death rate and greatest longevity can be expected for deer released when 1 to 3 years old. Also, in a Northern climate, delaying the release of all captive-raised deer until shortly after complete snow-melt in spring might increase their survival rate for the first few months in the wild.

Nonetheless, regardless of the climate, the available data suggest captive-raised bucks surviving translocation will be highly vulnerable to harvest by hunters. Relatively few of these deer survive longer than one year in the wild.

References

Jones, J.M., and J.H. Witham. 1990. Post-translocation survival and movements of metropolitan white-tailed deer. Wildlife Society Bulletin *18:434-441.*

McCall, T.C., R.D. Brown, and C.A. DeYoung. 1988. Comparison of mortality of pen-raised and wild white-tailed bucks. Wildlife Society Bulletin *16:380-384.*

Ozoga, J.J., R.V. Doepker, and R.D. Earle. 1992. Hunter harvest of captive-raised male white-tailed deer, Odocoileus virginianus, released in Upper Michigan. Canadian Field Naturalist *106:357-360.*

Chapter 6

TIMING OF THE RUT:

Differences in the North and South

Regardless of environment, the timing of deer births is critical to the species' survival. Breeding must occur so fawns are born when their survival chances are best. Natural selection minimizes poorly timed births.

With few exceptions, deer-hunting seasons occur shortly before, during or shortly after the whitetail's breeding season — a hectic period we hunters call the rut.

Whitetails in breeding condition are often recklessly more active, making them easier than normal to hunt. The timing of the breeding season is set by shortening days in autumn, or changing photoperiod. However, many environmental, biological and behavioral factors might interact to determine when or if a doe breeds. Therefore, knowing how certain factors influence breeding conditions in an area could be critical to hunting success.

Hunters can apply some basic principles to rutting behavior across the whitetail's extensive range. But they'll also see inherent differences. How a Northern whitetail responds to environmental pressures, social factors and nutritional changes sometimes mimics the responses of its Southern cousin. Then again, sometimes it doesn't. Research shows some factors that control the rut's timing in Southern deer have little or no effect

on rut behavior in Northern deer — and, probably, vice versa.

Basics

Regardless of environment, the timing of deer births is critical to the species' survival. Breeding must occur so fawns are born when their survival chances are best. Natural selection has minimized poorly timed births. Unusual traits that contribute to untimely breeding are soon lost from the gene pool because the resulting offspring generally die.

Professor Harry Jacobson, a long-time deer researcher at Mississippi State University, writes: "The renewal of life for white-tailed deer depends on favorable birthing times. In most regions whitetails inhabit, only certain periods of the year allow newborns and their mothers to thrive and survive. Unlike domestic farm animals, which breed year-round, deer require a restrictive breeding period, timed so that the resulting embryo becomes a completely developed fawn and is born at a time that favors survival. The mechanism by which breeding takes place at just the right time of year is an ingenious adaptation."

The pineal gland — a small, pea-sized gland deep within the brain — measures the amount of daylight and responds to changing photoperiod. In darkness, this "third eye" secretes a hormone called melatonin, which influences the release of sex hormones from the pituitary. It is the response of the pineal gland to shortening day length in autumn that ensures timely breeding so fawns are born on schedule in spring.

Narrow Northern Window

It's equally important to recognize that environmental pressures vary greatly by region. That means the timing and duration of the breeding season can vary regionally.

Professor Karl V. Miller, a researcher at the University of Georgia, calls the whitetail's breeding season a "window of opportunity." Its opening and closing varies by latitude. The whitetail's breeding window is generally narrow in the North, where it's tightly regulated by photoperiod. North of 36 degrees latitude, most whitetails breed between mid-October and mid-December. Peak breeding usually occurs in mid-November.

A doe will accept a male only during peak estrus, which lasts 24 to 36 hours. If she is not bred or does not become pregnant, her cycle might recur in 23 to 30 days.

If a Northern doe remains in peak physical condition but does not become pregnant, she might recycle a third time. In the North, however, a "negative energy balance" closes the breeding window once cold weather increases body heat-loss and snow cover reduces food availability. This doesn't mean Northern does don't sometimes breed unusually late. They do, often for unknown reasons.

Normally, we expect young does breeding for the first time to breed later than experienced does. Doe fawns in the North usually breed around mid-December, if at all. But even 1½-year-old does tend to breed later in the rut. On occasion, I've had healthy, mature enclosure does, which normally bred in the first week of November, not breed until March. I could not explain such phenomena.

The Wide Southern Window

By comparison, the Southern breeding window is potentially wide. A multitude of factors might combine to time breeding. Between 28 and 36 degrees latitude, for example, most whitetails breed between late September and late March. In some areas, peak breed-

No single factor is likely more influential in the timing of the rut than nutrition, which helps determine a doe's growth, the timing of her sexual maturity and, therefore, her breeding date, no matter the region.

ing occurs in November, but in other areas not until December or January. (Because the equator provides no seasonal photoperiod cues, deer in that region breed year-round.)

Some late-breeding, late-birthing schedules common in Southern herds are caused by nutritional shortages and slow growth rates. In other cases, delayed breeding schedules apparently are caused by a shortage of mature bucks, which tends to be hunting-induced.

In milder Southern climates, an unbred adult doe might come into estrus as many as seven times in one season. This considerable North/South difference is one reason for the South's potentially long whitetail breeding season. Therefore, in the South, late-breeding schedules might be advanced and better synchronized by changing deer harvest regulations. Those changes include carefully balancing deer numbers with available food and cover while allowing more males to reach maturity.

The Genetic Factor

According to Jacobson, however, some late breeding appears genetically linked and not easily altered. In Mississippi, for example, deer normally don't start breeding until November. Even when Michigan deer were transported to Mississippi, the Northern subspecies maintained its October and November breeding dates. Meanwhile, Mississippi penmates continued to breed in late December and January. Crossbred offspring of Michigan and Mississippi deer bred during the entire range of both parents.

Miller contends it isn't known whether the breeding window is controlled genetically or if it's set after conception or birth. If photoperiod cues are set after conception, Miller said: "The late breeding in some regions of the Southeast may be self-perpetuating. For instance, a fawn's timing would have been affected by when its mother's cues were set, and her mother's, and so on."

Nutrition

Although the rut's general timing is set by changing photoperiod, a doe's breeding date might be affected by many factors. No single factor is likely more influential than nutrition, which helps determine a doe's growth, the timing of her sexual maturity and, therefore, her breeding date, no matter the region.

On Northern range, malnourished does typically breed later than normal, which means late November or early December. These late-breeders are usually young, still-growing fawns and yearlings. However, this group might also include mature does on poor range, especially if they were burdened with nursing fawns. While these animals might achieve good physical condition and breed late on Southern range, they sometimes fail to breed on Northern range because of the narrow breeding window, especially when a harsh winter begins early.

Some early-born doe fawns that grow big and fat by autumn achieve puberty and then breed. Still, they generally don't breed until mid-December, or even later in some cases. This phenomenon can cause a protracted rut, even on Northern range.

Yearling does are also extremely sensitive to stress. When malnourished, Northern yearlings often fail to breed. Such was the case in Michigan's Cusino square-mile enclosure before we provided supplemental feeding. When living solely on natural forage, the enclosure's yearlings were grossly undersized. One-third of them failed to breed, and none conceived more than one fawn.

Although obesity is likely rare in free-ranging white-tails, an experiment by Michigan researcher Lou Verme at Cusino suggested it might also cause some does to breed late. Extreme obesity is known to disrupt reproduction in domestic animals. Fat might infiltrate the ovaries so much that it hinders follicular development. The result is irregular or cessation of estrus, and a delay or failure to breed.

Verme observed 2½-year-old does that did not raise fawns had become "hog fat" on energy-rich pellet diets, and did not breed until early December, about three weeks later than expected.

Costs of Female Subordination

Dominant animals don't have it as easy as one might expect. A dominant individual must expend extra energy fighting to maintain its high social status, which risks injury. This is true with does as well as bucks.

Subordination is also stressful and costly. One consequence of subordination, especially in high-density herds, is delayed breeding among low-ranking does. Social stress caused by maternal domination apparently causes a hormonal imbalance that interferes with a doe's reproductive functions. Such stress tends to increase progesterone production from the adrenal glands, which can block the effects of estradiol-induced hormone surges during estrus. That interrupts ovulation, and leads to late breeding.

Dominant animals don't have it as easy as one might expect. A dominant individual must expend extra energy fighting to maintain its high social status, which risks injury. This is true with does as well as bucks.

Yearling does (1½ years old) tend to remain subordinate to their mothers and, on average, breed about one week later than mature does. However, even 2½-year-old does that fail to raise fawns might revert to yearling behavior by seeking their mother's leadership (and domination), and continue to breed late. Therefore, even when well-fed, social factors might delay breeding among young does when doe densities are high. In our Cusino studies, social stress at densities exceeding 100 deer per square mile delayed the rut's peak by nearly a week, shifting it from around Nov. 16 to Nov. 22, even when the herd was optimally nourished. When poor nutrition is a factor, it's easy to see how the rut's peak could be delayed by several weeks, especially in the South.

Rut Activity: A Function of Age, Nutrition

Rubs, scrapes and other evidence of early buck rutting activity might indicate breeding among does. In the North, such activity usually starts in September and precedes active breeding by one or two months. In the South, bucks and does might be ready to reproduce at about the same time, possibly as soon as early September. Therefore, a flurry of scraping activity in late September might indicate some Southern does are in breeding condition.

Most rubbing and scraping is done by bucks 2½ years and older. Therefore, delayed and less-intense buck rutting activity can be expected in socially unbalanced herds because few mature bucks are present. Such a tendency might have nothing to do with the timing of doe breeding.

In my studies — even without mature bucks — yearling bucks only made 15 percent as many scrapes and half as many rubs as mature bucks. Further, while mature bucks started scraping in September, yearlings made no scrapes until late October, about one week before the first does bred.

In northern Georgia, researchers led by Miller recorded buck-rub densities ranging from 474 to 1,502 rubs per square mile. They also found rub density was closely related to the number of bucks in the herd older than 2½ years.

Interestingly, in the latter study, rub density and distribution changed each year depending on acorn abundance, a critical autumn deer food in the study area. More rubs were recorded in years of good acorn production, when rubs were also more concentrated in oak habitats.

Priming Pheromones

Buck signposts, in the form of rubs and scrapes, are visual and olfactory signals. That is, they're showy in nature and are scent-marked with various secretions. Unlike other communications, signposts are extensions of the animal, remaining functional for long periods, even in the maker's absence. Thus, signposts convey long-lasting messages that likely have physiological and psychological effects on other deer.

Miller and fellow Georgia researcher Larry Marchinton propose that signposting by dominant bucks plays a vital role in maintaining a herd's social harmony. These professors suggest that primer pheromones — which produce a physiological response — deposited by dominant bucks at rubs and scrapes help bring adult does into estrus early.

Even in northern Michigan, confining bucks and does together in autumn advanced mean breeding dates eight to nine days. The exact mechanisms involved were unknown, but observations suggested close, unnatural confinement of bucks with does had some type of biostimulating effect. It could have been caused by pheromones produced by males, which induced earlier ovulation.

The Mount Holly Study

Studies by professor David Guynn at Clemson University found that delayed and protracted whitetail breeding seasons can be advanced and shortened when nutritional and social factors are considered in herd management. They can, at least, in a Southern environment. In Guynn's Mount Holly study area in South Carolina, the herd was initially typical of many Southern herds: Deer densities were high, but bucks had been heavily exploited. The unbalanced adult sex ratio heavily favored females, and the breeding season was late and long (96 days), with some fawns born in September.

The researchers came in and selectively shot deer. Their goals were to better balance deer numbers with food and cover resources, to decrease the proportion of does, and to increase the proportion of bucks. Within five years, the rut at Mount Holly became more intense and shortened to 43 days. Mean conception dates shifted from Nov. 11 in the first year of study to Oct. 15 in the final year.

Improved nutrition was one reason for the earlier and shorter breeding periods. Also, a more balanced sex ratio likely contributed to less estrous recycling. However, increased biostimulation of females by

The obvious question is this: Can inexperienced young bucks handle the job of sires in herds where intensive harvesting removes most older males? The data from Guynn's study suggests they aren't reliable.

mature bucks was also considered important, because the availability of males to breed females could not by itself advance the breeding season.

Michigan Studies

According to studies by Miller and his co-workers, yearling bucks reach peak sex organ development and hormone production about one month later than prime-aged bucks. These findings closely mirror my studies that showed delayed scent-marking behavior by yearling bucks.

The obvious question is this: Can inexperienced young bucks handle the job of sires in herds where intensive harvesting removes most older males? The data from Guynn's study suggests they aren't reliable.

We put yearling bucks to the test in the Cusino enclosure by removing all older bucks for three years. This study was possible because we could live-trap all deer from the area annually, release surplus animals outside, and shape reintroduced populations according to our study's needs. Compared to mature bucks, yearling bucks fought more, even with does; failed to establish a strict dominance hierarchy before the rut; lacked a ritualistic courtship style, by literally chasing every doe in sight during the rut; and exhibited poor scent-marking behavior.

Still, despite sexual inexperience and seemingly inferior behavior, yearling bucks serviced most does on schedule, and produced as many offspring as could have been produced by mature sires. Surprisingly, we saw a tendency by yearling does to breed earlier when serviced by yearlings instead of mature bucks, while some older does conceived unusually late when bred by yearlings.

These finding, of course, differed considerably from those at Mount Holly. In the North, it appears the rut's timing is more closely regulated by photoperiod. It is influenced less by scent-marking, priming pheromones and biostimulation than in the South.

It's important to point out, however, that deer in our northern Michigan study were exceptionally well-fed. Had they been malnourished, the results might have been different.

Conclusion

The precise timing of the rut varies considerably from north to south across the species' range, depending on many poorly understood factors. Although the Northern rut is brief and rigidly controlled by photoperiod, poor nutrition and high herd densities can delay peak breeding by a week or two.

Southern herds seem more sensitive to social imbalances. When mature bucks are few, breeding in high-density, malnourished Southern herds becomes even more delayed and the rut more prolonged. Some believe this tendency for late-breeding and late-birth-

ing then becomes self-perpetuating.

Whatever the reason for late breeding, many late-born Southern fawns become small, poor-quality adults. Such a scenario in the North yields many small fawns ill-prepared for harsh winters, which leads to excessive winter-kill.

References

Gerlach, D., S. Atwater and J. Schnell. 1994. Deer. *Stackpole Books. 384 Pages.*

Miller, K.V., K.E. Kammermeyer, R.L. Marchinton and B. Moser. 1987. Population and habitat influences on antler rubbing by white-tailed deer. Journal of Wildlife Management *51:62-66.*

Miller, K.V., and R.L. Marchinton (Eds.). 1995. Quality Whitetails: The Why and How of Quality Deer Management. *Stackpole Books. 322 pages.*

Ozoga, J.J., and L.J. Verme. 1982. Reproduction and physical condition of a supplementally fed white-tailed deer herd. Journal of Wildlife Management *46:281-301.*

Ozoga, J.J., and L.J. Verme. 1984. Effect of family-bond deprivation on reproductive performance in female white-tailed deer. Journal of Wildlife Management *48:1326-1334.*

Ozoga, J.J., and L.J. Verme. 1985. Comparative breeding behavior and performance of yearling vs. prime-age white-tailed bucks. Journal of Wildlife Management *49:364-372.*

Ozoga, J.J., and L.J. Verme. 1986. Initial and subsequent maternal success of white-tailed deer. Journal of Wildlife Management *50:122-124.*

Verme, L.J. 1965. Reproduction studies on penned white-tailed deer. Journal of Wildlife Management *29:74-79.*

Verme, L.J., J.J. Ozoga, and J.T. Nellist. 1987. Induced early estrus in penned white-tailed deer. Journal of Wildlife Management *51:54-56.*

John Ford

Chapter 7

SHEDDING VELVET:

Nature's Annual Act of Murder

"The seasonal demise of antler skin is not innately programmed to the death of its cells, but must be attributed to external agencies. ... The shedding of antler velvet, therefore, is a case of murder, not suicide."
— *Richard Goss*

Depending on who's talking, antlers have been called magnificent ornaments, prized trophies, potent medicine, bones of contention, biological luxuries, and an extravagance of nature.

Whatever the poetic rhetoric, anatomically speaking, a buck's polished antlers are essentially dead bone. In fact, according to Richard Goss (1983), these bones are victims of "murder, not suicide."

Although experts might debate the issue, it seems ironic that antlers are most functional after they die. They are secondary sex characteristics that evolved hand-in-hand with other aspects of deer breeding behavior. To the beholder, dead (mineralized) antlers serve multiple purposes. But most importantly, large antlers are durable, showy structures — status symbols — that attract prospective mates, intimidate rival males, and sometimes serve as deadly weapons in the buck's competition for supremacy and breeding privileges.

To scientists like Goss, deer antlers are "fascinating curiosities that seem to defy the laws of nature." Deer antlers are so improbable, says Goss, "that if they had not evolved in the first place they would never have been conceived even in the wildest fantasies of the most imaginative biologists."

Hidden Answers?

In fact, so unusual are antlers, that they might help scientists solve many biological mysteries. Resting within the study of "antlerology" might be the secrets to combating cancer, regenerating lost body parts, or a host of other problems challenging the medical profession.

Contrary to speculation by pioneering French scientist Comet De Buffon, deer antlers aren't made of woody material, even though they are normally branched and shed their outer covering. Antlers are true solid bone with no marrow cavity, and they're unique in the mammal kingdom. They are grown only by members of the deer family, *Cervidae*. They are the only mammalian appendages that replace themselves, and their growth rate is phenomenal, averaging about ¼ inch daily in whitetails.

Antlers are actually two structures: the antler itself and the pedicle, or stump, where the antler develops. Before a deer can grow antlers, it must first grow pedicles. Antlers grow, mature, die, drop off, and are replaced annually. Pedicles, however, are permanently attached.

The annual cycle of antler growth and death is highly dependent on seasonal variations in the buck's amount of testosterone, a male hormone produced principally by the testes. The process involves a complex interplay between the testes, pineal gland, pituitary gland and hypothalamus of the brain in response to rhythmic, seasonal fluctuations in the amount of daylight (photoperiod).

Young bucks castrated during the first few months of their lives won't develop pedicles or antlers. In contrast, if adult bucks are castrated, their antlers are cast prematurely and new antlers will grow, but these antlers won't reach full maturation. Without testes, the male cannot produce enough testosterone to complete the antler cycle. As with antlered does, castrated bucks carry permanently viable antlers that remain velvet-covered, sometimes forming grotesque amorphous masses not unlike benign tumors.

Initially, pedicle development in the young male is closely linked to his rate of maturity, testes development, and his ability to produce a substantial amount of testosterone. Subsequent adult antler cycles are more closely programmed by seasons and light cycles, which control the rhythm of hormone production.

Antlers are actually two structures: the antler itself and the pedicle, or stump, where the antler develops. Before a deer can grow antlers, it must first grow pedicles.

Nurturing Velvet

The antler is an outgrowth of bone from the pedicle, while the skin overlaying the pedicle gives rise to antler velvet that covers and feeds the growing antler. Initially, a developing antler is fed not only by blood vessels within the velvet but by internal blood vessels originating within the pedicle.

Antler velvet differs from skin and hair that cover the deer's body. George Bubenik (1994) describes velvet as a "modified skin with modified pelage" or a special type of "fur." After the antlers drop off, velvet grows anew each year from the ring of skin surrounding the wound left by the cast antler.

Antler velvet is richly supplied with blood vessels and nerves, and is capable of enormous expansion, which is necessary to keep pace with the antler's rapid growth rate. Although growing antlers are soft and easily damaged, short hairs on the velvet stick out at right angles and serve as touch-sensitive feelers to warn of pending collisions, thereby helping to minimize damage.

Also, arteries supplying blood to growing antlers have unusually thick walls. When severed, the thick muscular walls quickly constrict, reducing blood loss.

The velvet skin has no muscles, but associated with each hair follicle is a sebaceous gland from which an oily secretion (sebum) is produced. This sebum is responsible for the shiny appearance of the velvet skin, which becomes more obvious when the velvet starts to shrink and die, forcing droplets of sebum to the surface.

Some researchers propose that the velvet-produced sebum serves as an insect repellent. Others speculate that the oily secretion contains pheromones that serve an important function in scent-marking. The late Anthony Bubenik (see Bubenik and Bubenik, 1990), for example, suggested that bucks smear the sebum produced by the velvet over their bodies, and then onto vegetation at head-height, leaving a strong scent track. To my knowledge, however, neither theory has been substantiated.

Why Does Growth Stop?

The completion of antler growth, antler mineralization and velvet shedding are closely linked to autumn's shortening days. By comparison, antler casting dates are more variable, and more strongly influenced by other factors. Sharply rising testosterone production induces such change, and causes dramatic alterations in buck behavior shortly before the breeding season.

Antler hardening seems to happen suddenly, but it is a gradual process. The antler's outer surface hardens quickly in the few weeks before velvet is shed. However, mineral deposition in the antler's interior is more gradual and prolonged. Bone formation starts internally in lower portions of the antler, and progresses from the base to the tips as antlers elongate.

Blood flow from the pedicle into the antler core becomes restricted by midsummer as the pedicles semi-mineralize. As a result, during its second half of growth, the antler is nourished primarily by the superficial temporal artery and about 12 of its major branches through the velvet. As the blood flow shuts off in these vessels, the bone gradually dies, dries and sheds the velvet, thus killing the antler. Even after the velvet sheds, artery impressions are visible in the antler bone as molded channels.

The final demise of antler velvet starts with a thickening and hardening of the arterial walls. That's caused by the deposition of mineral salts, which interfere with blood flow, a condition similar to arteriosclerosis. As a

INFANT ANTLERS

Bucks typically start growing their first antlers in spring when they're about 11 months old. However, some buck fawns grow prominent pedicles topped with small button, or infant antlers, less than ½ inch long, during autumn when they're 6 or 7 months old.

Infant antlers, which are essentially mineralized pedicle tips, are cast during winter before new antler growth starts.

The process of growing infant antlers is totally different from antler regeneration. "Because it is such a gradual process," says Richard Goss, "it is impossible to pinpoint the exact point when pedicle growth gives way to antler development. The (origin) of the first antlers is a phenomenon that is not conveniently classified. Although the histological events undoubtedly resemble those by which subsequent sets of antlers are regenerated each year, the process is not an example of regeneration because there has been nothing lost to be replaced. ... In this respect, the fawn's initial antler is a unique zoological structure."

Most buck fawns grow prominent pedicles when 4 or 5 months old.

Some buck fawns grow prominent pedicles topped with small button, or "infant" antlers, less than ½ inch long during autumn when they're 6 or 7 months old.

In the wild, however, only 5 percent to 10 percent of them reportedly grow polished button antlers. The incidence of infant antlers tends to be considerably higher for well-nourished, pen-raised animals.

Professor Harry Jacobson (1995) reported that 20 percent of buck fawns raised in the deer research facilities at Mississippi State University grew infant antlers. He noted, however, that none of the buck fawns rubbed-out before the end of January, and most not until February or March.

I found the incidence of infant antlers much higher in Upper

Michigan's Cusino deer enclosure (Ozoga 1988), where 84 percent of the supplementally fed buck fawns achieved polished antlers. Unlike in the South, however, the Michigan fawns polished their antlers from late November until early January, and then cast them by late February.

Reasons for the North-to-South difference in the timing of infant antler development is unknown. Quite likely, however, the accelerated physical development of Northern fawns is an adaptation that enhances their prospects for surviving harsh winters.

Clearly, infant antlers are indicative of an advanced rate of maturity and an achievement of puberty. Only well-nourished buck fawns that achieve some critical level of body weight and testes development ever produce enough male hormone for such advanced sexual development. Those that do probably exhibit velvet shedding, limited antler rubbing and other behavior patterns typical of young, sexually active bucks. Given the opportunity, they're probably capable of breeding.

— *John J. Ozoga*

result, blood flow decreases sharply as openings in the arteries constrict. According to theory, the sympathetic nervous system then responds by completely shutting off blood flow to the velvet, causing the starved velvet to die. Velvet death normally takes several weeks, but sometimes the strangulation of blood flow to the velvet occurs suddenly.

Given the circumstances surrounding velvet death, Goss concludes: "The seasonal demise of antler skin is not innately programmed to the death of its cells, but must be attributed to external agencies. ... The shedding of antler velvet, therefore, is a case of murder, not suicide."

Death and stripping of the antler velvet generally signal the death of the antler core itself. However, because the velvet might die before the antler tips harden, George Bubenik theorizes that velvet and antler death might be separate processes.

After Velvet Sheds

Even after shedding velvet, the innermost portions of the antler might remain porous, with a trickle of blood flowing to the antler base. That's why trophy antlers aren't officially measured until a given drying period elapses. Eventually, however, even the antler's spongy core dries out as it converts to solid bone. Then, the antler literally dies back to the pedicle junction. Such change over time probably explains why antlers become more brittle toward the end of the rut, immediately before they're cast.

As antlers harden, they shrink, as does the dying velvet, which tends to split lengthwise. In some cases, the dry condition might persist for days before the buck starts rubbing off the dead velvet. What prompts a buck to suddenly rub his antlers on vegetation or saplings to peel off the velvet is unknown

Because living velvet is well-supplied with nerves, some observers believe dead or dying velvet causes irritation or itching to the deer, thereby spurring the rubbing response. Even many scientists hold this view. Sometimes, however, rubbing might occur prematurely when the velvet is still living, which causes heavy bleeding, or before the antler fully hardens. The rubbing of living velvet has also been seen, however, after experimental denervation of antlers eliminates any possible sensations.

George Bubenik concludes that the rubbing of velvet occurs relatively independent of antler mineralization. He suggests it's primarily a behavioral response, triggered by sharply rising levels of male sex hormones, such as testosterone, that stimulate the central nervous system. Certainly, such is the case after bucks carry hardened antlers and use them to make rubs that serve as signposts. Some aggressive bucks even continue rubbing with their foreheads after casting antlers.

Normally, velvet is stripped from the antlers within 24 hours. But sometimes the cleaning process might take less than an hour or several days.

Occasionally the rub-out is incomplete, with live velvet left clinging to lower portions of the antlers for days or weeks. Such incomplete rubbing is especially common among injured, diseased or senile bucks, presumably because of low hormone production.

Strips of velvet left hanging from the antler base seem to irritate the buck, causing him to shake his head vigorously. In some cases he might eat the limp, dangling strips, or use his rear hoofs to carefully scratch away velvet that clings to the antler base.

Newly exposed antlers are nearly pure white but become darker in color after frequent rubbing. Some researchers claim dried blood on antlers stain them after the initial rub-off. However, because pen-raised bucks often carry abnormally light antlers, I'm inclined to believe the antlers of wild bucks are stained primarily from rubbing the bark of trees and shrubs.

The precise timing of velvet death varies among bucks, depending on their age, physical condition, dominance rank and other factors that determine seasonal rhythms in sex hormone levels.

Timing Varies

The timing of velvet shedding is closely regulated by the shortening day length in autumn, in tune with preparation for the breeding season. But the precise timing of velvet death varies among bucks, depending on their age, physical condition, dominance rank and other factors that determine seasonal rhythms in sex hormone levels.

Any stressful condition, such as poor diet, injury, disease, heavy parasite loads, extreme old age or social stress would likely suppress or delay a buck's seasonal rise in testosterone output, which would delay velvet shedding. Late-born yearling bucks, in particular, would tend to rub off velvet much later than other bucks. On the other hand, the most physically fit bucks would shed velvet first. Velvet shedding schedules might also vary regionally.

In Mississippi, Jacobson and R.N. Griffin (1983) reported that captive-raised bucks shed velvet from Sept. 4 to Oct. 12, with the average being Sept. 24. They also observed a wide variation in the shedding date from one year to the next, and saw some wild bucks carrying velvet antlers in mid-December. Under penned conditions, they saw no relation between the animal's age and velvet shedding date. Some yearlings were the first to rub off velvet, while others were the last.

On Northern range, bucks generally commence rubbing-out during the last week of August, with peak rubbing activity occurring in early September. Unhealthy mature bucks, or undersized yearlings that grow short spikes, might not rub out until mid-October. But, I've seen few sexually normal adult bucks in the Upper Great Lakes region carry velvet antlers into November. Therefore, aside from the more prolonged velvet shedding season found with Southern bucks, and despite the North's earlier rut, peak velvet shedding schedules likely vary by only a few weeks throughout most of the whitetail's range in the United States.

Studies conducted by Karl Miller and his coworkers (Miller et al. 1987), demonstrated that yearling and 2½-year-old bucks in the Southeast exhibited delayed elevations in testosterone production, and entered rutting condition later than older males. Normally, bucks 4½ to 8½ years old exhibit the earliest rise in testosterone and attain the highest levels of hormone production. This probably explains why young bucks, even in the absence of older bucks, tend to make fewer rubs and scrapes, and show delayed rubbing, as compared to older bucks.

Dominance-submissive relationships among bucks are also important in determining the order of velvet shedding in a deer population. Tests conducted at the University of Georgia (Forand et al. 1985) revealed that dominant bucks shed velvet earlier than subordinates, regardless of age. In the wild, older bucks normally dominate younger ones and shed velvet first. But even in the absence of older bucks, superior young bucks are the first to carry velvet-free antlers.

Conclusion

These findings illustrate the importance of behavior, and support the view that "winners" become psycholog-ically and physiologically stimulated. Bucks that win often become hormonally charged, shed antler velvet first, and become avid scent-markers. Logically, habitual "losers" suffer the reverse, depressing effects.

Whatever the precise timing of velvet shedding in your area, it's a prelude to coming events. Sharp seasonal changes in the whitetail's behavior are about to occur. Velvet shedding signals the death of antlers, an end to the tranquil days of summer, and the arrival of that hectic time of year we white-tailed deer enthusiasts call the pre-rut.

References

Bubenik, G.A. 1994. Antler velvet. Pages 46-47. in D. Gerlach, S. Atwater, and J. Schnell, eds. Deer. Stackpole Books, PA. 384 pages.

Bubenik, G.A. and A.B. Bubenik, eds. 1990. Horns, Pronghorns, and Antlers: Evolution, Morphology, Physiology, and Social Significance. Springer-Verlag, NY. 562 pages.

Forand, K.J., R.L. Marchinton, and Karl V. Miller. 1985. Influence of dominance rank on the antler cycle of white-tailed deer. Journal of Mammalogy 66:58-62.

Goss, R.J. 1983. Deer antlers: regeneration, function, and evolution. Academic Press, N.Y. 316 pages.

Jacobson, H.A. and R.N. Griffin. 1983. Antler cycles in white-tailed deer in Mississippi. Pages 15-22. in R.D. Brown, ed. Antler Development in Cervidae. Caesar Kleberg Wildlife Research Institute, Kingsville, Texas, 480 pages.

Jacobson, H.A. 1995. Age and quality relationships. Pages 103-111. in K.V. Miller and R.L. Marchinton, eds. Quality Whitetails: The Why and How of Quality Deer Management. Stackpole Books, PA. 322 pages.

Miller, K.V., O.E. Rhodes, T.R. Litchfield, M.H. Smith, and R.L. Marchinton. 1987. Reproductive characteristics of yearling and adult male white-tailed deer. Proceedings Annual Conference Southeast Association Fish and Wildlife Agencies 41:378-384.

Ozoga, J.J. 1988. Incidence of "infant" antlers among supplementally fed white-tailed deer. Journal of Mammalogy 69:393-395.

John Baccus

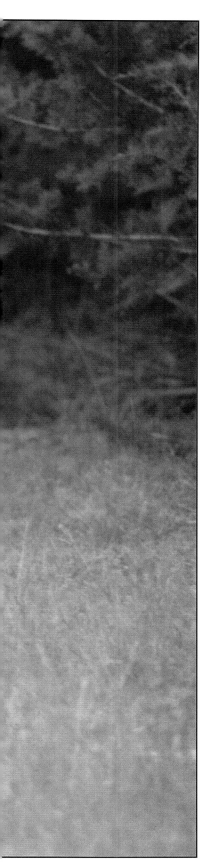

Chapter 8

WHITETAIL ODDITIES:

How Common are Abnormalities?

Certainly, not all deer are born equal. In fact, whitetails seem plagued with a host of deformities, the incidence of which varies greatly by area and often goes unnoticed.

Not all whitetails are born perfect. In fact, some of the whitetail's many physical deformities cause early death, and therefore, tend to go unnoticed. However, others are not so life-threatening, and they show up in the deer we shoot, if we know what to look for.

Three basic reasons account for most physical oddities in deer: Some defects have a genetic origin, and therefore, are hereditary. This covers most anomalies discussed in this article. Other abnormalities might be caused by physiological dysfunctions, which can be caused by malnutrition, disease, parasitism or other health problems. Still other oddities are caused by injuries.

In this chapter, I'll review some irregularities in deer, most of which are presumed to be coded in genes. Where possible, I've also considered how frequently some of these unusual deer are found.

Sources of Information

Records of abnormal deer are scattered throughout scientific and popular literature. Because most cases are based on casual observations, there is seldom a good indication of how frequently these unusual traits occur. There are exceptions, of course. A few studies in scientific literature supply data that show how frequently we might encounter various types of unusual deer in the wild. One study — written by Larry Ryel, a former biologist with the Michigan Department of Natural Resources, appeared in Volume 44 (1963) of the *Journal of Mammalogy*. Ryel's article, "The Occurrence of Certain Anomalies in Michigan White-tailed Deer," discusses the frequency of certain physical abnormalities.

Ryel examined records from 33,337 hunter-harvested deer in 1959, 1960 and 1961. In addition, biologists examined 2,649 accidentally killed does, and the 3,378 fetuses they carried. Ryel gleaned other records from DNR files, museum collections and various publications.

Ryel emphasized that his deer samples were not random, regarding time, space, sex or age. Of course, records of deer anomalies seldom are. Museums, in particular, seem prone to preserving the unusual. Also, many abnormalities, especially those involving teeth, are easily overlooked.

Nonetheless, given Ryel's large sample size, his data likely provide some idea of how frequently we might find certain anomalies in wild herds. Other records, however, reveal great regional variation in the frequency of oddities.

Fetus Anomalies

Prolonged shortages in nutrition during harsh winters often contribute to poor fetal growth, and sometimes cause death in the unborn. In these cases — which are relatively common on Northern deer range — the dead fetus will be reabsorbed by the doe's body or become mummified, and then passed later. Abortion is not common, even in malnourished white-tailed does. Even so, when the mother is well-nourished, deer fetuses seem remarkably free of disfiguring deformities.

Ryel found only one record of an abnormal deer fetus, which was two-headed. An earlier publication described the condition as follows:

"The doe was determined from the dentition to be about 6 years old. She was in poor physical condition, attributable to the general scarcity of winter deer food in the area. She was carrying two fetuses ... one a normal male weighing 192 grams, the other a two-headed female weighing 183 grams. The heads were joined in the occipital region with noses directed laterally. There was an ear on the lateral (free) surface of each head and a single ear in the 'V' formed by the union of the heads. Posteriorly, the body was that of a normal fetus with a single neck, trunk, and paired limbs."

The condition must be exceedingly rare. Although I examined one fetus with a grossly malformed head, I've never seen a two-headed fetus among the several thousand I've examined.

Other reports of fetal abnormalities are equally scarce, and generally come from studies conducted with penned deer. Michigan researcher Louis Verme, for example, reported a genetically related case involving a doe that transmitted leg defects to its offspring. Although this doe produced several healthy fawns, two offspring had deformed hind legs, which prevented them from standing and contributed to their early death. Because different bucks serviced the doe, Verme speculated the doe had passed along a mutant gene.

In 1997, a Maryland hunter killed a buck fawn that had one of the oddest genetic quirks ever documented — six legs.

Canine Teeth

While all species of deer have lower incisiform canines, white-tailed deer normally do not have upper (maxillary) canine teeth. Moose and mule deer don't either, but elk and caribou do. Because these tend to be tiny teeth, often hidden by gum flesh, they are easily overlooked in the hasty examination of fresh carcasses.

Ryel found no reports of upper canines among field-examined deer, but discovered a number of records among cleaned white-tailed deer skulls in museums. In the University of Michigan Museum of Zoology, he found six examples of upper canines among 360 skulls (1.7 percent), with a higher incidence (2.4 percent) among Upper Michigan specimens as compared to those from Lower Michigan (0.07 percent).

In New York, researchers found seven deer with upper canines among 1,729 deer examined (4 percent). Ryel also found one report of a Wisconsin fawn with upper canines, but none showed up during exams of about 10,000 hunter-harvested Wisconsin deer from 1950 to 1953.

Researchers have detected a tendency of increased incidence of upper canines in whitetails as one progresses southward. Upper canines seem especially common in Texas deer. For example, 10.2 percent of the Carmen Mountain whitetails (subspecies *carminus*) reportedly grow upper canines, while 17.9 percent of deer on the Welder Wildlife Refuge (subspecies *texanus*) had them.

The presence of upper canines in fawns suggests this trait develops early in life.

Under-Shot Jaw

Deer sometimes grow a short, or under-shot, jaw, a condition technically called *brachygnathia inferior*. The lower jaw (mandible) might be as much as 1 inch shorter than the upper. Although the upper and lower premolars and molars line up, the lower incisors work against the roof of the mouth instead of the upper jaw's callous pad. This condition has been observed in many deer species, and has been reported in about 0.4 percent of New York whitetails.

Ryel found records of 31 short-jawed deer from Michigan. The overall incidence of Upper Michigan deer with this jaw was 0.02 percent during Ryel's three-year study, while the Lower Michigan incidence was 0.15 percent, a significant difference.

Having a short mandible would seem to impair a deer's ability to feed, especially when grazing on low-growing herbaceous plants. However, because none of those deer examined seemed retarded in body development, and mature deer showed the condition, the short mandible does not appear to severely threaten survival.

Odd Lower Jaws

Although Ryel did not mention dental abnormalities other than upper canines and short mandibles, others have reported a variety of oddities in deer mandibles. While studying animal remains from American Indian sites in Florida, investigators found seven deer with extra teeth or unusually shaped teeth. They concluded that most of the abnormalities began during the tooth's early development or genetic makeup, but provided no clues about frequency of occurrence.

To my knowledge, Verme and I were the first to report deer with extra molars. We collected one such animal from the Cusino square-mile enclosure in 1966, and identified three more among nearby wild deer in 1967. All of these deer had a fourth molar between the third molar and the

posterior curvature of the lower jaw. In each instance, the teeth were mirror images of the third molar.

Verme concluded: "The distribution of these individuals suggest they were the progeny of one animal; that is, the result of a mutation recently introduced into this area's gene pool. Under the circumstances noted, my theory of a hereditary link for these deer is within the realm of possibility. The fact is, no other explanation quite suffices."

In Minnesota, researchers found 36 deer with abnormal mandible dentition. Thirteen were discovered during laboratory examinations of jaws from 142 deer killed by wolves and 259 killed by hunters. Most abnormalities involved extra teeth, teeth reduced in size and misshapen, or teeth missing altogether. Because the incidence of dental abnormalities was higher among wolf-killed deer than hunter-killed deer (5.6 percent vs. 1.9 percent, respectively), wolves seem to select deer with even minor physical deformities.

Melanism

Hair color in the normally brown whitetail might vary in a wide array of colors and patterns of white, brown, gray and black. It might range from white (albinism), through various degrees of white spotting, to nearly black (melanistic).

Melanism is caused by overproduction of melanin, a chemical responsible for dark pigmentation in animals. Melanistic animals have a dark, almost black coat. In whitetails, this tends to eliminate the normal white markings, particularly on the face. The characteristic white throat patch, the muzzle band, and inside ears are brown

Hair color of the normally brown whitetail can vary from all-white (albinism) to various degrees of white spotting (piebald) to nearly black (melanistic).

and sometimes even darker than the rest of the deer. The condition is particularly rare in whitetails, with no available estimates as to its frequency. Its genetic basis is unknown.

Ryel found no records of melanism in Michigan deer. However, noted wildlife photographer Leonard Lee Rue III reported a black spike buck was shot near Roscommon in Lower Michigan in 1965. There were earlier reports of three partly melanistic whitetails from the New York Adirondacks, two blue-black white-tailed bucks from Utah, and a melanistic doe from Wisconsin.

More recently, Michael Smith and his co-workers included an excellent photograph of a melanistic white-tailed fawn from Texas in their chapter "Population Genetics" in Lowell Hall's (1984) *White-tailed Deer Ecology and Management.*

Also, researchers John T. Baccus and John C. Posey of Southwest Texas State University reported unusually high numbers of melanistic whitetails in central Texas. From August 1989 through November 1995, they reported 218 melanistic deer in 3,768 deer sightings (5.8 percent) in seven central Texas counties. The highest percentage of melanistic deer (21 percent) in the population was in an area of eastern Hays and western Travis counties.

Baccus and Posey reported five melanistic color shades: seal brown, 54.5 percent; argus brown, 18.2 percent; bister, 16.9 percent; iron gray, 5.2 percent; and blackish-slate, 5.2

CAN YOU IDENTIFY THE ABNORMAL JAWS?

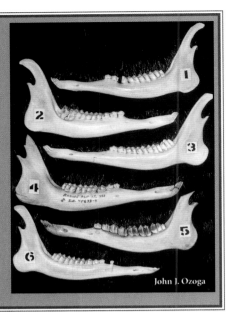

Deformities in the lower jaw of white-tailed deer are easily overlooked. Can you identify the abnormal jaws pictured here? If so, what makes them unusual?

I'll provide a couple of hints: All of these jaws are from adult deer, but only one is normal. The irregularities occur in the premolar and molar teeth. Normally, a whitetail has three premolars and three molars on each side of its lower jaw.

(Jaws courtesy of wildlife biologist Tom Cooley, Rose Lake Wildlife Pathology Lab, Michigan DNR.)

Answers:
(1) Malformed premolar.
(2) Extra molar.
(3) Only two premolars, but four molars.
(4) Normal jaw.
(5) Extra premolar.
(6) Extra premolar.
— *John J. Ozoga*

John J. Ozoga

---

percent. The pelage color of melanistic deer was based on comparisons of standard color plates with photographs and video tapes.

Albinos

Albino deer have a characteristic pink skin and pure white coat. The irises of their eyes are usually pink, but are sometimes a pale blue. Although rare, albinos occur more frequently than melanistic deer. Not all white deer are albinos, and there is no such thing as a partial albino. Unfortunately, many early records don't distinguish between the two.

Because albinism is a recessive genetic trait, inbreeding in captive herds can increase its incidence. True albinos have little or no melanin — the chemical that colors hair, skin and eyes — in their bodies. Their hair is white because it lacks pigment. The skin looks pink because the flowing blood shows through the deer's pale skin.

Albinos can't see well, and because there's no melanin in their eyes to block light, they have a particularly hard time in bright sunlight. They're also sensitive to exposure, and their white coat makes the young especially vulnerable to predation. Therefore, they often die at an early age.

According to an article in the March 1995 issue of *Deer & Deer Hunting* written by Richard P. Smith, 30 states and provinces have recorded albino deer sightings. Six states protect albinos by law. Albino whitetails tend to occur more frequently in Upper Michigan than in other parts of the country. Smith knew of at least 10 albinos in Upper Michigan during a nine-year period.

Two of 35,986 deer (0.006 percent) examined in Ryel's report were albinos, which is about the same rate that albinism occurs in humans. Both were shot illegally in Upper Michigan. One was a buck fawn, and the other a yearling doe.

All-White Deer

Other than the two albinos and some earlier reports scattered across Michigan, Ryel reported no all-white deer in his sample of about 36,000 deer.

George Shiras III, an early naturalist from Michigan, mentions efforts to perpetuate a strain of white deer on Grand Island in Lake Superior starting in 1915. An albino doe was also introduced into the captive herd. However, because most of the specimens were described as having "light blue-gray eyes and pearl-gray nose and hoofs," they probably were not true albinos. The herd died out for unknown reasons.

The largest herd of white deer currently lives inside the fenced-in Seneca Army Depot in New York. Although the animals' coats are white, they have brown eyes. Given protection from hunting, this population grew from a couple of white deer in the early 1950s to more than 100 by the late 1960s. White is now the dominant color phase in at least some segments of the population.

According to William Chapman, a professor at Utica College of Syracuse University, this herd of white deer might represent a unique genetic variety of whitetails. Unlike the recessive trait in albinos, preliminary studies indicate the gene for a white coat in the Seneca herd is dominant in males and females. While these deer are now concentrated in New York, investigators speculate that the range of this strain might extend from Michigan to North Carolina.

Piebalds

Partially white, or piebald, deer are the color mutation hunters are most likely to see, being far more common than melanistic, albino or all-white deer. Piebalds tend to be highly variable in color patterns, ranging from a few white spots to mostly white with a trace of brown. In albinos, none of the cells can produce melanin. In piebalds, at least some cells can produce pigment. This causes a spotting of coat colors, with some areas appearing normal and others white.

Besides unusual coloration, piebalds often have abnormal body proportions. Those with plump bodies, humped noses, and short legs and ears look almost goat-like.

In reviewing scientific literature, Ryel found a widespread occurrence of partially white deer. Of 24 recorded in Michigan, only two were females, probably because of limited antlerless deer hunting from 1959 to 1961. The incidence of partly white deer for those three years averaged 0.02 percent in Upper Michigan and 0.08 percent in Lower Michigan.

Wooly Coated Deer

Three deer with abnormal wooly hair have been reported: one each from Pennsylvania, Michigan and New York. All were females.

The New York deer was shot because, from a distance, it appeared to have mange. Instead, much of its body was covered with soft, silky, thin strands of short, curly hair that made it appear to have wooly underfur. A microscopic examination revealed three hair types. Two were normal, while the wooly hair was especially thin. It closely resembled sheep wool.

This condition, believed to have a genetic basis, must be extremely rare. No such specimens were detected among the nearly 36,000 deer Ryel examined, nor among 88,000 examined at New York check stations.

Manes

Another oddity sometimes observed in whitetails is the presence of a short, stiff mane that is 1 to 2 inches high and 6 or more inches long.

A New York buck examined by Rue had a mane extending from its forehead down the top of its neck to the shoulders. Rue said, "The ridge of hair looked just like the short-clipped mane of a show horse."

Rue also reported deer with manes from Tennessee and Wisconsin, and a surprisingly frequent number from Indiana.

Ryel reported two such animals from Michigan, both bucks, but only one in his three-year study, for an incidence of 0.003 percent.

William Ishmael, a Wisconsin biologist, spent some time tracking down reports of manes on deer. In the August 1992 issue of *Deer & Deer Hunting*, Ishmael reported 15 cases of deer with manes, but no reportable pattern of occurrence. He wrote: "Maned deer are not confined to one region. Nor are manes specific to one age or sex of deer. Manes occur on fawns and does as well as bucks. The manes come in different lengths, colors and textures."

Ishmael believes manes result from a recessive gene. He thinks these genes might be "leftovers" from some long-ago ancestor of the whitetail that was normally maned. A mane only surfaces, Ishmael believes, when the same recessive gene(s) is paired with a similar recessive gene from another deer, making manes incredibly rare.

Conclusion

Certainly, not all deer are born equal. In fact, whitetails seem plagued with a host of deformities that often go unnoticed. The incidence of the deformities varies greatly by area. Given nature's way, however, odd deer that are severely handicapped disappear early from the gene pool. Wolves even seem to be able to pick out individuals exhibiting subtle dental oddities, many of which would likely evade detection by the most astute hunter.

References

Baccus, J.T., and Posey, J.C. 1996. "Unusual Abundance of Melanistic White-tailed Deer in Central Texas: Public Perceptions and Management Implications." Abstract, 1996 Southeast Deer Study Group Meeting, Orlando, Fla.

Friend, M., and W. Hesselton. 1966. "A wooly coated white-tailed deer from New York state." Journal of Mammalogy 47:154-155.

Halls, L.K. Ed. 1984. White-tailed Deer: Ecology and Management. *Wildlife Management Institute, The Stackpole Co., Harrisburg, PA. 870 pages.*

Ishmael, W. 1992. "Maned Deer: How Common are They?" Deer & Deer Hunting 15(8): 90-92.

Krausman, P.R. 1978. "Dental anomalies of Carmen Mountains white-tailed deer." Journal of Mammalogy 59:863-864.

Mech, L.D., L.D. Frenzel, Jr., P.D. Karns, and D.W. Kuehn. 1970. "Mandibular dental anomalies in white-tailed deer from Minnesota." Journal of Mammalogy 51:804-806.

Rue, L.L. III. 1989. The Deer of North America: 2nd edition, updated and expanded. Outdoor Life Books. Grolier Book Clubs Inc. Danbury, Conn. 508 pages.

Ryel, L.A. 1963. "The occurrence of certain anomalies in Michigan white tailed deer." Journal of Mammalogy 44:79-98.

Smith, R.P. 1995. "Albinos in the Deer Herd." Deer & Deer Hunting 18(6):36-43.

Verme, L.J. 1968. "Possible hereditary defects in Michigan white-tailed deer." Journal of Mammalogy 49:148.

Wing, E.S. 1965. "Abnormal dentition in several white-tailed deer." Journal of Mammalogy 46:348-350.

Charles J. Alsheimer

Chapter 9

MAGNIFICENT MORPHOLOGIES:

Why Antlers Can Get Bizarre

The reasons for abnormal antler growth are often unknown and highly speculative, so confidently determining the causes of abnormal antlers — in any given buck, especially wild — is difficult to impossible.

From a zoologist's perspective, antlers are often viewed as "magnificent morphologies" and "complex processes." Complex processes, indeed, and, as a result, antlers are subject to frequent deviations from the norm.

Professor Richard Goss, a world authority on antler evolution and regeneration, says: "The more complicated a process is, the more chances there are for mistakes to occur."

Therefore, it's little wonder deer antlers vary so much in size and shape. No two antlers are exactly alike, although their similarities from side to side, or even from one buck to the next, are sometimes striking. And of the many questions asked of biologists, I suspect nothing draws more queries than the antler growth of white-tailed bucks.

Unusual antlers take many forms. Sometimes they're stunted or missing altogether, as in hummels, an antlerless adult buck. In other cases, antlers might be crooked, unbranched, excessively branched or carry an unusually high number of points. Even growth patterns, timing of maturation and schedule for casting are sometimes abnormal.

Occasionally, even females grow antlers.

The reasons for abnormal antler growth often are unknown and highly speculative. But scientists know three basic probable causes: One is genetic defects, which are therefore hereditary. The second is physiological problems from injuries, parasitism, disease, malnutrition or other health-related factors. These factors are called systemic conditions, and they alter bodily functions. The third factor is caused by injuries to the pedicle or growing antler.

In other chapters of this book, I discuss antler abnormalities in poorly nourished yearlings, old-aged bucks, extremely well-nourished buck fawns, and so-called antlered-does. Here, I'll look at other types of abnormal antler growth and the possible factors responsible.

The Role of Genetics

Many antler peculiarities such as configuration, rack shape and tine length are unquestionably hereditary. Many examples exist of bucks reproducing successive antler sets similar in appearance year after year. A buck's antlers tend to get a little larger and might add extra points with advancing age, but otherwise the successive racks resemble each other, barring injury or health-related abnormalities.

Just as the normal size and shape of antlers are inherited, so also are some irregularities. It's important to note, however, that antler symmetry normally decreases in all deer species as the animals grow older.

Goss also notes: "Only the important antler traits are strictly coded in genes. Unimportant details can be left to chance." Also, genetic antler anomalies are expected to occur on both sides, while one-sided defects are more likely caused by other factors.

Certainly, a buck with hereditary antler defects tends to reproduce those defects with each new set of antlers. It's my observation, though, that these abnormalities might not be evident until the buck grows his second or third set of antlers. Also, hereditary defects will likely be perpetuated and show up in future generations. However, it's difficult to determine which anomalies are genetic and which are not.

Remember, females might also carry genes for antler irregularities. Early European gamekeepers quickly learned that culling bucks with poor, abnormally shaped antlers did not necessarily remove poor antler genes from the population. Ultimately, such culling did little to improve trophy hunting.

A lack of brow tines on mature bucks, for example, appears genetically controlled, at least in bucks that repeat the condition each year. Most I've seen were missing both brow tines, which suggests a genetic trait.

Third antlers have also been recorded, with some sprouting from the eye orbit, or the top surface of the skull or snout. And some deer have grown two matched main beams on each side. Whether such deformities can be attributed to genetics is unknown.

Paired palmate antlers also seem to be hereditary. Several bucks I raised in Michigan's square-mile enclosure grew palmate antlers when 2½ years old, and the palmations became more pronounced as the bucks reached maturity. Nonetheless, damage to a growing antler might also promote unusually heavy, wide antler beams, which I'll discuss later. Drop tines off the main beam might be hereditary, or they might occur for other unknown reasons. Although scientists agree that drop tines occur most frequently on mature, well-nourished bucks, there seems to be no firm data to explain this occurrence in relatively few deer.

Of the several hundred bucks I raised, only one possessed what appeared to be genetically determined drop tines. These tines were first evident as small bumps when the buck was 2½ years old. Although the buck grew otherwise typical antlers in subsequent years, he grew an identically positioned pair of 3- to 4-inch drop tines each time. Several other bucks I raised grew single drop tines, but in each case it was a one-year occurrence, suggesting the growths were not caused by genetics.

Hummels

Bucks missing one or both antlers have often been reported in whitetails and mule deer, but it's more common among red deer, especially in Scotland. It has been estimated that one in 300 Scottish red deer stags don't grow antlers.

Researchers found an unusually high number of mule deer bucks in central Utah that didn't grow one or both antlers. Because all came from one drainage, investigators speculated it was hereditary.

In 1960, biologists recorded four white-tailed bucks missing one antler (one in 1,000) from widely separated areas in Michigan, but no such occurrences in 1959 or 1961. They couldn't explain the phenomenon.

Many late-born, malnourished or socially stressed buck fawns might grow small pedicles or none at all their first year. Although some abnormalities might be hereditary, they're more commonly caused by poor growth rates, insufficient sexual development or low testosterone levels. Most whitetails eventually overcome their delay in sexual maturity, and develop pedicles the next spring. Still, they tend to grow short, burr-free spikes when 1½ years old.

In Scotland, red deer males on poor range might not grow pedicles until they're 2 or 3 years old. Some only grow vestiges of small pedicles. If they don't produce a certain amount of testosterone, their pedicles and antlers don't develop. In other cases, some males grow pedicles but never antlers.

Interestingly, red deer hummels are fertile and capable of breeding, and they can produce viable offspring. Further, given good nutrition, their sons tend to produce normal antlers — ruling out any genetic link.

George Bubenik theorizes that poor nutrition contributes to hummels in Scottish red deer "because the antler growth centers (in the brain), or connections between pedicle and the antler growth centers do not develop sufficiently."

Velvet Antlers and Cactus Bucks

Normal testes development and related seasonal rhythms in testosterone production are essential if a buck is to grow normal antlers and maintain a normal antler cycle. Just as in castrated bucks and antlered does, the testosterone levels commonly lead to prolonged or permanent velvet antlers in otherwise normal-looking animals. Such hormone deficiencies might be caused by disease, ingesting toxins, nutritional deficiencies, testicular injuries or other factors that can alter a male's normal physiology.

Jack Ward Thomas and co-workers observed many white-tailed bucks suffering from gonadal atrophy in Texas' central mineral region. During the late 1950s and early 1960s, 3 percent to nearly 10 percent of that region's bucks suffered some unknown malady that left them infertile and their antlers permanently in velvet.

In the North, living velvet antlers tend to freeze back during winter. In the South, however, continually growing velvet antlers can lead to a massive, tumor-like growth known as a peruke. Deer that grow them are often called cactus bucks.

Certain diseases might also influence antler form. The lungworm, or *Dictyocaulus sp.*, for example, can cause spiral-shaped, or corkscrew, antlers in red deer. Other diseases might similarly affect antlers in whitetails.

Besides causing abnormally small antlers, poor nutrition might also lead to poor antler form. In large-antlered, well-nourished mature bucks, a sudden dietary shortage of calcium or phosphorus can cause the tines or main beams to collapse.

Contralateral Effects

Depending on the severity and timing of the damage, bodily injuries can profoundly affect antler size and form. An intriguing phenomenon is called contralateral effects, which means an injury to one side of a buck's body — usually a hind leg — causes an antler deformity on the opposite side. The effects might appear for several years after. When injuries cause or contribute to a permanent disability — such as with an amputated leg — the contralateral antler is usually shorter than normal throughout the buck's life.

The reasons for contralateral effects are unknown. In fact, some scientists refute the theory. Many times, uninjured deer, which appear normal and healthy, grow unequal antlers. Instances in which normal antlers are produced without injuries are also common.

Injuries can affect antler size and form. This phenomenon, called contralateral effects, means an injury to one side of a buck's body — usually a hind leg — causes an antler deformity on the opposite side. This buck's injury was so severe it affected both antlers.

"If true," says Goss, "it is difficult to explain ... except perhaps in terms of a compensatory response to counteract the imbalance caused by the original injury. A crippled deer would be expected to have an altered gait, the effects of which might result in compensatory changes in the growing antler owing to alterations in the flow or pressure of the blood supply."

Psychological Effects

Psychological stress can influence an animal's physiology and, thereby, affect basic body functions, including secondary sex characteristics and reproduction. As I wrote in an earlier chapter (see "Shedding Velvet: Nature's Annual Act of Murder," on Page 132), dominance-submissive relationships among bucks are important in the annual antler cycle. I wrote: "Bucks that win often become hormonally charged, shed antler velvet first, and become avid scent-markers. Logically, habitual 'losers' suffer the reverse, depressing effects."

While working with a herd of "white" red deer in Czechoslovakia, Ludek Bartos observed a strong correlation between a stag's antler size one year and his dominance rank the previous year. That is, top-ranking stags with large antlers were always replaced in the hierarchy by smaller-antlered stags. Only in the next year did the new alpha stag grow larger antlers, while the replaced stag grew smaller antlers.

George Bubenik observed that severe psychological stress can contribute to unnatural antler casting schedules, a condition I also observed at Cusino. Normally, a white-tailed buck will cast both antlers about the same time, often only hours or even minutes apart. When severely stressed, however, one antler might be retained several weeks, or even a month, longer than the other.

There seems little doubt psychological factors can greatly influence antler growth traits. To my knowledge, it's unproven if mental duress causes hormonal imbalances that contribute to abnormal antlers, but I think it's likely.

Pedicle Wounds

Before any deer can grow antlers, it must first grow pedicles on which the antlers form. Only the pedicle is capable of producing a normal, complete antler. Typically, the larger the pedicle, the larger the antler outgrowth.

Damage to the deer's forehead or pedicles is a powerful stimulus for abnormal antler growth. Injuries to forehead bones can cause out-of-season antler growth in bucks, and even initiate antler growth in does.

Pedicle injuries usually cause abnormal antler formations. In severe cases, they might even cause accessory antlers to grow from the injured pedicle or nearby skull bone. Still, determining which antler abnormalities result from pedicle wounds, and which result from hereditary or systemic conditions is difficult.

Accessory antlers caused by pedicle damage are usually malformed, shorter than normal and one-sided. In some cases, a split pedicle or antler bud can cause a third antler beam to grow. It might originate as a separate shaft from the antler base or as a short spike from the forehead or eye orbit. These accessory antlers tend to follow the usual replacement cycle, shedding velvet in autumn, casting in winter and regrowing in spring.

Velvet-Antler Injuries

The deer's nervous system plays a key, but mysterious, role in antler development. The growing antler is well-endowed with nerves, the principal function of which must be to allow the deer to avoid injury. Also, large-antlered bucks seem to possess a certain kinesthetic sense, which allows them to judge the position of their antlers to avoid bumping them. Even the velvet hairs

Donald M. Jones

It is tempting to blame genetic quirks for unusual antlers. However, a review of scientific literature reveals many possible reasons for abnormal antlers.

serve as sensitive feelers.

Inevitably, however, antlers are sometimes damaged while growing. A common injury is an antler fracture. Sometimes the break is so severe that part of the antler dangles loosely, held only by the velvet, which eventually drops off. If the blood supply is not severed, such broken parts might remain alive, fuse and continue to grow at a crooked angle. If the antler is only cracked, it can repair itself. Such damage usually causes conspicuous swelling along the shaft where the fracture occurred.

Studies have found that experimental denerving of growing antlers usually contributes to stunted antlers with abnormal forms. That's because deer cannot avoid bumping into things and injuring the soft antler.

Although major damage, such as fracturing the pedicle or budding antler, will usually heal fast, abnormal antler forms usually result. Massive damage, such as splitting the budding antler, might cause abnormally large, misshapen antlers with many extra points. In fact, early European gamekeepers reportedly sometimes shot the deer's velvet-covered antlers with bird shot to cause extra antler points to grow. Even today, deer farmers in New Zealand sometimes cut off the first growth of red deer spikes to induce branching — causing 8-point antlers to grow in just more than one year.

Trophic Memory Responses

The late Anthony Bubenik observed maximum antler development on the damaged side the year after injury, with continued abnormal enlargement on both sides in subsequent years. Because the effects of trauma occur primarily on the injured side, each antler likely has an antler growth center in the deer's central nervous system. Based on old evidence and experience, Bubenik proposed that trauma is remembered, a condition he called the "trophic memory response."

George Bubenik emphasizes that the term *memory*, as used here, "is not ideal." There is no mental effort to remember such injury, but somehow it is recorded in the brain and duplicated in subsequent years.

He notes the following:

1) Injuries to the pedicle and early stages of the antler cause the most pronounced changes in antler shapes.

2) The injury must involve nerves, as anesthetized deer in studies fail to show a response.

3) The response is slowly forgotten, if not reinforced, and antler form will eventually return to normal.

4) The more severe the injury, the longer the memory lasts.

5) Reinjury, which reinforces the memory, causes massive atypical antler growths.

Needless to say, nontypical trophies are rare in the wild. Even if a buck has the genes to sprout massive, nontypical antlers, those traits won't be expressed unless he lives a healthy life, is exceptionally well-nourished and lives long enough to reach maturity. Many pampered pen-raised bucks achieve such stature. One must wonder, though, how many nontypical trophies — pen-raised or wild — come to be so accidentally.

Conclusion

It is tempting to blame genetic quirks for unusual antlers. After all, some are. However, a review of scientific literature reveals many possible reasons for abnormal antler sizes, shapes and growth rhythms. Unfortunately, few studies have been conducted to unravel such mysteries. Instead, most records of antler abnormalities are based on single observations that are seldom duplicated experimentally. Even scientists who have done such research often disagree about why antler growth doesn't conform to expectations.

Given our understanding of such things, confidently determining the causes of abnormal antlers — in any given buck, especially wild — is difficult to impossible.

References

Brown, R.D., ed. 1983. Antler Development in Cervidae. *Caesar Kleberg Wildlife Research Institute, Kingsville, Texas. 480 pages.*

Bubenik, G.A. and A.B. Bubenik, eds. 1990. Horns, Pronghorns, and Antlers: Evolution, Morphology, Physiology, and Social Significance. *Springer-Verlag. N.Y. 562 pages.*

Goss, R.J. 1983. Deer Antlers: Regeneration, Function, and Evolution. *Academic Press, N.Y. 316 pages.*

Robinette, W.L., and D.A. Jones. 1959. Antler anoma- lies of mule deer. Journal of Mammalogy *40:96-108.*

Ryel, L.A. 1963. The occurrence of certain anomalies in Michigan white-tailed deer. Journal of Mammalogy *44:79-98.*

Thomas, J.W., R.M. Robinson and R.G. Marburger. 1964. Hypogonadism in white-tailed deer in the Central Mineral Region of Texas. Transactions North American Wildlife Conference *29:225-236.*

Wislocki, G.B. 1952. A possible antler rudiment on the nasal bones of a white-tailed deer (Odocoileus virginianus borealis). Journal of Mammalogy *33:73-76.*

Ian McMurchy

Chapter 10

A PUZZLE:

The Mystery of Antlered Does

With the exception of reindeer and caribou, female deer normally don't grow antlers. Nonetheless, females in all deer species have the capacity to grow antlers, and sometimes do when certain poorly understood circumstances arise.

It has been said that nature's exceptions are the germs of discovery. "If so," says Dr. Richard Goss (1983), one of the world's leading authorities on antler regeneration, "the study of those exceptional instances in which female deer grow antlers ... may yield clues to the fundamental nature of antler growth in general.

"The fact that female deer do on rare occasions grow antlers spontaneously is an intriguing phenomenon that demands explanation."

With the exception of reindeer and caribou, females in the deer family normally don't grow antlers. Nonetheless, females in all deer species have the capacity to grow antlers, and sometimes do when certain poorly understood circumstances arise. For mysterious reasons, however, female whitetails, muleys and roe deer tend to grow antlers more frequently than females in most other cervid species.

How common are antlered does? Where are they found most frequently? When do they occur? Why do they occur?

And what have researchers learned to help explain this phenomenon, which shows up surprisingly often in whitetails?

Scientific literature contains some documentation of antlered does. However, the subject is more complex than one might expect, and many questions remain unanswered.

How Common are They?

As with many aspects of antler growth, the causes and effects of the situation often leave scientists in disagreement. Further, sometimes a deer thought to be an antlered doe by a hunter might not be a female. While antlered female whitetails are not common in most herds, as scientific literature suggests, they are probably more common than most hunters realize.

In New York state, for example, biologist William Severinghaus (1956) estimated a frequency of one antlered doe per 2,650 white-tailed bucks harvested from 1941 to 1955. J.C. Donaldson and J.K. Doutt (1965) estimated a frequency of one antlered doe per 3,500 bucks after an intensive study of bucks harvested in

ARE SOME ANTLERED DOES 'FREEMARTINS'?

"The presence of antlers in female deer," says Richard Goss, "is a reminder of how fragile the distinction between the sexes can be. Although the gender of an individual is genetically determined, the extent to which sexual characteristics are in fact expressed may be affected by a number of physiological conditions."

The "freemartin" is a prime example of how the genetically determined sex of an animal can be modified even before birth. The freemartin is a female calf that's born co-twin to a male. In about 11 of 12 cases the female is sterile, because her reproductive system was modified by her brother's sex hormones.

Goss explains the complex phenomenon, which takes place in the womb, this way:

"Sometimes the placenta of such twins becomes fused, as a result of which their bloodstreams intermingle. When the male twin begins to develop its reproductive tract, the hormones produced can circulate into his sister's bloodstream and exert effects on the development of her reproductive organs. As a result of this, she may become a partially masculinized female and therefore infertile."

Although the freemartin typically occurs in cattle, Goss proposes that antlered-does might have been subjected to similar male hormonal influences before they were born.

Goss admits there is no proof freemartins occur in deer. However, he is quick to note antlered does occur most frequently in deer species that commonly produce twins, but are extremely rare among others that normally produce only a single fawn.

— John J. Ozoga

Pennsylvania from 1958 to 1961. In Michigan, L.A. Ryel (1963) reported nine antlered does among 8,605 adult does (one antlered doe per 956 bucks) shot from 1959 to 1961. Likewise, W.T. Hesselton and R.M. Hesselton (1982) estimated that one in every 1,000 to 1,100 female whitetails produce antlers.

Without question, however, the most amazing documentation of antlered female whitetails was made by William Wishart (1985) in Camp Wainwright, a 232-square-mile military reserve in eastern Alberta. While monitoring hunter harvest of whitetails, Wishart recorded an incidence of antlered does 15 to 40 times higher than anything reported by earlier investigators.

From 1968 to 1982 Wishart reported that 1,182 adult whitetails were examined from Wainwright, including 665 bucks and 517 does. Eight of the adult does had antlers, ranging from about 0.6-inch to nearly 9½ inches long. All of the does' antlers were still covered in velvet at a time when all bucks had polished antlers. This amounts to an astonishing rate of one antlered doe for every 65 adult does or one antlered doe for every 83 adult bucks.

What's Their Sex?

Earlier, I mentioned that the sex of some antlered deer might be difficult to determine. While that might seem improbable, researchers have identified a variety of morphological and physiological conditions in whitetails that sometimes complicate accurate sex determination.

George Wislocki (1954) pioneered antler research in this country. Based largely on 19th century European research of roe deer, Wislocki proposed that so-called antlered does fall into various groups, depending on the status of their reproductive tracts, as follows:

(1) No recognizable pathology and a seemingly normal female reproductive tract.

(2) Diseased or degenerated ovaries, usually of unknown cause.

(3) Degenerated ovaries caused by old age.

(4) True hermaphrodites having both ovaries and testes, but possessing male or female external sex organs, or both.

(5) Pseudohermaphrodite (also called cryptorchid males) with abdominal (internal) rudimentary testes and no recognizable ovaries.

Antler Possibilities

Descriptions of doe antlers include velvet-covered pedicles only, or small button antlers, small velvet-covered spikes with occasional branching, and hard polished antlers — which usually occur in bucks.

In Michigan, Ryel described the antlers of 20 antlered does, all of which were in velvet. In six cases, however, he mentions only the presence of "buttons," which he described as "velvet-covered incipient antler pedicles." Whether some of these button-antlered does carried only pedicles or both pedicles and diminutive antlers is unknown.

European investigators observed that the relative size and characteristics of doe antlers varied. These variances depended on the type of the deer's reproductive tract. Does with ovaries, for example, showed the least amount of antler development. True hermaphrodites generally had a greater amount of antler development, while pseudohermaphrodites showed the greatest antler development.

Breeding Capabilities

Some antlered does are capable of breeding, carrying fetuses and rearing fawns, and some are not. Generally, fertile does carry velvet-covered antlers. It's important to note that comparatively high levels of testosterone are required to promote antler hardening (maturation) and velvet stripping. As in the case of male castrates, otherwise sexually normal female whitetails seldom achieve such elevated levels of male sex hormone production. Hence, they tend to carry permanent velvet-covered antlers.

On the other hand, "antlered does" with polished antlers are more likely to be hermaphrodites or pseudo-hermaphrodites — or females with serious reproductive problems. Most likely, their high production of male hormones, combined with low production of female hormones, prevents them from breeding and producing fawns. Researchers suggest, however, that even true hermaphrodites might be fertile and produce offspring in some species.

What causes antlers to grow on otherwise normal female whitetails is unknown. Some researchers suggest the ability to produce antlers might be inherited. Others believe a short-time imbalance in sex hormones is involved. Still others propose that accidental injury to the doe's forehead can cause antler growth.

Although there seems to be little scientific data for wild deer, the so-called antlered doe with polished antlers probably exhibits sharp seasonal changes in male hormone production and probably casts antlers annually. Given the proper circumstances, such an animal would presumably grow new antlers each year. Also, subsequent antlers would probably possess a flared base, called a cornet. Some researchers believe a cornet signifies antler regrowth, as opposed to growth of the first antlers, which supposedly lack cornets.

True antlered does more commonly carry velvet-covered antlers lacking a cornet. Generally, it's difficult to determine where the pedicle ends and the antler begins. Such a condition hints that pedicle and antler growth occurred as one continuous process, as in buck fawns that grow infant, or button, antlers.

Even the permanently attached, velvet-covered antlers of does might change size and shape. Freezing during winter sometimes causes the tips to break off, but regrowth the next summer might add length or change the antler's configuration.

Close Examinations

Clearly, in order to accurately judge the reproductive status of a deer presumed to be an antlered doe, it's necessary to examine its reproductive tract. The mere presence of external female sex organs doesn't necessar-ily mean the animal is a true female. Even then, it might be difficult to determine the type of intersexuality.

In the Pennsylvania study, Donaldson and Doutt examined the reproductive tracts of 28 deer first assumed to be antlered does. Of that group, 17 were judged to be functional females, and two were pregnant. Three animals had female lower reproductive tracts, but with malformations in the upper tract. The uterus, tubes or ovaries were missing or much smaller than normal. One animal had a male lower genital tract and carried polished antlers. Four animals were cryptorchid males — a term the authors preferred instead of pseudohermaphrodite — with female-type external sex organs but with unde-scended testes buried in body fat. One animal with polished antlers had an adrenal tumor, and one was a true hermaphrodite.

The antlered does from Camp Wainwright included four with paired spikes, three with one antler each, and three with small branched antlers. According to Wishart, milk was easily expressed from the does' nipples, and they all "clearly belonged to the fertile velvet-spike group."

Induced Antler Growth

Researchers have induced antler growth in female deer in various ways. (For more detail see Goss 1983, and Bubenik and Bubenik 1990.) Wislock first caused white-tailed does to grow antlers by removing their ovaries and injecting single "priming" doses of testosterone. Later, Bubenik stimulated pedicle growth in white-tailed does by administering drugs that blocked the production of the female hormone estrogen. He then followed up with injury to the forehead bones to produce antler growth.

What causes antlers to grow on otherwise normal female whitetails is unknown. Some researchers suggest the ability to produce antlers might be inherited. Others believe a short-time imbalance in sex hormones is involved. Still others propose that accidental injury to the doe's forehead can cause antler growth.

Wishart couldn't explain the unusually high incidence of antlered does at Camp Wainwright. However, most of those he examined were old — averaging 6.1 years — which could be a factor. Older does more likely have degenerated ovaries, adrenal tumors or other maladies that cause hormonal imbalances. Such imbalances are possibly responsible for producing male characteristics. Adrenal tumors, in particular, can cause increased production of male sex hormones and produce masculine traits in females of other species.

Genetics could also have been involved at Wainwright. There, female whitetails might have possessed inherited traits that more likely predisposed them to growing antlers. There is one documented case of a free-ranging antlered muley doe in Colorado that produced a daughter that also grew antlers.

Most antlered does appear large and healthy. In fact, Donaldson and Doutt suggested antlered does might be larger than normal. In their study, for example, does with antlers dressed out at an average of about 115 pounds compared to 94 pounds for non-antlered females. Wishart observed a similar relationship.

The growth of pedicles and antlers depends on short-term elevations in the secretion of testosterone. Because we know the ovaries of rats, mice and other mammals produce limited amounts of male hormone, Wislocki speculated that ovarian production of male hormones might sometimes trigger antler growth. He suggests antlered female deer with functional ovaries might have secreted male hormones or progesterone during pregnancy, and that these hormones triggered the pituitary gland to prompt antler growth. Such a short burst of male sex hormone could stimulate antler growth and produce permanently fixed velvet-covered antlers, but still not interfere with subsequent breeding and fawn rearing.

The Injury Factor

Although probably rare in nature, injury to the forehead bones of female deer can prompt the growth of pedicles and subsequent antlers. In the late 1800s, a tame (normal) female roe deer grew a single antler, about 4 inches long, after accidentally driving a piece of broken glass into her scalp.

It has been observed that administering testosterone to does sometimes produces pedicles, but not antler growth. It is then necessary to surgically "injure" the pedicles to cause antler growth. Interestingly, however, if one pedicle is injured but not the other, only the injured side will produce an antler. This implies, therefore, that the nervous system is also somehow intricately involved.

Donald M. Jones

With the exception of reindeer and caribou, females in the deer family normally don't grow antlers. Nonetheless, females in all deer species, including mule deer like those pictured above, have the capacity to grow antlers, and sometimes do when certain poorly understood circumstances arise.

(George Bubenik has demonstrated that wounding of the pedicle does not prompt antler growth if the female deer is deeply anesthetized.)

The timing of antler growth in wild does has been poorly documented. When a hormone imbalance is responsible, most female whitetails seem to grow their antlers at the normal time of year — that is, commencing in April or May. However, because injury is a powerful stimulus for antler growth, George Bubenik proposes that accidental injury to the forehead bones might cause a female deer to grow antlers at any time of the year.

It's interesting to note that some true female deer grow only one antler, but others grow a paired set. Is it possible, therefore, that forehead injuries more often spur the growth of single antlers, while an imbalance in hormone production more likely causes two antlers to grow?

Trauma and wound healing are especially important in the cycle of a deer antler. As a result, several scientists speculate that deer antlers evolved as a special adaptation in response to continuous forehead injury. According to fossil evidence, the deer's early ancestors had only hair-covered, bony protuberances that grew from their skulls. When used as weapons, these structures were probably vulnerable to repeated injury. If so, natural selection might have favored animals capable of healing the wound sites in such a way so as to replace lost parts, thus giving rise to antlers.

Conclusion

Granted, the development of antlers in does is, as Goss declared, "an intriguing phenomenon that demands explanation." But with the possible involvement of intersexual characteristics, the subject is more complicated than most of us can handle.

Is the unusual antlered specimen you bagged really an antlered doe? Or is it part buck and part doe? On the other hand, maybe you merely bagged a buck disguised as a doe. In any event, if your so-called "antlered doe" has polished antlers you should suspect it's not a true female.

But even the experts might have difficulty determining the sexual status of your antlered prize.

References

Bubenik, G.A. and A.B. Bubenik, eds. 1990. Horns, Pronghorns, and Antlers: Evolution, Morphology, Physiology, and Social Significance. *Springer-Verlag, N.Y. 562 pages.*

Donaldson, J.C., and J.K. Doutt. 1965. Antlers in Female White-tailed Deer: A 4-Year Study. Journal of Wildlife Management 29:699-705.

Goss, R.J. 1983. Deer Antlers: Regeneration, Function, and Evolution. *Academic Press, N.Y. 316 pages.*

Hesselton, W.T., and R.M. Hesselton. 1982. White-tailed deer. Pages 878-901 in J. A. Chapman and G. A. *Feldhamer, eds.* Wild Mammals of North America. *The John Hopkins University Press, Baltimore, Md.*

Ryel, L.A. 1963. The Occurrence of Certain Anomalies in Michigan White-tailed Deer. Journal of Mammalogy 44:79-98.

Severinghaus, C.W. 1956. Antlered does. New York State Conservationist 10:32

Wishart, W.D. 1985. Frequency of antlered white-tailed does in Camp Wainwright, Alberta. Journal of Wildlife Management 49:386-388.

Wislocki, G.B. 1954. Antlers in female deer, with a report of three cases in Odocoileus. Journal of Mammalogy 37:486-495.

George Barnett

The Herd's Future

A JOINT EFFORT

Both man and animal play a role in the perpetuation of a healthy whitetail herd: the deer through its survival instincts and fertile reproductive abilities, and man through his hunting practices and habitat manipulations.

Seldom is the process achieved without death and hardships for the herd. Pressure on the herd — whether from overpopulation, a lack of food, poor habitat or prolonged hazardous weather — alters the whitetail's life. Deer adapt and change, and hunters modify their land-management and hunting practices in careful attempts to ensure the whitetail's future.

By studying the wealth of research into whitetails and applying that knowledge to create flexible hunting regulations, hunters ensure the continued health of America's No. 1 big-game animal.

Chapter 1

A PRESSURED HERD:

The Whitetail's Response to Social Pressure

Researchers have only scratched the surface in their quest to better understand and apply basic principles of deer sociobiology. One thing is clear: Preliminary findings clearly show hunter-induced mortality, or lack thereof, can seriously alter the social environment of whitetails.

In his famous book, *A Herd of Red Deer*, Fraser Darling concluded: "Where a species is of social habit, I would emphasize the necessity of taking sociality fully into account in observing and interpreting behavior. ... The life-history of the red deer would be an empty and meaningless thing divorced from the sociality which is the very foundation of their existence."

Obviously, the same can be said of white-tailed deer. In fact, because whitetails are highly social creatures — and responsive to social pressure — some researchers contend a firm understanding of their social behavior is critical to proper herd management.

Anthony Bubenik: Pioneer Deer Sociobiologist

The practical need for a better understanding of white-tailed deer social behavior was brought to my attention in the early 1970s. Anthony Bubenik, an internationally recognized researcher and authority on ungulate sociobiology, then warned that behavioral factors might influence the well-being of certain hoofed mammals, including whitetails, just as easily as nutritional factors affect them.

Bubenik said free-choice hunting and the virtual elimination of major predators have seriously reduced the quality of ungulate populations. He also cautioned that today's big-game harvest systems permit cropping too many healthy prime-age animals — the so-called social governors of their populations. This mortality sharply contrasts with the selective culling by natural predators of young, old and unhealthy animals.

Bubenik often criticized traditional North American big-game harvest strategies. "Social aspects of species, each belonging very often to different social types, are not considered at all in North American management principles," he argued. "Game production is the main goal and its techniques are so similar to extensive farming that veterinarians, agriculturists and foresters would be more useful than wildlife biologists."

The basis for Bubenik's concerns rests on the premise that all mammals have evolved social systems to minimize tension and strife among individuals. Such organization promotes a state of social well-being and assures physical fitness within the population.

The Agonistic Balance

Theoretically, overharvest of prime-age ungulates upsets a population's agonistic balance. That is, when mature animals are too few to dampen the aggressiveness of younger animals, strife, excitement and confusion can become dangerously intense and energetically costly to their society. Social disorder ultimately leads to higher than normal food requirements, low productivity, poor physical condition of individual animals, poor survival and, ultimately, severe damage to the environment.

Logically, the whitetail's societal organization originated as an adaptation to ecosystems in which the animal evolved, and, therefore, is essential to their healthy existence. Conceivably, deer harvest strategies that disrupt behavioral patterns — caused either by insufficient or excessive cropping among sex and age classes — might eventually harm the population.

Biologists have only recently investigated interactions between the whitetail's social behavior and population dynamics. For example, Karl Miller and I reviewed some of the published data on deer sociobiology, and published our findings in the book *The Science of Overabundance: Deer Ecology and Population Management*, edited by William McShea, H. Brian Underwood and John Rappole.

Although the subject of deer sociobiology is poorly understood, we found plenty of evidence to support Bubenik's contention that behavioral factors can influence the well-being of whitetails just as readily as nutritional constraints.

Cusino Enclosure Studies

Our initial studies in the square-mile enclosure at Upper Michigan's Cusino Wildlife Research Station were aimed at evaluating the pros and cons of supplementally feeding deer to achieve densities higher than the habitat could support naturally. However, we also had the opportunity to look more closely at whitetail social organization, and determine the consequences of density stress as the well-fed herd increased rapidly in size.

The enclosure studies were a unique compromise between studying free-ranging whitetails and deer that are closely confined in small pens. Although the enclosure population ranged freely over the square-mile area, we were able to live-trap, blood-sample, measure, weigh and tag each deer. Detailed field observations permitted us to determine doe-fawn relationships, and closely monitor the growth of family units as deer density and social pressure increased.

The most valuable data we gathered were from X-rays

Bill Lerner

As the yearling male approaches sexual maturity, at 16 to 17 months of age, he is harassed, dominated and rejected by his mother and female relatives. In all likelihood, a subdued male will be rejected to a low social rank within the family group.

completed on the enclosure's does. Fetuses, 80 to 140 days old in March, could be counted on the radiograms, and aged with precision. This allowed us to calculate probable breeding and birthing dates, determine potential fawn production, and, when combined with field observations, assess fawn-rearing success for each doe. All this was accomplished under tightly controlled nutritional and herd composition conditions — something not possible in other studies of free-ranging deer.

When left unchecked, the supplementally nourished enclosure herd increased from 23 deer in Spring 1972 to 159 deer by Fall 1976 — about 10 times the area's normal carrying capacity. This growth rate occurred despite considerable mortality of fawns, and some adult deer died from handling injuries and poaching. Such a high rate of increase, 50 percent to 70 percent annually, or about 20 percent higher than normal, clearly demonstrated the prolific nature of well-fed whitetails.

Despite high deer density during the final year of the study, we saw no behavioral or physiological signs of an impending population crash, as some investigators predicted. Instead, once the test herd surpassed 100 deer per square-mile, we detected more subtle changes, such as delayed breeding and lower fawning rates among young does, and high newborn fawn losses (63 percent) among first-time mothers. Surprisingly, 22 percent of the yearling bucks grew very short spikes during the final year of study, despite being fed unlimited amounts of high-quality feed year-round.

Territorial Behavior

It's important to note the chief factor slowing the deer population's growth rate in the final years of the Cusino study was the steady rise in newborn fawn mortality.

Indirect evidence suggested most fawns died shortly after birth and losses were indeed density-dependent. That is, because does with newborn fawns are extremely antagonistic and defend a territory (10 to 20 acres in size) for about one month, crowding at peak deer density limited fawn-rearing space, disrupted maternal behavior and contributed to increased fawn deaths.

We concluded heavy newborn fawn mortality resulted from imprinting failure — mother to young or vice versa — or outright abandonment of otherwise healthy offspring by inexperienced and socially stressed mothers. Therefore, this situation represents an effective self-regulation mechanism even where food shortage is not an important factor in deer welfare.

George Schwede confirmed the territorial behavior of does during his studies in Virginia. However, David Hirth found little evidence of such behavior on savannah grasslands in South Texas. These contrasting results exemplify the behavioral plasticity exhibited by whitetails, depending upon environmental circumstances.

Short Spikes

Physiological development of males was also affected by increased density in the Cusino studies. At high densities, yearling bucks grew especially poor antlers, despite good nutrition.

The precise mechanisms involved are poorly understood. However, we believe that some socially-stressed buck fawns experienced a serious physiological setback, and a sex hormone imbalance, which impaired antler pedicle development. Undersized pedicles then gave rise to smaller-than-normal antlers. This resulted in short spikes for many of the yearling bucks.

Effects of Social Isolation

In the final year of study, the enclosure herd was reduced from 159 to 44 deer to mimic severe exploitation of antlerless deer. In some family groups, we removed all but one member, calling these lone individuals isolates. In other groups, we retained three to 12 related does per group, and referred to them as socials. This treatment was possible because mother-daughter

lineage had been determined previously through observations of marked animals.

Our objective was to determine how the surviving doe or fawn, deprived of her kin, would respond to drastic social change. We theorized that intensive harvesting of antlerless deer might break down the highly organized family group structure, cause social disruption and impair the reproductive performance of socially isolated does.

We were wrong!

During a three-year period, such annual treatment did not influence the date of breeding or number of fawns produced by yearlings and even does 3½ years old and older, regardless of their social status. However, 2½-year-old isolates consistently outperformed socials of the same age by breeding earlier in the rut, conceiving larger litters with more female progeny and rearing a greater proportion of their young.

Therefore, we learned intensive harvesting of antlerless deer did not hinder fawn production, and in at least one age class, it actually stimulated more births and better survival.

Female Suppression

The Cusino studies clearly demonstrated that density stress and social subordination — independent of nutrition — can alter a doe's rate of physical maturation and reproductive performance. What hasn't been determined is whether territorial behavior associated with fawning can regulate populations at high densities. However, observations suggest that some high-density, unhunted deer populations might achieve stable densities, due in part to increased newborn fawn mortality associated with territorial behavior at fawning time.

Female white-tailed deer social organization is a matriarchal group consisting of multiple generations of related does and their offspring that shares a common ancestral range. Where deer are well-nourished and adult does suffer minimal mortality, family groups can become large and complex. Such a matriarchal social unit might consist of the matriarch, her daughters, grand-daughters and even great-great-granddaughters.

As we watched the enclosure deer population grow in size, it became apparent the female whitetail's social organization allows for rapid exploitation of favorable food and cover, and permits deer to make maximum use of even limited space. However, it was equally evident that older, more dominant, does suppressed the reproductive success of younger does.

In late summer and early autumn, yearling does and nonproductive older does reunite with their respective mothers and their new fawns to form the classic family group. Out of necessity, the nonproductive does willingly assume subordinate social roles under the leadership of their mothers.

We found significant differences when we examined the reproductive performance of 2-year-old does that successfully raised fawns vs. those of the same age that did not raise fawns. The young does that failed to raise fawns bred an average of one week later than those that reared fawns and conceived more males. Normally, one would expect just the opposite, because lactating does would be under greater nutritional stress. However, because the enclosure deer were supplementally fed, social stress apparently became more important.

We speculated behavioral subordination produced certain physiological consequences and hormonal imbalances that delayed estrus among subordinate does. Psychological stress, for example, tends to increase progesterone production from the adrenal glands, which can block the effects of estradiol-induced hormone surges during estrus, which delays ovulation. In that event, delayed copulation could also account for a preponderance of male progeny.

Pressured to Disperse

Young bucks also experience the effects of social pressure. Due largely to intra-family strife, 80 percent to 90 percent of sexually active yearling bucks disperse from their ancestral range shortly before breeding starts each autumn.

As the yearling male approaches sexual maturity at 16 to 17 months of age, he is harassed, dominated and rejected by his mother and female relatives. Like his sister, the young male can avoid serious attacks from female relatives and unite with the family group, but only if he displays submissive, feminine posturing. In all likelihood, however, such a subdued male will be relegated a low social rank within the family group and will probably become a psychological castrate if he remains with female kin during the rut.

Dispersal behavior by male whitetails probably helps maintain an optimal balance between the amount of inbreeding and outbreeding. It tends to minimize the adverse effects of mother-son and brother-sister inbreeding, but still allows for breeding among distant relatives, thereby perpetuating desirable, genetically linked adaptive traits.

Our enclosure study indicated that social pressure induced by older female relatives is the primary stimulus prompting yearling bucks to leave their birth range. Therefore, a high dispersal rate and long dispersal distances among yearling bucks can be expected as the density of does increases. The corollary, of course, is yearling buck dispersal rates and distances traveled should decrease when young bucks are relieved of such stress.

The presence of older bucks and their signposts also tends to suppress the rutting activity of younger bucks. This suppressor effect might result in lowered testosterone levels in younger bucks, thereby reducing their aggressiveness and libido.

Studies conducted in Virginia by Stefan Holzenbein and Larry Marchinton demonstrated the importance of maternal domination in prompting dispersal among yearling whitetails. When comparing the movements of young bucks raised by their mothers vs. bucks that were orphaned several months after being weaned, these researchers found that few orphaned bucks dispersed from their natal home ranges as yearlings. On the other hand, most doe-raised males dispersed as expected. Also, as a group, the orphans exhibited better survival rates, which demonstrates that many unforeseen risks are involved when deer move to new areas.

Male Suppression

The presence of older bucks and their signposts also tend to suppress the rutting activity of younger bucks. This suppressor effect might result in lowered testosterone levels in younger bucks, thereby reducing their aggressiveness and libido. The behaviorally suppressed young buck also expends less energy, experiences less rut-related weight loss, and, therefore, grows to greater size at maturity before assuming a sire role in a herd.

In a three-year experiment, we simulated the complete harvest of antlered deer in our enclosure studies by reintroducing only 9-month-old buck fawns at trap-out. Our purpose was to evaluate the reputedly poor breeding performance of yearlings vs. the presumed virility of prime-age bucks.

As expected, we observed gross differences in rutting behavior of yearlings vs. mature bucks. As the young males became sexually mature, they easily dominated strange does but remained submissive to older female relatives.

Compared to mature bucks, the young "social floaters" fought more (even with does) and lacked the ritualized courtship and scent-marking behavior characteristic of older bucks. Because the young bucks failed to form a strict pre-rut dominance hierarchy, we believe all of them did some breeding.

Nonetheless, despite their obvious sexual inexperience and seemingly inferior behavior, yearlings serviced most does "on schedule" and produced as many offspring as mature sires. These results, however, differ from those of studies conducted in the South.

Biostimulation

The research of David Guynn and his coworkers on the Mount Holly Plantation in South Carolina, for example, demonstrated that the presence of mature bucks and their signposts stimulate and help synchronize estrus among does. Such "biostimulation" tends to have a much more significant impact on whitetail breeding in Southern herds than it apparently does in the North.

In the Mt. Holly study, the deer population was initially out of balance socially, as is typical of many Southern deer herds. The bucks had been heavily exploited, but deer density was high. There existed an unbalanced adult sex ratio heavily favoring females, and the breeding season was long — 96 days. In fact, some fawns weren't dropped until September.

During a five-year period, the researchers selectively killed deer to better balance deer numbers with existing food and cover resources, to decrease the proportion of does and to increase the proportion of bucks. Within five years, the rut became more intense and was shortened to 43 days. Mean conception dates shifted from Nov. 11 in the first year of study to Oct. 15 during the final year.

Similar results were reported by Harry Jacobson on Davis Island, Miss., where selective harvesting resulted in moving the peak of the rut three weeks earlier.

According to Miller: "In these two studies, improved nutrition certainly was fundamental to the changes, but sociobiological factors apparently also were involved. It appears likely that the increased numbers of mature bucks play a direct role in the earlier and shorter breeding season. Another possible factor is a reduction in the number of females remaining unbred during their first or subsequent estrous cycles. The availability of bucks to breed does on their first heat could account for a shorter breeding season but not an earlier one."

Miller also contends that ... "signposts have a strong priming effect on the does' estrous cycles, and they may be a significant factor in the shorter and earlier breeding seasons observed on quality managed areas in the Southeast."

In summer and early autumn, yearling does and nonproductive older does reunite with their mothers and new fawns to form the classic family group. Out of necessity, the nonproductive does assume subordinate social roles under the leadership of their mothers.

In the North, where photoperiod changes much more abruptly, the breeding window is narrow. Where such conditions prevail, social factors seem to have less impact on the rut's timing.

Conclusion

Researchers have only scratched the surface in their quest to better understand and apply basic principles of deer sociobiology. One thing is clear: Preliminary findings clearly show that hunter-induced mortality, or lack thereof, can seriously alter the social environment of whitetails. Studies also show social stress can affect the physical and reproductive condition of deer just about as effectively as habitat quality and nutrition. However, because whitetails are so highly adaptable and regionally diverse in behavior, their response to social pressure is not always predictable.

References

Miller, K.V., R.L. Marchinton, and J.J. Ozoga. 1995. Deer sociobiology. Pages 118-128 in K.V. Miller and R.L. Marchinton (Eds.) Quality Whitetails: The Why and How of Quality Deer Management. *Stackpole Books*, Harrisburg, PA. 322 pages.

Miller, K.V., and J.J. Ozoga. 1997. "Density Effects on Deer Sociobiology." Pages 136-150 in W.J. McShea, H.B. Underwood, and J.H. Rappole (Eds.) The Science of Overabundance: Deer Ecology and Population Management. *Smithsonian Institution*. 402 pages.

Chapter 2

GENDER EQUALITY?

Why Sex Ratios Vary in Whitetails

White-tailed deer manipulate the sex ratio of their offspring in response to various environmental factors. Researchers disagree, however, about why such variations occur.

We expect animal populations to produce approximately equal numbers of male and female offspring. And, in the long-run, it generally happens. However, abundant evidence suggests that certain animals, including white-tailed deer, manipulate sex ratio in response to various environmental factors. Investigators disagree, however, about why such variations occur. They also argue about the adaptiveness involved in producing more males or more females.

Studies have shown that whitetails sometimes produce a high number of male offspring, but in other situations they produce an excess of females. The exact mechanisms involved are poorly understood. However, the doe's age, nutritional intake, and various aspects of her behavior are likely to be important factors that influence the sex of her fawns.

Young does — doe fawns and yearlings — and old does tend to produce an excess of male fawns under natural conditions. Prime-aged does, however, usually produce more females. Also, single fawns are more likely males, whereas females tend to be more common among twins and triplets.

These general trends vary, however, depending on nutritional and social factors that prevail at the time of breeding. Generally, well-fed herds in comfortable social arrangements tend to produce more female fawns, while more males are conceived by poorly nourished or density-stressed animals.

Examining the Factors

Professor Harry Jacobson of Mississippi State University suggests sex ratios rest primarily in a doe's hormonal levels at conception. Jacobson writes (1994): "These hormones cause higher probability of one sex or the other because they affect the uterine environment and thus the relative motility of sperm. It is the sperm cell that determines the sex of offspring depending on X or Y chromosome presence. Perhaps these hormones cause changes in acidity within the uterus, which make the X-chromosome sperm swim faster or slower, and thus reach the ova earlier or later than the Y-chromosome sperm."

The implication is relatively simple: The doe's physiological status at the time she breeds largely determines her fawns' sex. The factors that might determine her status when she breeds, however, are complex.

Even the doe's psychological state can influence her physiology, and consequently the sex of her fawns. Behavioral stress, for example, tends to alter hormone production from the adrenal gland, which can create a hormone imbalance. The adrenal gland can secrete significant amounts of progesterone when a doe is stressed, which could block the effects of estrous-related hormones. Such an imbalance could delay ovulation and/or decrease the doe's mating urge. Thus, delayed copulation would influence the fawn's sex.

Therefore, untimely behavioral stress at breeding time could counter otherwise favorable circumstances.

What Research Shows

When reviewing literature about sex ratio variations in white-tailed deer, my former co-worker Louis Verme (1983) reported that doe fawns, when bred at 7 to 9 months of age, bore 62.5 percent male fawns. Meanwhile, yearling does produced 52.6 percent males, prime-age does — those 2½ to 7½ years old — produced 50.2 percent males, and older does produced 53.6 percent male fawns. He found that undernourished does produced fewer fawns and more males, while healthy does carried larger litters with more females.

Although earlier studies revealed male fawns normally predominate in deer, Verme concluded that such data largely came from high-density herds on impoverished range. He also suggested that recent intensive deer management efforts and habitat improvement practices have created more favorable situations in many herds. Therefore, these same herds now produce more females.

Based on his review, Verme concluded that an excess of male fawns would be expected when the bulk of the breeding stock consists of pubertal doe fawns and yearlings, in herds of low density or scattered distribution, among animals nutritionally deprived during the rut, and in instances of extreme density that lead to strife.

In contrast, Verme proposed that more female births would prevail in stable or increasing populations on good range and where seasonal food restrictions caused infertility or heavy neonatal mortality, which can lead to compensatory productivity during the next breeding season.

What About Timing?

The timing of breeding might also influence fawn sex ratio. Investigators in Utah (W.L. Robinette et al., 1977), for example, observed that 65.9 percent of early-born mule deer were males, compared to 47.6 percent males among late-born fawns. The researchers concluded that because the study area had poor summer range, early breeding does were in poor health. Late-breeders were presumably in better condition because they had more time to build body reserves while on superior winter range.

Robert Downing (1965) recorded a highly unbalanced sex ratio of 24 male to six female fawns in a Georgia enclosure. He speculated this was related to the order does bred, wherein the buck's first matings resulted in more male progeny, but subsequent services resulted in more females. However, studies conducted with captive deer have failed to

support this theory.

In our studies at the Cusino Wildlife Research Station in Upper Michigan, we learned that captive does become restless around estrus. We also found that the timing of a doe's mating relative to the onset of her estrous-related activity influenced the sex of her fawns (Verme and Ozoga, 1981). For instance, does that bred comparatively late in estrus — from 49 to 95 hours — produced, on average, 81 percent male fawns. That was especially true with first-time breeders that seemed apprehensive about mating. By comparison, prime-aged does normally bred early in estrus — from 13 to 24 hours — and conceived only 14 percent males.

Obviously, then, doe-to-buck ratios and the availability of bucks to breed does promptly and on schedule become important factors in determining the whitetail's reproductive performance. Theoretically, if a doe shows a preference for a certain buck as her mate, even the age structure of the male population might help determine sex ratios in fawns. A shortage of bucks — especially mature bucks — could lead to estrous recycling, late-births and an excess of poor-quality male fawns by winter. That would be especially true in areas with poor habitat and/or high female deer densities.

The Cusino Experience

While conducting research in Cusino's square-mile deer enclosure, we had an opportunity to regulate the herd's size and composition. We closely monitored the productivity of individual does and examined the role that social behavior played in their reproductive performance.

Female whitetails live in a matriarchal society. A doe's rate of physical and behavioral maturity determines her reproductive performance, and, ultimately, her fawn-rearing success will determine her social standing within the herd.

In whitetails, the birth of females is essential in perpetuating the family group or, in the case of daughters, in forming their own social unit. Generally, older, maternally experienced does within a clan are most dominant. They also tend to control the most favorable habitat and maintain the best physical condition. As a result, prime-aged matriarchs tend to breed first, conceive multiple litters and produce a disproportionate number of females. Obviously, for a doe to become a matriarch, she must produce surviving daughters.

In contrast, subordination tends to have a strong suppressor effect on a doe's reproductive performance. Except under the most favorable conditions, it would be difficult for doe fawns or yearlings to establish a family group. Instead, these young does would be better off to produce males, which would disperse to new range where they might become dominant breeder bucks.

Even 2-year-old does that fail to raise fawns often revert to subordinate female behavior by seeking close association with their mother. In our enclosure studies (Ozoga and Verme, 1986), these 2-year-olds behaved (socially) more like yearlings. Compared to does of the same age that successfully reared fawns, maternally inexperienced 2½ year olds bred a week later and conceived an excess of (64.7 percent) male fawns — reproductive traits similar to does breeding for the first time. On the other hand, the maternally experienced and more socially independent 2½-year-olds conceived only 38.9 percent males, the lowest proportion of males recorded for any doe age class.

Normally, adult does not nursing fawns in summer enter the rut in better-than-average physical shape. They breed earlier and conceive larger litters, with more female progeny than does burdened with nursing fawns. In our studies, however, that was not the case among 2½-year-old does. Although the unsuccessful mothers were heavier, and therefore presumably physically superior compared to does of the same age that nursed fawns, maternally experienced does demonstrated more advanced reproductive traits. In other words, differences in fawn-rearing success, and resultant maternal experience, were the primary factors influencing the sex ratio of offspring during the doe's second mating.

Dispersing Mothers

From an adaptive standpoint, it's important to note that second-time mothers generally disperse varying distances to establish new fawn-rearing territories. That expands the clan's range during times of bountiful food and cover. The production of female fawns on the new range could be viewed as adaptive, in that production of females accelerates the formation of a family unit.

In contrast, the unsuccessful 2-year-old doe likely remains with its mother on ancestral range for an additional year. The delayed birth of the second litter and the tendency to conceive males — which ultimately disperse — minimizes mother-daughter competition for limited fawn-rearing space. It also preserves the matriarch's traditional fawning territory.

It isn't the young doe's age by itself that determines the sex ratio of her fawns. Her rate of physical and behavioral development, and her fawn-rearing success, are more important. That is, a yearling doe that conceived fawns when it was 6 or 7 months old, and then reared them, would be reproductively and behaviorally more advanced than a doe of similar age that had not raised fawns.

Researcher Dale McCullough also argues that the herd derives distinct benefits by producing male fawns — especially if they are large and healthy — when habitat doesn't favor population growth. According to McCullough (1979),

when a doe is surviving with limited resources, she benefits by annually producing only one fawn, preferably a male. Because males normally disperse from their natal range, a male reared by a doe in poor habitat might more likely find favorable habitat elsewhere, while relieving his mother of added competition for limited resources. Also, a healthy male fawn might someday become a dominant buck and sire many offspring, thereby increasing the probability of passing on maternal genes.

Which Fawn 'Costs' More?

Much of the current argument about the adaptiveness of producing one sex over another rests with deciding which sex is more "expensive" to produce. Some investigators suggest that because male fawns are larger and have greater nutritional needs, they are most expensive. If so, the mother should produce more males only when range conditions are good, when she can afford the high cost of nourishing an expensive mate — which obviously isn't the case.

In whitetails, however, other researchers propose that females might be the most expensive sex because they tend to remain on their mother's range longer than sons. Although most yearling males disperse — thereby freeing the mother of added competition for available food and cover — daughters normally don't look for new fawning grounds until they're ready to raise their second litter. As a result, because daughters normally compete with the mother for resources one to several years longer than do sons, they might be more expensive in the long run.

Conclusion

Noted scientist Tony Peterle (1975) proposed that deer should have developed certain sociobiological traits during evolution that would control their population in response to constantly fluctuating, patchy food resources. The whitetail's matriarchal society and the ability to vary the sex ratio of its progeny appears to be a good example of such adaptiveness.

To date, research supports the contention that "local resource competition" accounts for the production of male-biased sex ratios among nutritionally stressed does. The production of fawns by younger does and female-biased sex ratios among progeny of well-fed mature does, on the other hand, should logically occur when conditions are most favorable for population growth.

References

Downing, R.L,. 1965. *An unusual sex ratio in white-tailed deer.* Journal of Wildlife Management 29:884-885.

Jacobson, H.A. 1994. *Reproduction. Pages 98-108 in Gerlach, D.S. Atwater, and J. Schnell. Deer.* Stackpole Books, Mechanicsburg, Pa. 384 pp.

McCullough, D.R. 1979. *The George Reserve Deer Herd.* University of Michigan Press, Ann Arbor. 271 pp.

Ozoga, J.J., and L.J. Verme. 1986. *Initial and subsequent maternal success of white-tailed deer.* Journal of Wildlife Management 50:122-124.

Peterle, T.J. 1975. *Deer sociobiology.* Wildlife Society Bulletin 3:82-83.

Robinette, W.L., N.V. Hancock, and D.A. Jones. 1977. *The Oak Creek Mule Deer Herd in Utah. Utah Division of Wildlife Resources Publication 77-15. 148 pp.*

Verme, L.J. 1983. *Sex ratio variation in Odocoileus: A critical review.* Journal of Wildlife Management 47:573-582.

Verme, L.J., and J.J. Ozoga. 1981. *Sex ratio of white-tailed deer and the estrous cycle.* Journal of Wildlife Management 45:710-715.

Len Rue, Jr.

Chapter 3

LIFE HOLDS ON:

Why Survival Begins in the Womb

Newborn deer die from many maladies, including accidents, abandonment, predation, parasitism and disease. But the mother's nutritional intake is the most crucial factor in the newborn's fate.

Most animals produce more young than can be expected to survive, and white-tailed deer are no exception. Many factors might interact, however, to determine how many fawns are born and how many survive to weaning age.

For some reason, many fawns fail to survive more than a few weeks after birth. In some instances, they live less than a few days. But the losses vary greatly. Losses might be small in some areas in some years. In other years, reproductive failure might be nearly 100 percent in the same area, and the reasons why aren't always clear.

What Kills Newborns?

Almost invariably, the highest death rates for newborn fawns occur in poor habitat where food and cover are inadequate. This typically follows severe winters, or wherever deer are overpopulated. Fragile and vulnerable newborn deer succumb to a host of maladies, including accidents, abandonment, predation, parasitism and disease. But the mother's nutritional intake — especially during the last third of pregnancy and shortly after giving birth — is by far the most crucial factor in the newborn's fate.

If the pregnant doe's diet is inadequate, she draws on her bone and body tissues to nourish her rapidly growing fetuses. A doe that is severely depleted tends to give birth to weak, undersized fawns, most of which die in a few days. Also, evidence suggests malnourished mothers sometimes behave abnormally (because of hormonal imbalances), and do not properly tend or defend their young, and might even abandon them.

Based on studies at the Cusino Wildlife Research Station in Upper Michigan, researcher Lou Verme (1962) found 92 percent of fawns born to does that were malnourished throughout pregnancy died within 48 hours of birth. When winter diets were poor and spring diets good, the does lost 35 percent of their fawns. By comparison, about 95 percent of the fawns survived if the does were well-fed throughout winter and spring. Survivors, on average, weighed about 8 pounds at birth, while those that died weighed about 4 pounds. Five pounds seemed to be the cutoff point.

In Verme's studies, malnourished does rarely absorbed or aborted fetuses, but some fawns were stillborn. Most fawns were born alive, but many died shortly after because of

four kinds of nutritive failure, including:
  ✔ Fawns born in poor, weakened condition.
  ✔ Fawns too small to reach the standing doe's teats.
  ✔ Does would not permit fawns to nurse.
  ✔ Does did not produce milk.

Other investigations conducted by Murphy and Coates (1966) found the amount of protein in the diet of pregnant does greatly influenced newborn survival. Penned does that received a diet of 13 percent crude protein didn't lose any fawns after birth, while a group fed a 10.4 percent crude protein diet lost 25 percent of its fawns. Furthermore, a group fed only 7.4 percent crude protein lost 42 percent of its fawns within a few days of birth.

The Doe's Milk

Because no dead fawns had milk in their stomachs, researchers believed the primary cause of death was delayed or inadequate milk production by the does.

Compared with cow's milk, deer milk is richer in fat, protein, dry solids and energy. Given a good milk supply — 6 to 8 ounces per serving two or three times daily — healthy fawns gain nearly one-half pound per day. They double their birth weight in about two weeks and triple it within a month. In the process, they change from meek "hiders" to strong runners. Therefore, early in life, the fawn's best strategy is to conserve energy and maximize its growth rate. This hinges on the mother's favorable nutrition and her ability to produce plenty of milk.

Detailed studies of deer milk's chemical composition (Youatt et al., 1965) revealed its nutritive value changes little with the doe's diet. If a doe receives insufficient nutrition, however, her milk production decreases. Therefore, does living in poor habitat might have a hard time producing enough milk to nourish twins or triplets. As a result, poorly nourished fawns develop slowly, are vulnerable to predation for a longer time, and are generally smaller than normal when weaned.

Nutritional Stress

A detailed study of winter nutritional stress on maternal-care traits in whitetails was conducted by Ed Langenau and John Lerg (1976) at the Houghton Lake Wildlife Research Station in Lower Michigan. Many earlier studies suggested some does refused to nurse their fawns, even though they produced milk. Therefore, Langenau and Lerg tried to determine if the doe's winter nutrition (during pregnancy) influenced her maternal behavior after she gave birth.

They used 30 pen-raised does in their study, assigning each to one of three nutritional levels January through March: unlimited feed, 75 percent of full feed, 50 percent of full feed.

All does received full rations during other seasons and were allowed to breed in autumn when 1 and 2 years old. The researchers then monitored the does' behavior and their fawns during the first few days after birth.

During the two-year study, 89 fawns were born alive and two fetuses were stillborn. Eleven fawns died within 72 hours. All but one of these fawns were from does on poor winter diets. All of these deaths — except two stillborn fetuses and one fawn too small to nurse — were attributed directly to a lack of maternal care.

The researchers recorded only minor differences in the behavior of fawns born to low-diet vs. high-diet mothers. However, 27 percent of does malnourished in winter abandoned their newborns, while well-fed mothers abandoned only 2 percent of their fawns.

Maternal Rejection

The most common newborn fawn mortality came from "maternal rejection syndrome." Langenau and Lerg wrote: "Does which failed to nurse or care for their young displayed fear and aggressive postures toward fawns, birth fluids and afterbirth. This lack of initial mother-young bond caused fawns to increase the amount of care-soliciting behaviors such as bleating, running at the doe, and time out of the bed. This response of the fawns probably reinforced the fear and aggressive behavior of the does."

The lack of an initial doe-fawn bond was critical. Without the important bond, fawns never nursed, and died from starvation. With twins, both were usually abandoned.

Crowding can also lead to abnormal maternal behavior and unusually high newborn fawn mortality, even with well-fed deer. Because does with newborns are antagonistic and defend a territory for about one month, high herd densities might leave young subordinate does without adequate fawn-rearing space. That lack of solitude and the resulting psychological stress might cause heavy fawn mortality as young, inexperienced mothers abandon otherwise healthy fawns.

This phenomenon of fawn rejection or abandonment by malnourished or socially stressed does probably has a firm physiological basis. In either case, abnormal maternal behavior likely stems from insufficient production of prolactin. This is a hormone produced by the pituitary gland that induces milk secretion and promotes the maternal instinct.

In the wild, any young, abandoned fawn is doomed. Once its mother fails to respond to its bawling and the fawn starts wandering alone, it's an easy target for predators.

Verme (1977) devised a way to predict annual newborn fawn birth weights, and chances for survival, based on their weight and age. He did this by studying fetuses from road-killed pregnant does. He calculated that newborn fawn losses in Upper Michigan, from nutritional factors alone, varied from 10 percent after mild winters to as much as 75 percent after severe ones. The most devastating winters brought prolonged adversity.

Defensive Does

Does, however, will often protect their young tenaciously. Scientific literature contains many examples of white-tailed does attacking and defending young fawns against predators. However, in my studies, maternally experienced does were far more successful than young does in rearing fawns when threatened by black bears (Ozoga and Verme 1986).

When black bears entered the Cusino square-mile deer enclosure in spring, they killed about 22 percent of the fawns. However, prime-age does lost only slightly more fawns when bears were present (17 percent) than they did when bears were absent (11 percent). Two- and 3-year-old does, however, suffered heavy fawn mortality when bears were present. The 2-year-olds lost 32 percent of their fawns, while 3-year-olds lost 58 percent. When bears were absent, the losses were 13 percent and 4 percent, respectively. Also, experienced does rarely lost single fawns or both members of twin litters. Meanwhile, complete litter failure with young does was not uncommon.

Canine Predation

When whitetails live in wolf country, fawn survival also varies in relation to the mother's age, concluded researchers David Mech and Ronald McRoberts (1990). As in my studies of black bear predation, these Minnesota researchers found that older white-tailed does were better able to protect their fawns from wolves.

Coyotes are probably one of the most significant predators of newborn whitetails. In the Southwest, they frequently account for about half the deaths of newborn fawns. Even there, however, B.K. Carroll and D.L. Brown (1977) found annual fawn mortality varied with the amount of rainfall in spring and early summer.

Rainfall determines deer nutrition and fawn hiding cover. Fawn losses ranged from 10 percent during years of heavy rainfall to as much as 90 percent during drought years.

Coyotes are far less successful in killing newborn fawns in the Midwest and Great Lakes regions. Does there are typically well-nourished, and dense ground vegetation provides ideal hiding cover. No predation occurred among 33 radio-collared fawns in a Minnesota study, while coyotes and domestic dogs killed an estimated 21 percent and 20 percent, respectively, of the fawns in south-central Iowa and southern Illinois.

Maternal Defenses

While conducting research on Columbian white-tailed deer in Oregon, Winston Smith (1987) observed considerable variation in the degree of maternal defense shown by does. Sometimes does aggressively charged and struck at dogs that Smith used to find fawns. Other times, however, the does remained out of sight. Smith also observed that does with twins sometimes defended one of their fawns more diligently than the other.

The mother's outright defense of her fawns requires a lot of energy, not to mention risking injury or death. Therefore, Smith speculated that sometimes a doe's defense of her fawns was worth it, and sometimes it wasn't. That hinged heavily on the physical condition of the doe and her fawns.

Smith proposed that healthy does could afford to defend healthy fawns. Such early action could be important in predicting the fawn's chances for survival. In his study, does defended larger siblings more aggressively than smaller ones.

Smith concluded that "natural selection should favor some optimum level of fawn defense based on the risk incurred by the parent and the expected benefit derived by the offspring."

Conclusion

Clearly, nutrition during late winter and spring powerfully influences newborn fawn survival. Also, the effects of malnutrition are sometimes difficult to separate from those of predation when determining the cause of excessive fawn mortality.

Healthy whitetails are well-endowed with inherited antipredator strategies that help minimize the fawn's detection and improve its survival prospects.

On the other hand, malnutrition increases fawn vulnerability and, sometimes, a breakdown in the mother's maternal behavior and her defense against predators. Therefore, when predators and scavengers are present, it's difficult to determine the events leading up to a young fawn's death. In most cases, all that remains are scattered fragments of evidence.

References

Carroll, B.K., and D.L. Brown. 1977. *Factors affecting neonatal fawn survival in south-central Texas.* Journal of Wildlife Management 41:63-69.

Langenau E.F., and J.M. Lerg. 1976. *The effect of winter nutritional stress on maternal and neonatal behavior in penned white-tailed deer.* Applied Animal Ethology 2:207-223.

Mech, L.D., and R.E. McRoberts. 1990. *Survival of white-tailed fawns in relation to maternal age.* Journal of Mammalogy 71:465-467.

Ozoga, J.J., and L.J. Verme. 1986. *Relation of maternal age to fawn-rearing success of white-tailed deer.* The Journal of Wildlife Management 50:480-486.

Smith, W.P. 1987. *Maternal defense in Columbian white-tailed deer: When is it worth it?* The American Naturalist 130:310-316.

Verme, L.J. 1962. *Mortality of white-tailed deer fawns in relation to nutrition.* Proceedings, National White-tailed Deer Disease Symposium. 1:15-38.

Verme, L.J. 1977. *Assessment of natal mortality in Upper Michigan deer.* Journal of Wildlife Management 41:700-708.

Youatt, W.G., L.J. Verme, and D.E. Ullrey. 1965. *Composition of milk and blood in nursing white-tailed does and blood composition of their fawns.* Journal of Wildlife Management 29:79-84.

Bill Lerner

Chapter 4

EARLY BREEDERS:

Why Can Some Doe Fawns Breed?

Early-born doe fawns that grow to be big and fat by autumn are likely to achieve puberty and breed, especially in low-density herds. Even then, harsh weather, social pressures and other forces might interrupt breeding.

White-tailed deer are among the most prolific deer species. One reason is females can breed at a young age and produce offspring shortly after their first birthday. Mule deer are inherently less productive, in part, because their fawns seldom breed.

Breeding in 6- to 8-month-old female whitetails is fairly common in rich environments. This special trait allows its populations to explode in favorable conditions.

Whether a female whitetail reaches puberty and breeds in her first year might depend on many poorly understood factors. Birth date, genetics, day length, nutrition, climate and social pressures are just a few factors likely involved. Despite considerable research, however, investigators still debate the phenomenon.

The George Reserve

The George Reserve deer herd is a classic example of how fast whitetails multiply when conditions allow doe fawns to achieve puberty and breed.

The nearly two-square-mile fenced enclosure in George Reserve is in south-ern Michigan. It's operated by the University of Michigan as an outdoor laboratory. Six deer, including two bucks and four presumably pregnant does were put into the reserve in 1928. Within five years a drive-count census revealed a herd of 160 deer.

At the time, biologists marveled at this reproductive rate, and it became a land-mark in the budding wildlife management profession. Amazingly, when Dale McCullough, who was in charge of the reserve's deer research for years, re-examined the data, he realized the introductory herd probably had grown even faster.

McCullough said drive-counts in the reserve's early years were made by crews too small for effective censuses. Based on newer evidence, McCullough calculated the 1934 deer herd at about 180, not 160. He also estimated the population peaked at about 222 in 1935.

McCullough tested his estimates by reducing the reserve's herd to 10 deer in 1975. He then closed hunting. By 1981, the herd had soared to 212. Further, the population followed a growth curve nearly identical to the original herd's

DOE FAWNS PRODUCE LARGE NEWBORNS

On Northern range, it's crucial that fawns grow rapidly. They must attain large body size and store abundant fat reserves by late autumn, because few runts survive harsh winters.

Because most doe fawns breed in December, their offspring are usually born in July. This could be a serious disadvantage — especially if they're undersize at birth — should the next winter be severe. Late-born fawns have less time to grow and fatten before winter.

One would intuitively expect small, immature does to produce smaller newborn fawns than a mature doe. This handicap would also decrease survival of the doe fawn's offspring.

Surprisingly, however, studies at Michigan's Cusino Wildlife Research Station show the opposite. That is, late-born offspring of doe fawns tend to be larger at birth than the early-born fawns of mature does.

In an article in the *Journal of Wildlife Management* (1985), Louis Verme compared the birth weights of 18 single fawns produced by doe fawns to the birth weights of their mothers. The doe-fawn offspring, which were born between June 12 and Sept. 7, weighed an average of 8.6 pounds at birth. By comparison, the doe-fawn mothers — which were progeny of mature does — that produced these fawns were all born between May 22 and June 8, and weighed an average of 7.2 pounds at birth. That's a significant difference. A similar relationship was found among adult does, wherein late-fawning does produced larger newborn.

Because these deer were born and raised in the same penned environment and received the same nutrition, Verme concluded differ-

ences in newborn weights were not influenced by nutrition. Instead, he suggested, "The most plausible explanation is that late fawning doe fawns were in a different physiological state during the latter part of pregnancy in comparison to earlier fawning adult does."

In whitetails, various endocrine hormones fluctuate by season. Growth hormone and prolactin, for example, which are important for growth, reach peak levels in summer. Verme theorized that higher concentrations of these hormones stimulated exceptional growth in fetuses carried by late-breeding does.

If Verme's hypothesis is correct, this tendency would partly, if not completely, nullify the growth advantage of early-born fawns — especially on rich Midwestern farmlands.

— *John J. Ozoga*

from 1928 to 1935.

Ironically, the reserve's herd was not achieving its maximum breeding potential! McCullough observed that reproductive success declined as the herd's density increased. Had the initial rate of increase continued, the herd could have grown to 300, instead of the estimates of 222 in 1935 and 212 in 1981.

Because few deer died inside the reserve, McCullough concluded that reproductive success declined and slowed herd growth. Much of the productivity decline occurred because doe fawns didn't breed at higher herd densities. McCullough determined that doe fawns breed only under superb conditions, when herds are well below carrying capacity and most fawns survive.

McCullough also observed that production of triplets by adult does and breeding by fawn does occurred at about the same herd densities. Therefore, he believed the occurrence of triplets among adult does might be a useful clue to breeding of doe fawns in wild herds.

Good Nutrition Important

Biologists generally agree fawns must be well-nourished to achieve puberty and breed. Therefore, a high incidence of pregnant fawns indicates good range condi-

tions where healthy herds are maintained below carrying capacity.

To achieve puberty and breed at ages 6 to 8 months, fawns must be born on schedule — generally in late May or early June — and reach a certain critical body size. In the North, that size is about 80 to 90 pounds. For smaller Southern species, it's about 70 pounds. That doesn't mean all animals reaching or exceeding these weights breed and reproduce. Protein is required for body growth, and energy-rich foods appear especially important in producing female hormones.

In Virginia, researchers learned female fawns on high-energy diets had higher progesterone levels than fawns on low-energy diets. These differences in hormonal levels affect the female's sexual maturity and the eggs' release from the ovaries, and thus, the fawn's ability to breed. Dietary protein apparently had no effect on attaining puberty.

Regional Differences

Not all large, well-nourished doe fawns breed, even when they live in low-density areas. The highest fawn pregnancy rate is in the Midwest. More than half of doe fawns typically breed in agricultural areas of Illinois,

Iowa, Kansas, Missouri, Nebraska, North Dakota, Ohio and South Dakota, as well as the southern regions of Minnesota, Wisconsin and Michigan.

In Iowa, researchers found more than 70 percent of the doe fawns bred, and that they carried an average of 1.25 fetuses. While most conceived only one fawn, many carried twins and some even triplets!

Fewer doe fawns breed in Southern states. Only 10 percent to 40 percent reportedly breed in the Southeast, even on the best range. Likewise, less than 16 percent of doe fawns likely breed in Texas' Llano Basin.

Doe fawns are also less likely to breed near the whitetail's northern range limits. There, climate and range quality can vary greatly each year over relatively short distances, and even the same area.

In New York's Adirondacks, only about 4 percent of doe fawns breed. But in southern New York, where forage quantity and quality is better, more than 36 percent of doe fawns become pregnant. Likewise, in southern Michigan more than half of the doe fawns usually breed each year. In comparison, less than 5 percent become pregnant in Upper Michigan. Similar trends appear in Wisconsin and Minnesota.

While some differences are caused by variations in nutrients, some researchers believe other environmental factors — such as temperature and day length — could play a role.

Genetics might also be a factor in some areas. However, genetics don't explain the different breeding potential found between fawns in northern and southern Michigan. The ancestral stock of southern Michigan's George Reserve came from near the southern shore of Lake Superior in Upper Michigan.

Photoperiod Effects

Most — if not all — of the whitetail's seasonal physiological events such as antler growth, body growth, coat molt, fattening and reproduction are controlled by or cued to seasonal changes in daylight, or photoperiod. This has led to speculation that regional differences in daylight amounts might affect puberty attainment in young deer.

Researchers in southern Michigan studied doe fawns raised in light-controlled chambers to evaluate photoperiod's effects on puberty. Fawns raised on 16 hours of light and eight hours of dark were placed in two test groups at age 4 months. One group was switched to eight hours of light in mid-October. The other group remained on 16 hours of light until December, and then switched to eight hours of light.

The researchers found the timing of pelage change, changes in growth rates and onset of puberty were affected by the start of the 8-hour day. Fawns experiencing an earlier switch to short days were physiologically more advanced than those on prolonged daylight. Seven of eight early short-day fawns achieved sexual maturity in January or February, while none of the eight in the extended daylight group sexually matured.

Contrasting Results

We studied the relationship of photoperiod to puberty in doe fawns at the Cusino Wildlife Research Station in Upper Michigan. Interestingly, we had very different results.

At Cusino, we subjected one group of 4-month-old female fawns to extended photoperiod by using overhead lights to illuminate outdoor pens to simulate longer days. Our "control" animals were also confined outdoors, but with natural daylight length. The study's photoperiod phase lasted nine weeks. A mature buck was then placed in each pen until March.

During the study, 19 of 29 test fawns bred. Sixty-one percent of the long-day fawns bred, compared to nearly 73 percent of the natural-day fawns. One long-day fawn conceived twins, but all others bore singletons. Similar reproductive performance between these groups refutes the idea that extended photoperiod improves reproductive performance in doe fawns. Factors other than photoperiod must cause poor breeding success in Northern doe fawns.

We found only one striking difference in reproductive performance between doe-fawn groups in our study: widely varying estrous dates according to experimental treatment. That is, long-day fawns had a prolonged breeding season, extending from Nov. 24 until Feb. 20. Eight of them bred during January and February. By comparison, all fawns exposed to natural daylight bred on or before Jan. 20.

Interestingly, despite comparable birth dates and newborn weights, doe fawns that became pregnant — irrespective of treatment — in the Cusino studies averaged more than seven pounds heavier by Sept. 21 compared to nonbreeders. Fawns that bred also demonstrated greater skeletal growth during the study.

Fat to Lean Biomass Ratio

Obviously, doe fawns must be fat and skeletally large to achieve sexual maturity. Under varying nutrition levels, it's equally possible to find large, lean fawns and small, fat ones, none of which could be expected to breed. We suspect, therefore, that doe fawns must achieve a certain critical fat to lean body composition to achieve puberty.

The timing and extent of fat deposits seem to play an important role in attaining puberty. Reduced photoperiod tends to trigger such important seasonal events as pelage change and fattening. Therefore, long-day fawns in our Cusino studies probably did not achieve the critical fat/lean body composition necessary to induce puberty until after they were switched to natural daylight. This, in turn, likely accounted for their delayed puberty and breeding.

PRECOCIOUS BUCK FAWNS

Some buck fawns achieve puberty and are capable of breeding. Buck fawns have been known to impregnate doe fawns in captivity, but their role as sires in the wild is unknown.

Polished antlers among fawns are considered a sign of sexual maturity. The male hormone testosterone (produced primarily by the testes) is essential in fawns for pedicle and antler development. High testosterone levels result in polished antler buttons, or infant, antlers.

Only 5 percent to 10 percent of the buck fawns in most wild herds reportedly achieve sexual maturity, based on the presence of polished antlers. Pen-raised buck fawns might develop polished antlers by late October or November, but most do not reach sexual maturity until December or even January. Because most wild fawns killed by hunters are harvested and examined before mid-December, the percentage of fertile buck fawns could be much higher than expected in some populations.

About 37 percent of 130 buck fawns collected in January from the Crab Orchard National Wildlife Refuge in Illinois were presumed fertile. This relatively high level was obviously influenced by excellent nutrition. However, investigators concluded that male fawns with late birth dates had a minimal chance of achieving puberty.

While it's generally assumed the same proportion of each sex reaches puberty as fawns, observations from the Cusino enclosure suggest otherwise. Of 19 buck fawns present in the enclosure during 1984 and 1985, 16 (84 percent) grew infant antlers. Most achieved hardened pedicle tips and polishing during early December, but some occurred as early as Nov. 27. All cast their miniature antlers before March. At the same time, only one of 14 (7 percent) doe fawns became pregnant.

Therefore, a high incidence of infant antlers among male fawns might not indicate frequent breeding among female fawns in the same population. Even when born on schedule and provided excellent nutrition, other factors might suppress the breeding activity of young bucks and does.

— *John J. Ozoga*

We concluded that body weights of wild Upper Michigan doe fawns essentially become stable in midautumn because of marginal nutrition and the onset of harsh weather. In other studies, as little as a 10 percent reduction in caloric intake for fawns in autumn seriously curbed their fattening and skeletal growth. Therefore, on Northern range, a natural decrease in high-energy foods, rather than decreasing daylight, probably halts the fawn's sexual development.

Enclosure Studies

Despite such findings, we couldn't stimulate frequent breeding among supplementally fed doe fawns in the square-mile Cusino enclosure. Although the well-fed doe fawns averaged more than 80 pounds by late November (with some exceeding 100 pounds), and they undoubtedly had good fat/lean biomass ratios, only one of 208 became pregnant in 12 years. This occurred despite high productivity in mature does and high frequencies of triplets.

Therefore, the lack of breeding among the enclosure fawns suggests selective pressures other than genetics, photoperiod, nutrition and climate were involved.

Social Effects

It's important to note that Cusino's enclosure deer lived more natural social lives than pen-raised deer. Mature bucks in constant close contact with young females — which often occurs in small-pen studies — is unnatural. I guess that differences in social behavior largely account for the gross differences in breeding performance of penned vs. enclosure doe fawns.

Several possible social factors might explain why pen-raised fawns bred while enclosure fawns did not, despite comparable weather conditions and nutritious diets. The unnatural confinement of bucks with doe fawns in pens might have a biostimulating effect, which induced breeding. As I've mentioned in other articles, confining bucks and mature does together in autumn tends to advance mean breeding dates by eight to nine days. It's possible the close (unnatural) contact with sexually active bucks also stimulated and advanced puberty's onset in pen-raised doe fawns.

Orphaning

Another possibility is orphaning — severing mother-young bonds. Pen-raised fawns were separated from their mothers at age 4 months. Enclosure fawns, however, remained with their mothers and other female relatives throughout the breeding season.

Domination by older females tends to suppress the reproductive performance of younger females. We learned, for example, that a release from maternal domination improves the reproductive performance of 2-year-old does. The critical ratio of fat to lean biomass controlling sexual maturity probably occurs earlier in orphaned fawns than fawns subjected to the constant psychological stress of maternal domination.

A Texas study confirmed that orphaning plays a key role in doe-fawn breeding, even in a Southern environment. Two of four doe fawns deliberately orphaned in midautumn subsequently bred, while none of five control deer achieved puberty.

McCullough surmised that herd reduction in the George Reserve contributed to improved nutrition, better physical condition and, hence, increased pregnancy rates in doe fawns. On the other hand, one might argue that fawns were freed from maternal suppression as the herd was purposely decimated by a mid-December hunt, and that social factors were more important than nutrition in triggering puberty in doe fawns.

A Michigan Experience

While southern Michigan deer numbers increased dramatically the past several decades, the incidence of doe-fawn breeding declined. The reasons, however, aren't clear.

Southern Michigan's deer harvest increased from about 7,000 in 1963 to 78,000 in 1982, which reflects about a 10-fold herd increase. Meanwhile, pregnancy rates in doe fawns declined from 60 percent to about 47 percent.

Lou Verme argues that harvest rates did not keep pace with the steadily expanding southern Michigan herd. As a result, he claims, "as the [southern Michigan] deer population increased, proportionately fewer doe fawns

were orphaned because the annual harvest, although considerable, did not increase as a percentage of the available productive does taken through hunting." Therefore, he contends the decreased pregnancy rates among doe fawns stems from social factors — namely, increased maternal domination — and not nutritional constraints.

Lowered fertility probably likewise occurred in southern Wisconsin doe fawns in recent years, despite liberal antlerless seasons designed to check population growth. Conversely, breeding rates among doe fawns in a South Carolina herd reportedly increased as deer densities were reduced through heavier antlerless harvests.

These trends support the hypothesis that biosocial factors, coincident with herd eruption or decline, can influence pregnancy rates in doe fawns as readily as nutrition.

Conclusion

Clearly, doe-fawn breeding is a complicated phenomenon. Whether a doe fawn breeds seems to depend on many factors, the effects of which remain poorly understood.

Certainly, early-born doe fawns that grow to be fat and skeletally large by autumn are most likely to achieve puberty and breed, especially if they're in a low-density herd. But even then, harsh weather, social pressures and other unknown forces might come into play and interrupt breeding.

References
Abler, W.A., D.E. Buckland, R.L. Kirkpatrick, and P.F. Scanlon. 1976. Plasma progestins and puberty in fawns as influenced by energy and protein. Journal of Wildlife Management 40:442-446.

Budde, W.S. 1983. Effects of photoperiod on puberty attainment of female white-tailed deer. Journal of Wildlife Management 47:595-604.

McCullough, D.R. 1979. The George Reserve deer herd: population ecology of a K-selected species. University of Michigan Press, Ann Arbor. 271 pages.

McCullough, D.R. 1982. Population growth rate of the George Reserve deer herd. Journal of Wildlife Management 46:1079-1083.

Ozoga, J.J. 1987. Maximum fecundity in supplementally fed northern Michigan white-tailed deer. Journal of Mammalogy 86:878-879.

Verme, L.J. 1991. Decline in doe fawn fertility in southern Michigan deer. Canadian Journal of Zoology 69:25-28.

Verme, L.J., and J.J. Ozoga. 1987. Relationship of photoperiod to puberty in doe fawn white-tailed deer. Journal of Mammalogy 68:107-1110.

Charles J. Alsheimer

Chapter 5

SMALL BODIES, SMALL RACKS:

The Short-Spike Phenomenon

The old adage, "The head grows according to the pasture, good or otherwise," holds true throughout the whitetail's range. Theoretically, short-spike yearlings should be almost nonexistent.

Yearling bucks (1½ years old) cannot grow antlers of Boone and Crockett proportions. But when born early in the year and well-nourished, they can develop respectable racks of eight or more points. In some areas, however, you're more likely to see spiked yearlings, some that carry miniature antlers hardly visible above the hair. In some states, a legally harvested buck must have at least one 3-inch antler. Generally, this measurement is from the base of the skull to the tip of longest antler, meaning it includes about one-half inch or so of pedicle bone on the skull of an average yearling.

The original intent of these laws was probably to protect antlerless deer, including button-buck fawns, from harvest. Hence, in states where the 3-inch antler law prevails, short-spike bucks can only be harvested if the hunter holds a permit for antlerless deer. These regulations might sometimes cause problems for wildlife managers, particularly when short-spike adult bucks are abundant. Under such conditions, many bucks with sub-legal-sized antlers are shot and tagged with permits intended for does or fawns.

As a result, fewer female deer than expected are harvested. That could leave the post-hunt herd larger than desired, which could contribute to over-browsing and unnecessary habitat damage.

Button-Bucks

Let's not confuse short-spike adult bucks with button-buck fawns. Buck fawns sporting small, polished antlers — usually less than one-half inch long — usually indicate excellent living conditions for deer. But short-spike adult bucks frequently result from nutritional shortages, and indicate poor physical development. Healthy buck fawns tend to grow prominent antler pedicles, or stumps, on which the antlers form, by late autumn. Some even develop small, polished antler caps, or infant antlers, which are mineralized tips of the pedicles, when 6 to 7 months old. The growth of the pedicle and these infant antlers is a continuous process, in that antler growth starts when pedicle growth is complete.

You will find little documentation of infant antlers on young whitetails in scientific literature. However, most biologists contend that about 5 percent of buck fawns can be expected to produce polished button antlers by the time they are 6 to 7 months old. I believe the frequency of infant antlers might be considerably higher in well-nourished deer populations. For example, I found 84 percent of supplementally fed buck fawns raised in Upper Michigan's square-mile Cusino enclosure during 1985 and 1986 produced polished button antlers (Ozoga 1988). Although some of these buck fawns rubbed off velvet during the last week of November, most did not polish their miniature antlers until early December. All had cast their antlers by late February. Therefore, most antler-bearing fawns would be overlooked where deer hunting seasons end by December.

Wildlife managers expect to see fewer than 25 percent spikes among yearling bucks in well-nourished, well-managed white-tailed deer herds. Theoretically, short-spike yearlings should be almost nonexistent.

Antler Basics

When discussing initial antler development in deer, whether they are fawns or yearlings, two considerations are crucial: (1) before any deer can grow antlers it must first grow pedicles on which antlers form, and (2) body growth takes precedence over antler growth. This means proper pedicle development plays a critical role in antler growth. Any dietary shortage can have strong negative effects on subsequent antler size.

The age at which the pedicle is first distinguishable depends on the species and its environment. In some species, such as elk and caribou, the pedicle bases appear in the fetus during the second half of gestation. In white-tailed deer and mule deer, however, pedicles develop after birth, and usually don't become pronounced bumps until the fawn is about 4 or 5 months old. That's when the healthy young male's testes develop and start producing sufficient quantities of the male hormone testosterone, which stimulates the laying down of additional bone at the pedicle site.

Young deer must be born on schedule, however, and be properly nourished to achieve a certain threshold body weight before the testes produce enough testosterone to start pedicle formation. In the absence of testosterone, or the presence of the female hormone estrogen, no pedicles form and antlers fail to develop later.

The Nutritional Factor

Wildlife managers expect to see fewer than 25 percent spikes among yearling bucks in well-nourished, well-managed white-tailed deer herds. Theoretically, short-spike yearlings should be almost nonexistent. However, you are apt to encounter considerable debate among biologists on this subject, including varied reasons (and sometimes excuses) for a higher-than-accepted occur-

rence of small-antlered adult bucks. Nonetheless, the common rule is that yearling buck body size and antler size go together; if they are small-bodied you can expect them to carry small antlers.

During an early investigation, William Severinghaus and his co-workers (1950) reported more than 50 percent of yearling bucks they examined from New York's central Adirondack region carried spike antlers shorter than 3 inches. And although their sample sizes were small, 15 percent and 6 percent respectively of the 2½- and 3½-year-old bucks developed only sub-legal spikes. By comparison, they found only a 3 percent short-spike rate among yearlings from the western Adirondacks, where deer had much better nutrition. Quite often, a high incidence of short-spiked yearling bucks is linked to deer overabundance and resultant poor food conditions. For example, we found an unusually high frequency of short-spike yearling bucks harvested from certain areas of Michigan during 1992. About one-third of the yearling bucks taken from Dickinson County in the Upper Peninsula carried sub-legal spikes. Short-spike rates ranged from 10 percent to 17 percent in six other northern Michigan counties. In all cases, the unusually high frequency of short spikes could be linked to areas of high deer density (in excess of 50 deer per square mile) on Northern range.

A high incidence of short-spike antlers, however, is not limited to areas of especially high deer densities. Nor is it a phenomenon only in the North. But the old adage, "The head grows according to the pasture, good or otherwise," holds true throughout the whitetail's range.

Steve Shea and his co-workers (1992a) found range nutrition so poor for whitetails in the flatwood habitats of northwestern Florida that 78 percent of the yearling bucks grew spike antlers less than 5 inches long. Further, herd reduction did little to improve the deer's nutritional plane. Even when deer density was lowered, body size and antler size among yearling bucks did not improve. Researchers generally agree that a buck's antler development depends on one or more of four factors: age, nutrition, genetics and timing of the fawning season.

The Effects of Stress

In the case of yearling bucks, I would add one more factor: social stress. I'm convinced that excessive social stress, caused by frequent conflict among individuals, can disrupt basic physiological functions in young males in particular, and lead to an imbalance of certain hormones. This might ultimately suppress antler development — even when animals are born on schedule and well-fed.

We saw the effects of crowding stress in the Cusino enclosure at times of high herd density (Ozoga and Verme 1982). When deer density surpassed 100 deer per square mile, social stress resulted in delayed breeding, lower-than-normal fawning rates, and unusually high newborn fawn losses among young does. And despite being fed unlimited amounts of high-quality artificial feed year-round, 22 percent of the yearling bucks grew short, sub-legal spikes. Naturally, we expect to see elevated stress in high-density deer herds where deer might compete savagely for food and space. And that's when many yearling bucks reportedly grow only short spike antlers — even though the reasons might be obscure.

However, it's also likely that increased social stress might occur in deer herds socially out of balance because of improper harvesting practices. A shortage of prime-age bucks, for example, could be disruptive during the breeding season when the presence of older, more dominant bucks ensures harmony and social order. On the other hand, high doe densities during the fawning season could lead to extreme competition among deer for space at a time when fawn-rearing does are especially antagonistic. I believe some deer managers are missing the boat when dealing with, and attempting to explain, the unusually high incidence of short-spiked yearling bucks in herds they manage. Biologists do not always carefully ponder the basic reasons behind such abnormalities, and do not take advantage of the wealth of information therein. I admit, however, that we need more research on the subject.

Yearling bucks that are unhealthy or delayed in sexual maturity commonly carry short spikes. That's pretty much established fact. However, the precise reasons for the predicament vary greatly by region, depending on many factors. Even within a given area, short-spike yearlings might be plentiful one year but scarce the next. Looking closely at why they occur could provide important clues to help managers remedy the situation.

Short-Spike Variations

Generally, we see two types of short-spike antlers among yearling bucks: those with a burr and those without. The burr, also called a cornet, is the flared base of the antler most prominent on the antlers of older bucks. While both of these short-spike conditions among yearlings indicate unfavorable living conditions, they result from different troublesome life histories.

Short-spike antlers lacking a burr are generally short, straight shafts of bone, small but fairly uniform in diameter, with a rounded tip. As in the case of infant antlers, burrless spikes carried by yearling bucks are virtually elongated pedicles. Such a condition suggests the yearling buck did not achieve favorable pedicle develop-

ment, or had no pedicles before his first winter. Consequently, he had to play catch-up the next spring by adding more pedicle bone before growing antlers — all within three to four months. Therefore, yearling bucks with burrless short-spike antlers generally indicate delayed maturation caused by late birth, poor nutrition during its first six or seven months, or possibly physiological problems associated with social stress. Yearling bucks with short, burrless spikes tend to be smaller than average for their age, and their delayed antler cycle often results in unusually late velvet shedding. These retarded bucks might be sexually active, but they tend to have low dominance rank, and probably seldom breed when the local herd contains older, larger bucks. Depending on nutritional conditions, they might not overcome their poor start in life. If nutrition remains poor, they will likely never become a large-bodied, large-antlered buck, even at maturity. Conversely, a stunted young animal might compensate later in life if nutritional conditions improve sharply.

We also see bucks with short, sub-legal spikes with a burr, or cornet. These short structures are wide at the base because of the flared cornet, but tend to come to an abrupt, sharp point. Therefore, they differ greatly in shape, and are also more heavily stained than short, burrless spikes. George Bubenik, a leading authority on antler development, says: "We don't really know why and how they (cornets) developed. No experimental study has been so far performed."

Bubenik notes, however, that cornets usually develop during late stages of antler growth, generally after at least two-thirds of the antler beam length has been achieved. He suggests the reason for the cornet is probably to provide additional protection to the blood vessels around the pedicles during fights. He emphasizes that some members of the deer family living in Northern environments do not develop cornets until they form their second antlers, probably because of the low level of male hormone production during the usual time of cornet formation. Furthermore, because a high level of testosterone depends on good nutrition, cornets might not develop in older, malnourished bucks.

Late Bloomers

As noted earlier, body growth takes precedence over antler growth in younger animals. In northern Michigan, Duane Ullrey (1982) found high protein and adequate energy supplies during March, just before the start of antler development, are especially important for antler growth in yearling bucks.

Given what we know about antler development, we can generally assume that a yearling buck with cornet-equipped short spikes was born in May or June, and he found reasonable nutrition during his first seven months. Either that or he lives in an area with fantastically good nutrition, which enabled him to overcome the handicaps of late birth. Further, he probably achieved favorable body size by autumn and developed good-sized pedicles before winter; he might also have grown infant antlers. However, he probably experienced serious nutritional shortages later in life, either during late winter or the next spring, or more likely both seasons. On Northern range, well-developed fawns that barely survive winter, and then find poor food conditions from March through June, likely grow this type of short-spike antler. These animals might be fairly large-bodied and, provided good nutrition in subsequent years, are likely to grow respectable antlers at maturity.

While genetics certainly are a factor in buck antler development, I believe some hunters and managers often employ the "inferior genetic stock" idea to excuse an abundance of stunted, miniature-antlered bucks.

A Matter of Inheritance

There is no denying antler development is somewhat hereditary. The studies of Donnie Harmel (1982), conducted in Texas, demonstrated that a buck's body and antler size can be greatly influenced by genetics. Spiked yearling bucks, which he studied, more often sired spiked sons than fork-antlered yearling sires. Nonetheless, even the spiked progeny in Harmel's studies carried antlers that averaged more than 6 inches long, suggesting good nutrition minimized the occurrence of short spikes.

Furthermore, the doe also plays an important role in antler genetics. Research with penned deer revealed some does consistently reared large-antlered sons, whereas other does more commonly produced small-antlered sons.

While genetics certainly are a factor in antler development, I believe some hunters, and managers, too, often employ the "inferior genetic stock" idea to excuse an abundance of stunted, miniature-antlered bucks. In reality, poor nutrition, late-births or social stress are more often responsible. Aside from a possible genetic link associated with unusually late-breeding that results in late fawning — as proposed by professor Harry Jacobson for certain areas in Mississippi — there is little reason to believe short-spike antlers, burred or burrless, are an inherited trait. That is, I doubt if a "short-spike antler gene" exists.

Managing Efforts

Late-born fawns are common in Southern states, where deer exhibit a long breeding season, and heavy buck harvesting often precedes the breeding season. As a result, a shortage of bucks can lead to doe recycling and late-season breeding, as Jacobson and his co-workers (1979) demonstrated for some areas of Mississippi. Buck fawns born during August and September are less

likely to achieve favorable body or antler size by yearling age, and many are likely to carry short burrless spike antlers. Therefore, harvest strategies designed to bring the herd's size and composition into better nutritional and social balance will normally advance breeding dates, improve the deer's physical condition, and reduce the occurrence of burrless short-spike yearling bucks.

In some areas, however, the combined negative effects of inherent late births and poor range nutrition might seriously compromise management efforts to advance maturation rates and improve the physical development of yearling bucks. As noted by Shea and his co-workers (1992b) in northwestern Florida, most fawns are born in August and September. These late-born animals are then subjected to extremely poor nutrition because of low-quality forage that grows on poorly drained, acidic and infertile soils, which impairs their growth rate. In other words, in some areas, low-density deer herds with more balanced adult sex and age ratios might not mean fewer or no burrless short-spiked yearlings.

On Northern range, the whitetail's breeding season tends to be short. In Michigan, for example, 80 percent to 90 percent of adult does breed in November and give birth in late May or June (Verme et al. 1987). Nearly half of adult does are pregnant by the time firearms season starts Nov. 15, thus minimizing the adverse effects of a buck shortage that soon develops because of hunter preference for antlered deer.

If late-breeding were the primary reason for short-spike bucks in Northern states, they should be most prevalent where a high proportion of doe fawns breed. Doe fawns typically breed in December or January, and give birth considerably later than adult does. This is not the case in Michigan. Most short-spike adult bucks are found in northern Michigan, whereas most pregnant doe fawns are found in southern Lower Michigan.

One phenomenon we commonly see in Michigan is a wide difference in body size among young bucks within certain populations. In Menominee County of Upper Michigan, for example, some yearling bucks might be exceptionally large and carry excellent 8-point racks. Others might be as small as some buck fawns and carry burrless short spikes. These variable conditions are most pronounced in areas of excellent deer habitat, but where high deer densities (sometimes greater than 100 deer per square mile) lead to excessive competition among pregnant does for fawn-rearing space.

Under extremely crowded conditions mature, dominant does control the best fawning habitat. They also are most successful in raising fawns, and tend to raise large males that grow into superior yearling bucks. Meanwhile, subordinate does are forced to use marginal habitat where their fawns grow poorly, if they survive. In autumn, increased aggressive interaction among deer merely adds to an already bad situation, further stressing undersized fawns and suppressing their growth. Some of these stressed buck fawns don't even grow pedicles before the onset of winter.

Herd Density

Somewhat different circumstances prevail throughout the whitetail's range where high deer numbers live on relatively poor soils. There, decades of high deer densities have greatly altered the composition and abundance of certain vegetation. Because deer are selective feeders, their intensive browsing pressure has drastically reduced or even eliminated the most nutritious forage in some areas. As a result, the capacity of such land to naturally support healthy deer has steadily declined and many, if not most, young bucks now demonstrate poor growth rates and carry especially poor antlers. The frequency and type of short spike antlers carried by yearling bucks in any given area can vary annually, depending upon many factors. A poor acorn crop, unusually early — or late — snow cover, or any other disturbance that limits the availability of nutritious food and curtails the growth of young deer earlier than normal, or delays their recovery in spring, can set the stage for an abundance of short-spike bucks. In Southern states, or

during mild winters in Northern states, many stunted fawns survive to become short-spike yearlings the next autumn. In contrast, poor autumn food conditions followed by severe winters might contribute to heavy starvation losses on Northern range, especially among small fawns, thereby lowering the incidence of short-spike yearling bucks.

Conclusion

Despite the potential complexity of factors, a high incidence of short-spike yearling bucks in a herd normally signals something is wrong. Generally, the deer population is nutritionally and/or socially out of balance.

The presence of short-spike bucks older than yearling age is a clear sign that deer are poorly nourished. Keep in mind, however, that deer overabundance leading to nutritional or social density stress is almost always linked to an overabundance of female deer. Conversely, a scarcity of mature bucks can be socially disruptive and yield similar consequences.

The ultimate solution to the short-spike dilemma lies in upgrading the whitetail's quality of life by restoring the herd's nutritional balance and social harmony. And, with few exceptions — some of which we discussed above — this can generally be accomplished by increasing the antlerless harvest and allowing more bucks to reach maturity. This should be done in conjunction with habitat manipulation designed to improve forage and cover quality for deer.

References

Harmel, D.E. 1982. Effects of genetics on antler quality and body size in white-tailed deer. Pages 339-348 in R.D. Brown, ed., Antler Development in Cervidae. *Caesar Kleberg Wildlife Research Institute, Kingsville, Texas. 480 pp.*

Jacobson, H.A., D.C. Guynn Jr., R.N. Griffin, and D. Lewis. 1979. Fecundity of white-tailed deer in Mississippi and periodicity of corpora lutea and lactation. *Proceedings of the Southeastern Association of Fish and Wildlife Agencies 33:30-35.*

Ozoga, J.J. 1988. Incidence of "infant" antlers among supplementally fed white-tailed deer. Journal of Mammalogy 69(2):393-395.

Ozoga, J.J., and L.J. Verme. 1982. Physical and reproductive characteristics of a supplementally fed white-tailed deer herd. Journal of Wildlife Management 46(2):281-301.

Shea, S.M., T.A. Breault, and M.L. Richardson. 1992a. Herd density and physical condition of white-tailed deer in Florida flatwoods. Journal of Wildlife Management 56(2):262-267.

Shea, S.M., T.A. Breault, and M.L. Richardson. 1992b. Relationship of birth date and physical development of yearling white-tailed deer in Florida. Proceedings of the Southeastern Association of Fish and Wildlife Agencies 46:159-166.

Severinghaus, C.W., H.R. Maguire, R.A. Cookingham, and J.E. Tanck. 1950. Variations by age class in the antler beam diameters of white-tailed deer related to range conditions. Transactions of the North American Wildlife Conference 553-568.

Ullrey, D.E. 1982. Nutrition and antler development in white-tailed deer. Pages 49-59 in R.D. Brown, ed., Antler Development in Cervidae. Caesar Kleberg Wildlife Research Institute, Kingsville, Texas. 480 pp.

Verme, L.J., J.J. Ozoga, and J.T. Nellist. 1987. Induced early estrus in penned white-tailed deer. Journal of Wildlife Management 51(1):54-56.

Other Recommended Reading: Bubenik, G.A., and A.B. Bubenik. 1990. Horns, Pronghorns, Antlers: Evolution, Morphology, Physiology, and Social Significance. Springer-Verlag, New York. 562 pp.

Goss, R.J. 1983. Deer Antlers: Regeneration, Function, and Evolution. Academic Press, New York. 316 pp.

Bill Lerner

Chapter 6

A MANAGEMENT TIMELINE:

Where Whitetails Are Headed

Deer management issues in the 1970s seemed simple, almost predictable. Deer numbers were low, just about everyone wanted deer, and deer lived mainly in the deep woods. Now, deer are everywhere, and everyone responds to them differently.

Of the world's many large grazing species, white-tailed deer have the most genetic diversity — the raw material by which a species evolves and adapts to changing conditions. That trait accounts for the whitetail's ability to live in many habitats, its vast geographic range, and its unpredictable nature or so-called plastic behavior.

In fact, everything about whitetails — including hunting — seems to involve adaptations to changing conditions, the timing and direction of which defy prediction.

Once a symbol of the wilderness, whitetails have expanded their range and now populate nearly every conceivable habitat niche. Whitetails not only live in forest habitat, they also live on farmlands and suburban woodlots. Each situation presents its own special hunting opportunities and management dilemmas, many of which were unheard of a few decades ago.

In this chapter, I'll look at what's happened in the whitetail's world during the second half of the 1900s, and make some brief predictions about its future.

Granted, my perspective is based on my home region — the upper Great Lakes — but many of these trends occurred across the whitetail's range.

The Panic of 1965

My career as a wildlife research biologist with the Michigan Department of Natural Resources began during the early 1960s. That was just after deer populations peaked in the late 1940s and early 1950s, and just before the "Panic of '65." In those days, deer hunters traditionally headed north to hunt, because the Midwest's farm belt held relatively few deer. This was also about the time deer herds in the upper Great Lakes region plummeted, and biologists were accused of decimating deer herds through over-harvesting.

Unfortunately, many hunters seemed oblivious to social and habitat changes that had occurred around them.

"I've hunted from the same stump for 25 years," many hunters insisted. "The woods are the same, but the deer are gone, and doe shooting is to blame."

They hadn't noticed the brush had grown into pole-sized trees, which provided little browse and shaded out sun-loving herbaceous growth. They also hadn't noticed that winter deeryards were seriously overbrowsed, and that other browse had grown out of the deer's reach. Nor did they acknowledge that widespread winter-kill during a siege of severe winters claimed more deer annually than the legal harvest.

I recall a frustrated Ralph MacMullen, former director of the Michigan DNR, saying: "Things gotta get better. They can't get much worse."

But things got worse. The region was battered by more severe winters in the late 1960s and early 1970s. Between 1964-65 and 1971-72, five out of eight winters in northern Wisconsin were considered severe — a pattern that prevailed across the region.

Despite what some considered radical regulations and overly aggressive hunting during the 1980s, deer herds still boomed. In 1989, for example, Michigan held about 2 million whitetails. That number rose to nearly 2.2 million by 1995, when the combined harvest by gun- and bow-hunters reached nearly 479,000.

The Michigan deer herd continued to decline, dropping from a high of around 1.4 million in 1949, to an all-time low of less than 500,000 by 1970. The annual deer harvest hit a low of around 59,000 in 1972. That same year, more than 600,000 Wisconsin hunters took home less than 75,000 deer, and Minnesota closed its deer season.

Day in Court

In 1971, disgruntled Michigan hunters gained the sympathetic ear of state Rep. John Payant, who challenged Michigan DNR deer management in court. Payant, citing the newly adopted Environmental Protection Act, filed suit to stop the DNR from issuing permits to allow hunters to take 447 antlerless deer in Upper Michigan's Dickinson County during the 1971 firearms season.

In dismissing the suit, the court's judges found that the DNR's testimony overwhelmingly contradicted the plaintiff's charge that antlerless deer harvests could impair or destroy the herd.

The judges wrote: "The testimony further establishes that large numbers of deer have died in recent years due to the harshness of the winters, lack of food and consequent starvation; and that not only will the taking of a limited number of antlerless deer result in harvesting deer that would die anyway, but it also is beneficial to the remaining deer in that they have a better chance of survival and are in better condition to propagate the herd."

The Boom Period

Needless to say, deer numbers, hunting opportunities and harvest rates have risen sharply throughout the upper Midwest since those bleak years of the early 1970s. But so have the problems associated with abundant deer.

Winter conditions and the quality of winter habitat are important regulators of the North's deer densities, but those factors are minor influences on Southern herds. Several factors in the 1980s and early 1990s sparked huge growth in Northern Forest herds. These factors included more timber harvesting, state-funded programs to improve deer range, conservative antlerless harvesting and an increase in supplemental feeding of deer.

Meanwhile, in agricultural regions, farming practices changed. Fewer acres were tilled, and society saw a general trend toward more casual farming and more land set aside for recreation. From 1960 to 1984, 55,000 farms in Michigan alone were abandoned, a reduction of 4 million acres of tillable land. As more farms turned casual, more land was converted to brushy vegetation, habitat favored by whitetails and other wildlife.

Deer herds boomed nationwide. As deer became more abundant, the antlerless deer harvest became more liberal, regulations changed, and hunters harvested a larger percentage of the herd. In 1977, Michigan hunters harvested 16 percent of the available deer. That number increased to 22 percent in 1995, when 38 percent of the harvest was antlerless. Next door, Wisconsin hunters consistently harvested 25 percent to 43 percent of the herd during the early 1990s, 55 percent of which were antlerless in 1995.

Despite what some considered radical regulations and overly aggressive hunting during the 1980s, deer herds still boomed. In 1989, for example, Michigan held about 2 million whitetails. That number rose to nearly 2.2 million by 1995, when the combined harvest by gun-hunters and bow-hunters reached nearly 479,000. The same year, Wisconsin recorded a peak harvest when hunters tagged 472,196 deer from a herd of about 1.5 million. Further, 500,000 Minnesota hunters harvested a state record of 243,068 deer in 1992.

But no longer are all hunters satisfied with mere numbers. In many regions hunters now harvest 80 percent to 90 percent of the available bucks each year. This has caused many hunters to complain about a lack of older bucks. In 1991, Michigan reduced the buck bag limit from four to two for the combined seasons. Recently, there has been considerable pressure to drop the second buck tag altogether, and initiate quality deer management to increase the proportion of older bucks.

Increased Competition

Despite gradually decreasing interest in hunting nationwide, deer hunting interest in the upper Midwest has risen steadily along with the expanding herds.

When the first issue of *Deer & Deer Hunting* magazine came out in 1977, Michigan had about 177,000 bow-hunters and fewer than 14,000 muzzleloading hunters. By 1995, those numbers had risen to more than 379,000 and 177,000, respectively. At the same time, the number of firearm hunters has varied from 693,880 to 740,440. Wisconsin has experienced similar trends.

License sales, however, don't translate perfectly into individual hunter numbers. That's because many individuals buy archery and firearms licenses. Ed Langenau, Michigan's big-game specialist, said: "The number of separate individuals who hunt deer in (Michigan) increased 57 percent from about 515,000 in 1963 to 817,730 in 1992. At the same time, the average number of days spent deer hunting each year per hunter increased from about six to 16. Thus, the frequency and intensity of deer hunting has increased during these decades."

Langenau's concern is that the increased interest has created intense competition between bow- and gun-hunters.

"For instance, some claim it's unfair the archery season is twice as long as the firearms season," Langenau said. "Bow-hunters have 77 days to hunt, compared to a combined 33 for the regular firearms and muzzleloading seasons. On the other hand, it might appear unfair that firearms hunters harvest most of the deer (73 percent), which is more than their share in terms of group size (57 percent), or days spent afield hunting deer (52 percent)."

New and Old Issues

Dennis Voigt, a ministry research biologist in Ontario, predicts the demand for deer hunting and viewing will rise substantially in the future. He also expects several new deer-management issues to arise. "For example, hunters are likely to demand more opportunities for trophy hunts, various types of weapon hunts and multiple bag-limit hunts," he said.

Deer baiting has also become an issue with hunters, and it's especially divisive in Michigan. A Michigan survey revealed 41 percent of the respondents hunted over bait in 1991, up from 29 percent in 1984. The amount of bait distributed annually increased from 16.3 bushels to 40 bushels per hunter during that time, and totaled more than 13 million bushels in 1991.

Hunters surveyed in 1991 were more tolerant of others using bait (45 percent approved, 31 percent were undecided and 24 percent disapproved) than in 1984. However, the report said: "There is still a potential for controversy and disagreement among hunters. Michigan deer hunters have strong and divergent opinions about this and other hunting methods, such as crossbows, tree stands and others."

David Schad, Minnesota's chief deer biologist, said Michigan's baiting problems — which include littering, bad public perceptions and competition and territorialism between hunters — heavily influenced Minnesota's decision to ban deer baiting in 1991.

Langenau believes hunters and state agencies should consider themselves one group of deer hunters, "rather than a long list of subgroups with special interests that splinter themselves by arguing over the equitable distribution of (deer)." He also discourages complex regulations that attempt to ensure each subgroup harvests its "fair share."

Social Problems Rising

Unfortunately, social problems caused by high deer densities have also risen. Over the past 25 years, much of the expanding human population has spilled out of cities and into deer habitat. Most deer now live on private property. With increasing numbers of deer and people interacting daily, it's no surprise conflicts have increased. Urban deer populations are causing economic losses, nuisance problems, and threats to human health and safety through Lyme disease and deer-vehicle accidents.

Deer also present challenges in farm country. More than 500,000 deer now inhabit southern Wisconsin's farmlands, where deer caused at least $37 million in agricultural damage in 1984 alone. Of 14 states studied by the U.S. Department of Agriculture, Wisconsin was found to have the most severe deer damage to corn, estimated at $15 million in 1993. In the past few years, Wisconsin's abatement and compensation program has spent more than $12 million to prevent or pay for crop damage caused by deer.

About 600,000 deer live in southern Lower Michigan, where only about 70,000 lived in 1970. The region's deer harvest now exceeds that of Upper Michigan's. In 1995, deer-related crop losses in Michigan totaled $31.9 million. As a result, the Michigan Farm Bureau threatened a class-action lawsuit against the Michigan DNR unless the deer herd was trimmed to its population goal of 1.3 million.

While there were only 10,742 deer-vehicle accidents reported in Michigan in 1972, that number swelled to 62,503 in 1995 (34,469 in southern Lower Michigan), causing in excess of $50 million in damage. Wisconsin placed its deer-vehicle accidents at 38,000, in 1990, costing an estimated $92 million in property damage and personal injury.

The Urban Affair

Cornell University's Daniel Decker and Milo

Richmond reported: "Urban deer management has fast become one of the most urgent and controversial wildlife management problems of the decade."

Although some urban deer problems date to the 1950s and '60s, most have developed since about 1970. In reviewing the history of urban deer problems, Michael Conover of Utah State University questions why this phenomenon occurred. He acknowledges that deer populations are higher, but suggests deer might have made behavioral adjustments to changing conditions during the past century. Part of those changes is the fact deer are protected outside the hunting season in rural areas and year-round in urban settings.

The long-range outlook for deer-human conflicts in urban settings is not encouraging. Few effective deer-control strategies can handle such touchy issues. Given people's compassion for wildlife, and more backyard deer feeding, such problems will probably escalate.

Conover writes: "Deer apparently have learned the contradictory lesson that while a low density of humans in rural areas may pose a threat, at least in the fall, a high density of humans in urban areas does not."

Decker and Richmond believe "urban deer/people management may be one of the biggest wildlife management 'problems' facing the profession." The main reason, they say, is because "urban deer managers face larger, more vocal, and politically active publics that range from animal-rights extremists to animal-welfare advocates to wildlife-use proponents, and finally to people who dislike deer altogether." Most are not sympathetic to recreational hunting.

The long-range outlook for deer-human conflicts in urban settings is not encouraging. Few effective deer-control strategies can handle such touchy issues. Given people's compassion for wildlife, and more backyard deer feeding, such problems will probably escalate.

Forest Changes

Traditionally, deer populations in Northern Forests have undergone a boom-and-bust rhythm, depending largely on logging, winter weather and forest successional trends. Since the mid-1970s, pulpwood production alone has increased 250 percent in parts of Upper Michigan and northern Wisconsin. These operations create extensive areas of ideal summer deer range. In some cases, however, especially on private land, heavily cut white cedar and hemlock have not regrown, thereby degrading vital winter thermal cover. Recreational development has also eaten up important winter deer habitat, as has an overabundance of wintering whitetails.

Given that scenario — good summer range but poor winter range — most deer managers envision even more dramatic ups and downs in regional deer numbers.

Record deer herds were hit hard across the North Woods during the severe winter of 1995-96. Dead-deer surveys in Upper Michigan placed winter losses at nearly 200,000, a loss comparable to an estimate for northern Wisconsin. About 100,000 deer also died in northern Lower Michigan, and another 104,000 died in northern Minnesota despite costly emergency feeding.

Those tough winters, combined with modest antlerless and excessive buck harvests, pushed Northern deer populations closer to goal levels. Hence, lower deer numbers and reduced buck hunting success were expected throughout the northern Great Lakes.

People who started hunting during the past two decades probably won't like these lower deer numbers. After all, they have high expectations because they're accustomed to hunting high-density herds. Therefore, biologists will probably be under considerable political pressure to back off on antlerless deer harvests. In some cases, they'll also be asked to conduct expensive emergency deer feedings. Unfortunately, such practices only help build herds to unrealistic high numbers, from which they'll only crash later.

Conversely, if biodiversity advocates have their way, we'll most certainly see fewer deer on public lands across the North in the future. That's because these folks want to reduce deer damage to certain regenerating forest types and sensitive herbaceous species.

Quantity Up, Quality Down

As deer densities increased from the mid-1970s to early 1990s, deer quality declined. Northern Michigan bucks, in particular, are now typically younger and smaller, a natural progression when deer are nutritionally and socially stressed and bucks are overhunted. Antlered bucks have traditionally been heavily exploited across the whitetail's range. It's not uncommon for yearling bucks to make up 70 percent to 80 percent of the buck population. Further, less than 2 percent of those bucks will reach age 4½. In lower Michigan, for example, only one buck in 1 million dies of old age.

In the 1970s, about half of Michigan's best bucks came from the Upper Peninsula, and the rest were almost split between northern and southern Lower Michigan. In those days, about 40 percent of bucks killed in the U.P. were yearlings, of which less than 30 percent were "spike-horns," and nearly 15 percent were 4½ and older. Many remote areas were lightly hunted, or not hunted at all, and about one buck in 5,000 died of old age.

All that changed in the 1990s, with more hunters, better access and more ATVs. No area seemed remote anymore, and mature bucks were scarce. Yearling bucks comprise about 60 percent of the U.P. buck harvest. More than half have spike antlers, and many of the spikes measure less than 3 inches. Further, less than 4 percent of U.P. bucks are 4½ years or older, and only about 25 percent of Michigan's top bucks now come from the U.P. About 70 percent of the state's biggest bucks now come from its southern farmlands, where well-fed bucks can reach record-book status by age 3½.

The incidence of short-spike antlers has also risen sharply in northern Wisconsin, where the long-term average was about 15 percent. A record was set in the state's Central Forest in 1992 when about 37 percent of yearling bucks had short spikes.

Unfortunately, even farmland yearling bucks declined in quality as herd sizes increased. In the mid-1980s, only about 5 percent of Michigan's farmland yearlings had spikes. Now, about 20 percent of them do, and the year-lings' average number of points have decreased from 5.9 to 5.3, while average beam diameters went from 22.7 to 21.4 millimeters.

Decreasing antler size among yearling bucks is a clear sign of nutritional and social stress caused by crowding and overbrowsing. Such stress is especially pronounced in areas where deer densities exceed 50 per square mile of range, but some areas have twice that many deer.

Interestingly, as southern Lower Michigan's deer densities rose, pregnancy rates among doe fawns declined. In the mid-1950s, 60 percent of farmland doe fawns were bred, but that rate dropped to 47 percent by the mid-1980s.

Conclusion

In comparison with today, deer management issues in the 1970s seem simple, almost predictable. Deer numbers were low, just about everyone wanted deer around, and deer lived mainly in the deep woods. Now, deer are every-where, and everyone responds to them differently. Some people want more deer, some want fewer, some will settle for fewer deer but want better quality, and some people don't seem to want any deer at all.

Given the current effects of large deer herds, one wonders how much agricultural damage, deer-vehicle collisions, health problems and habitat degradation the public will tolerate.

Fewer farmland deer seem a certainty, with hunters playing the lead role in reducing deer densities. Meanwhile, deer populations in Northern forests will probably continue their boom-and-bust patterns, controlled primarily by the quality of winter range and weather severity.

However, I see no easy solutions to the urban deer problems. I also believe deer hunter numbers in the future will follow the path of deer abundance: fewer deer will probably mean fewer hunters.

All things considered, white-tailed deer might once again have their day in court. Only next time, I hope deer hunters and deer managers will be on the same side.

Charles J. Alsheimer

Chapter 7

FAWN HARVESTING:

A Logical Alternative for Northern Range

Harvesting fawns on Northern range makes good biological sense. It's a logical alternative to massive winter deer mortality and further deeryard degradation. It could be safely implemented even in areas with low deer numbers where no antlerless hunting currently exists.

The quality of winter habitat and severity of winter weather are the critical factors regulating deer populations on Northern range.

In the Upper Great Lakes region, mild winters allow deer populations to build to unusually high numbers only to crash during the next severe winter when herds are stressed by starvation and predation. Such boom-and-bust trends have probably prevailed since whitetails extended their range northward behind receding glaciers.

The whitetail's young of the year — still considered fawns in winter — are the pawns squandered in nature's wicked game of winter survival. In good times — mild winters — fawns flourish and represent a high percentage of the herd. In bad times — harsh winters — they're the first to die, sometimes by the hundreds of thousands across the North Woods.

Why Shoot Fawns?

I can think of some good biological reasons for hunters to shoot more fawns on Northern range:

✓ Fawns generally represent the herd's most numerous single age class. More fawns typically survive to weaning age than are needed to replace adults that die.

✓ Fawns contribute relatively little or nothing toward reproduction the next year. Therefore, their harvest has little impact on annual recruitment.

✓ Fawns are always under-represented in the annual harvest. Given a choice, hunters will shoot an antlered buck or a doe instead of a small-bodied fawn.

✓ Fawns are the most likely deer to die in harsh winters. Even in years of high reproductive success, there is no guarantee a high proportion of fawns will survive their first winter and be available for harvest as yearlings.

Being Small: Good or Bad?

Fawns typically are smaller than adults, which presents advantages and disadvantages. Professor Duane Ullrey, an animal nutritionist at Michigan State University, suggests the smaller body size of fawns

Richard P. Smith

When winters are rated less than severe, fawns represent 80 percent to 90 percent of winter mortality. When coupled with browse-depleted winter range, losses can be staggering in high-density herds where many malnourished fawns enter winter.

entering their first winter might be adaptive. According to Ullrey: "A deer which is healthy but small will not require as much energy (in absolute terms) for maintenance during this period of extreme weather stress and food deprivation as a deer which is healthy and large."

Aaron Moen, a professor at Cornell University, argues that fawns entering winter at below-average weights encounter physical laws operating against survival. Moen writes, "More heat is lost by convection (air movement) from a square meter of surface of a small deer than from a square meter of surface of a large deer."

The critical body weight for fawns is somewhere between 77 pounds and 88 pounds. Animals weighing less than those weights lose considerably more body heat to cold exposure, and are less likely to survive extended cold weather while on a browse diet. By comparison, larger deer are more metabolically efficient at conserving energy.

Moen acknowledges many other factors in this equation, some of which tend to be compensatory. "Small fawns, for example, are at a disadvantage in snow because their legs are shorter than those of large deer," he writes. "Small fawns, however, are less likely to be pregnant, so their energy requirements do not include the

metabolic costs of pregnancy. Smaller, subdominant animals may have a lower energy requirement because they do not have to maintain a high social position in the herd. The energy requirement might be lower because they need not be as alert as older deer; they can rely on older deer to signal approaching danger. These are interesting considerations, but it is doubtful these factors compensate enough to equalize the effect of weight on the metabolic efficiency of small and large deer."

In the South, small fawns might often result from late births. In fact, these fawns might have metabolic advantages because of lower food requirements, and survive in a region where mild winters are normal. Small fawns in the North, however, are more often the product of poor summer and autumn nutrition. For them, poor nutrition in snow-free months is invariably followed by stressful and impoverished food conditions in winter. Few stunted, and comparatively lean, fawns survive such hardship.

Feeding Trials

As part of their adaptation for winter survival, whitetails restrict food consumption in midwinter. They also limit their movements and experience physiological changes, which reduces their metabolism.

Winter feeding patterns depend on many factors. Even when given all they want to eat — regardless of quality — healthy whitetails consume about 30 percent less food from January through early March. However, feeding tests at Michigan's Cusino Wildlife Research

Station revealed a deer's level of nutrition in autumn can influence winter feeding behavior. In our studies, adult does fed submaintenance (30 percent less than normal) rations in October and November followed the expected winter food intake pattern, with depressed feeding activity in midwinter. But they consumed 20 percent to 30 percent more white-cedar browse than normal throughout winter.

We saw similar winter feeding patterns in fawns subjected to poor nutrition when 5 to 6 months old. Fawns on marginal and poor diets (30 percent and 50 percent less than normal, respectively) in October and November, gained little weight, or in some cases lost weight by December. By comparison, fawns on full rations gained about 18 percent in body weight.

Later, when provided unlimited white-cedar browse, all fawns — regardless of autumn diet — followed the normal winter feeding pattern. They fed heavily in early winter and reduced their food intake in midwinter. Overall, however, fawns that received inadequate nutrition in autumn consumed more cedar browse and became inactive in winter. Even so, regardless of autumn diet, all fawns survived the 100-day winter test period when given unlimited white-cedar browse.

Autumn Fattening

Fawns fed poor diets in autumn were considerably smaller and leaner at the start of winter than fawns fed unlimited, high-quality feed during the same period. Even so, despite poor growth, fawns on marginal or poor autumn diets accumulated considerable fat. We concluded that fat accumulation in Northern deer is mostly controlled by hormones. That is, undernourished young animals sacrifice growth, if necessary, to build fat reserves in preparation for winter.

From a wildlife manager's perspective, fat fawns at the start of winter might not necessarily signify good range conditions. Healthy fawns will be large in skeleton as well as fat, while malnourished fawns might still be fairly fat, but stunted in skeleton.

Diet Promotes Fattening

Our studies also revealed a protein-rich diet isn't vital to fawns in autumn. The amount of dietary energy is more important. Even a small deficiency in digestible energy can slow a fawn's growth rate and decrease its fat levels.

Fawns receiving unlimited nutrition in autumn lost about 16 percent of their weight in winter when fed only cedar browse. By comparison, fawns on marginal and poor autumn diets lost 13 percent and 5 percent, respectively, of their body weight.

This difference in weight loss undoubtedly was attributable to the initial difference in fat reserves among fawns. Those well-fed in autumn built heavy fat stores and had energy to burn in winter. By compari-son, small, lean fawns had little surplus fat and experienced greater body heat loss from cold exposure. To survive winter, they had to consume more cedar browse than normal, plus become extremely energy-conservative. In a natural setting, that would require ideal winter habitat and/or an extremely mild winter, which seldom occurs in the North.

Regardless of autumn diet, female fawns normally accumulated more fat than males. We suspect male reproductive hormones are somehow involved in the disparity of stored fat. Still, that doesn't necessarily mean female fawns are more likely to survive tough winters. Numerous other behaviorisms and physical laws also determine a fawn's prospects for surviving winter.

Northern whitetails have evolved many adaptations for winter survival. It appears stressed fawns also undergo physiological changes that make them hardier than usual. The point is, no amount of fat will allow a young whitetail to survive a lengthy, tough winter without food, whereas even small, lean fawns might survive, given a reasonably good winter diet. Reducing the size of the wintering herd could make the difference.

Winter Mortality

The recent winters of 1995-96 and 1996-97 were deer killers across the Upper Great Lakes. Nearly 400,000 whitetails died in Upper Michigan alone. Roughly 50 percent were fawns.

When winters are rated less than severe, fawns represent 80 percent to 90 percent of winter mortality. When coupled with browse-depleted winter range, losses can be staggering in high-density herds where many malnourished fawns enter winter. In Upper Michigan, for example, the annual deer toll during mild winters in the late 1980s and early 1990s matched or exceeded the area's legal harvest, which ranged between 40,000 and 55,000 deer annually.

Ironically, such winter mortality occurs mainly in late winter and early spring — after each dead deer has consumed large amounts of valuable browse and further degraded winter habitat.

Fawn Tagging Studies

Studies in Upper Michigan's Petrel Grade Deeryard revealed high natural fawn mortality in their first winter. Although fawns represented only about 30 percent of the yard's herd, they accounted for about 60 percent of the mortality at winter deeryard cuttings. Of 145 male fawns we live-trapped, tagged and released in winter, only 47 (32.4 percent) were ever reported killed by hunters. We had no information on female fawns because the area had so little antlerless harvesting. More recently, biologists in central Upper Michigan also found a 32 percent recovery rate after examining more than 250 male fawn tagging records from several deeryards.

Certainly, not all tagged animals shot by hunters are reported, and some bucks probably survive their first winter only to die later of other causes. Nonetheless, the evidence suggests that, on average, only about 50 percent of all fawns survive their first winter in Upper Michigan.

Telemetry Studies

Studies by professor Timothy VanDeelen — now with the Illinois Natural History Survey, at Champaign, Ill. — revealed comparatively high winter fawn death rates in Upper Michigan's Whitefish Deeryard even in mild winters. During three mild winters — 1992, 1993 and 1994 — 32 percent of buck fawns and 28 percent of doe fawns fitted with radio-collars died from natural causes in their first winter.

In northern Wisconsin, Orrin Rongstad — a professor emeritus from the University of Wisconsin-Madison — also found overwinter fawn mortality rates highly variable. In some mild winters, none of his radio-collared fawns died. But in some severe winters, as many as 44 percent died.

The "Bambi" Complex

From a management standpoint, I believe it's unfortunate we call young-of-the-year deer "fawns." Even when they're 7 or 8 months old, and even when some are sexually mature, they're still fawns in the eyes of biologists, well-schooled hunters and other segments of the public. Educated hunters typically distinguish deer as fawns, yearlings or adults in autumn. On the other hand, I'm amazed some hunters, who know little about deer biology, recognize only bucks and does. For them, female fawns become "small does," while a male fawn is a "button buck." Even knowledgeable hunters resort to such terms to deflect possible criticism for shooting a fawn.

The term "fawn" carries a stigma. The public often envisions them as innocent, spotted creatures, hardly able to toddle on wobbly legs. And, regardless of size, to some, the term fawn is synonymous with "Bambi," and who could shoot such an innocent creature?

The idea that fawns should be harvested on Northern range is nothing new. In 1975, Rongstad issued a University of Wisconsin extension news release titled "Shoot Fawns to Help the Deer Herd."

Rongstad criticized hunters for not shooting more fawns, suggesting starvation losses and waste would be reduced on Northern range if hunters selectively shot more fawns. He added: "Because hunters with antlerless permits shoot larger animals, the ages of the animals hunters kill differ from the age structure of deer dying during a severe winter. So, killing a deer during the hunting season doesn't necessarily prevent one from starving in winter."

In fact, Rongstad proposed that hunters who shoot a

The idea of shooting a fawn sometimes raises an eyebrow or two with the general public. Most people perceive fawns as teetering infants with spots and spindly legs. However, harvesting fawns can be a logical alternative to massive winter deer mortality.

fawn should be rewarded, not condemned. "They're helping the deer population", he argued, "more so than hunters who kill larger, older animals instead."

Despite the solid biology behind his fawn-harvesting proposal, Rongstad was blasted by the ecologically ignorant press from coast to coast. Even some wildlife professionals slammed Rongstad, not on biological grounds, but for political reasons. The sentimental and emotional public just wasn't ready, neither were deer managers, who were then more concerned with providing quantity than quality. Deer hunters, some more concerned with trophies for the wall or large venison supplies for the freezer, weren't ready, either.

Conclusion

Harvesting fawns on Northern range makes good biological sense. It's a logical alternative to massive winter deer mortality and further deeryard degradation. It could be safely implemented even in areas with low deer numbers where no antlerless hunting currently exists.

Such a harvest mimics natural mortality, makes wise

use of a vulnerable and precarious surplus, and has little impact on the size of next year's herd. Harvesting a sizable portion of the annual fawn crop would lessen browsing pressure in critically important deeryards, while maintaining a prime-age nucleus in the herd that's capable of maximum reproductive output.

Surprisingly, neither right-minded hunters nor trained biologists have pushed for selective fawn harvesting on Northern range — not even in the face of recent massive winter losses.

I can't help but wonder: Will the day ever come when scientific reasoning, not emotions, determines deer management direction?

References

Halls, L.K., Ed. 1984. White-tailed Deer: Ecology and Management. Wildlife Management Institute, *The Stackpole Co., Harrisburg, Pa. 870 page.*

Moen, A.N. 1973. Wildlife Ecology. *San Francisco: W.H. Freemand and Co. 458 pages.*

Ozoga, J.J. 1972. Aggressive behavior of white-tailed deer at winter cuttings. Journal of Wildlife Management 36:861-868.

Ozoga, J.J., R.V. Doepker, and R.D. Earle. 1992. Hunter-harvest of captive-raised male white-tailed deer Odocoileus virginianus, released in Upper Michigan. Canadian Field Naturalist *106:357-360.*

Verme, L.J., and J.J. Ozoga. 1980. Influence of protein-energy intake on deer fawns in autumn. Journal of Wildlife Management *44:305-314.*

Verme, L.J., and J.J. Ozoga. 1980. Effect of diet on growth and lipogenesis in deer fawns. Journal of Wildlife Management *44:315-324.*

Wegner, R. 1988. Death in the deeryard. Deer & Deer Hunting *Volume 11, Issue 3, Number 63: 8-16, 18-22.*

Chapter 8

BOVINE TUBERCULOSIS:

A Bitter Lesson in Deer Management

During the late 1990s, Michigan's Club Country had the infamous and humiliating distinction of harboring whitetails infected with bovine tuberculosis, or TB. However, with everyone's cooperation, TB in Michigan whitetails can be eradicated.

Traditionally, Lower Michigan's northeastern corner has been called the "Club Country." It has also been known as Michigan's deer-food shortage area — the state's first such area.

This four-county area has been overpopulated with whitetails for decades because of artificial feeding and inadequate antlerless harvests. Frankly, it has been a longtime sore spot in Michigan's deer management program.

Michigan's Club Country has had the infamous and humiliating distinction of harboring whitetails infected with bovine tuberculosis, or TB. Never before in North America has this disease been self-sustaining in free-ranging wildlife, which presents a unique and serious situation with many complex considerations.

The Club Country

While the situation is unusual, its origins are obvious. It's nothing more than a consequence of carrying far more deer than the natural habitat can support in healthy condition. The problem was brewing for a long time and won't be resolved easily or quickly.

Hunting clubs in northern Michigan played a vital role in restoring Michigan's deer herd early this century. According to the late Ilo Bartlett, the 25,000-acre Turtle Lake Club — in the heart of the TB area — was organized in 1884. As deer increased on club lands in the 1920s, smaller clubs sprang up. The club approach spread until more than 500 square miles of nearly solid club land covered Alpena, Alcona, Oscoda and Montmorency counties.

Because deer in this region were usually overprotected, the herds continued to increase and soon overpopulated winter range throughout Club Country. Deer starvation in winter first appeared in Alpena County in 1930. By then, 100 square miles of deer range was overpopulated and overbrowsed. By 1936, the starvation area had spread to include about 500 square miles. By 1948, the problem area exceeded 3,000 square miles and included much of northeastern Lower Michigan.

Bartlett estimated as many as 50,000

whitetails died annually from starvation in Club Country during severe winters in the 1930s, 40s and early 50s. Those estimates are probably conservative. Systematic dead-deer surveys revealed losses exceeding 25 deer per square mile on the Turtle Lake Club during the hard winter of 1958-59. When applied across 3,000 square miles, winter losses would have approached 75,000.

Given the combination of low deer harvests and depleted winter range, Club Country deer cycled through boom-and-bust patterns. The herds built to unusually high numbers during mild winters, only to crash during tough winters because of starvation. Eventually, winter range became so poor it could not naturally support deer in a healthy condition even in easy winters.

Michigan DNR

Pea-sized tubercles on the inside lining of a deer's rib cage are one of the more easily visible signs of TB. The disease is spread through the air and on moist food items, primarily by close contact with infected animals.

Setting the Stage

In an effort to curb declining deer numbers, club members began artificially feeding deer in the 1960s. Each winter, well-meaning landowners fed deer hundreds of tons of oats, corn, carrots, apples, sugar beets, pumpkins, cabbage, hay and pellet feed. The feeding helped prevent mass starvation. Unfortunately, it produced high deer densities that not only prevented winter habitat from rebounding, but also devastated summer range.

As a club member told me in the early 1980s, "I think we created a monster." He was right.

Dave Arnold, a former deer specialist, said: "The Club Country became virtually mined by the deer. Reproduction of desirable species is absent from many wintering areas. Browsing on spruce and balsam (starvation rations) is common, even in uplands."

Arnold also noted that feeding went hand-in-hand with overprotection. He wrote: "Even if club memberships are not protectionists, even if they have no aversion to 'doe shooting,' they usually shoot only antlered bucks and only a few because the number of 'members per acre' of club land is frequently sparse. ... As a result, the deer in the Club Country are made up of older animals, which have a lower productivity rate than animals on heavily hunted areas more accessible to the general public."

By the 1950s, Club Country whitetails were among Michigan's unhealthiest deer. They were also among the state's smallest deer in body and antler. The combination of unhealthy, highly stressed deer crowded at artificial feeding sites set the stage for transmitting TB.

What is Bovine TB?

Tuberculosis is a serious respiratory disorder caused by several bacteria of the *Mycobacterium* family. These consist of three main types: human, avian and bovine. Human and avian TB are the most host-specific. Bovine TB, also called cattle TB, is the most infectious, afflicting most warm-blooded animals, including humans.

Tuberculosis is spread through the air and on moist food items, primarily by close contact with infected animals that cough or sneeze. Therefore, the disease's spread is enhanced when stressed, unhealthy animals are crowded together.

According to Dr. Steve Schmitt, a veterinarian with the Michigan Department of Natural Resources: "It's thought the maintenance of bovine TB in Michigan white-tailed deer is directly related to supplemental feeding and the increased densities this practice creates. ... Under these circumstances, inhalation of the bovine TB bacteria or consumption of feed contaminated with bovine TB by coughing and exhalation is much more likely to occur than in a free-ranging (wild) cervide (deer or elk) population."

Signs of the disease might not be easily seen. Sometimes, small (pea-sized) tan or yellow lumps might be present on the inside of the rib cage. The lungs might also have these nodules throughout the tissue.

Animals can transmit TB to humans, and vice versa. This is extremely rare, however, and there is no record of humans catching TB from deer in Michigan. Nonetheless, it's wise to wear heavy rubber gloves while gutting deer. Also, all meat from any animal in the four-county area must be thoroughly cooked until it's no

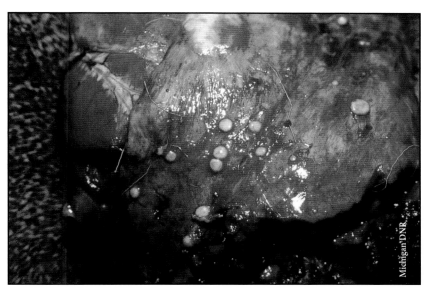

TB tubercles can also be found on the lungs and mesentery of the small intestines. Although there is no record of humans catching TB from deer in Michigan, it's wise to wear heavy gloves when gutting deer.

longer pink and all juice from the meat is clear, not red or pink. However, if the lungs or rib cage look abnormal, avoid the meat and contact the DNR.

TB History in Michigan Deer

Before 1994, only eight wild whitetails or mule deer in North America had been reported with bovine TB. One of these was a Michigan Club Country whitetail shot in 1975.

In November 1994, however, a hunter shot a deer in Club Country near Alpena that had internal lesions and abscesses on the lungs and rib cage. The hunter notified the Michigan DNR, which sent a biologist to examine the deer. The DNR determined the deer had bovine TB. A survey of hunter-killed deer within a 10-mile radius of the infected deer was undertaken in 1995. Based on cultures taken from lymph nodes in the heads of 354 whitetails, 18 deer tested positive for bovine TB.

Similar surveys in 1996 and 1997 included examinations of road-killed deer and others found dead. As of March 1998, more than 8,600 deer had been examined from Alpena, Montmorency, Oscoda, Alcona and Presque Isle counties, and 149 tested positive for bovine TB — 1.8 percent.

Ongoing exams of thousands of deer from Michigan's 83 counties found three TB-infected deer outside the five-county area in November 1999. None of the nearly 200 elk Michigan tested had shown signs of TB.

Bovine TB is known to affect a variety of wildlife, and several species in other counties have been implicated as a reservoir for the disease. Therefore, opossums, raccoons, coyotes, bobcats, badgers and red foxes have also been tested. Several coyotes and at least one bear and raccoon had tested positive before 1999.

Threat to Livestock

Bovine TB in wild deer presents a special threat to domestic livestock. Therefore, Michigan's Department of Agriculture examined area livestock for the disease. Testing is necessary to determine public health risks and maintain the integrity of Michigan's bovine TB-free accredited status.

Testing for bovine TB and surveillance of livestock herds in the five-county area began in March 1995. It will continue until the department determines there is no longer a risk of spreading bovine TB from wild deer to domestic livestock.

As of November 1998, 150 herds comprising more than 5,400 head of cattle, goats, pigs and llamas had been tested for bovine TB. Four of those herds were under quarantine pending further diagnostic testing. However, only one infected cow had been found.

That caused the state's TB-free status to be suspended in late June 1998. Other states will likely require TB testing before cattle from Michigan can be sold. Previously, Wisconsin and Virginia had already required tests of Michigan-produced cattle. That development was expected to cost Michigan livestock producers millions of dollars. In fact, the Michigan Farm Bureau estimated the cost of losing the TB-free status would amount to $170 million over 10 years.

Even so, authorities emphasize that consumers shouldn't worry excessively about the safety of their milk and meat supply. Since 1965, all Grade A milk in Michigan has been pasteurized to assure its safety. Likewise, all beef sold for public consumption must pass federal inspections.

Captive Deer Surveillance

The Michigan Department of Agriculture has implemented a program for TB testing in all captive deer herds in the critical five-county area. As of November 1998, six herds had completed testing programs, 11 herds were under quarantine pending completion of testing, and five herds were under review for development of test plans. The owners of quarantined herds cannot move live animals from the premises.

In October 1997, two TB-positive deer were found among 55 deer slaughtered in a 1,500-acre enclosure in Presque Isle County. A plan was initiated to kill all deer (about 700) in the enclosure.

The incidence of TB-positive whitetails nearly doubled within the four-county Club Country area from 1996 to 1997, going from 1.24 percent to 2.23 percent. The rate was even higher within a newly established deer management unit — DMU 452 — which covers a major part of the Club Country, increasing from 2.33 percent in 1996 to 4.47 percent in 1997.

This increase, coupled with finding infected deer in the enclosed facility, led Michigan Gov. John Engler to direct the departments of agriculture, natural resources and community health to work together to eradicate bovine TB from state deer herds.

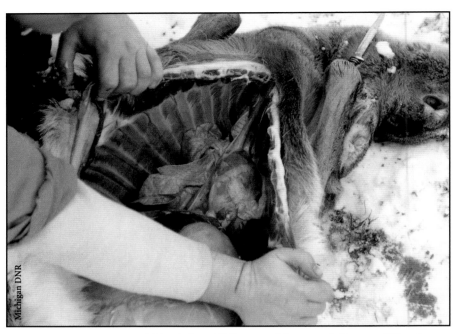

This photo exhibits normal lungs and rib cage. If the deer had been infected with TB, small tan or yellow nodules might have have been visible.

Eradication Strategy

Engler identified several actions for the state's eradication strategy:

1. Develop wild deer herd harvest quotas consistent with eradication of bovine TB.

2. Develop and implement methods for farmers to eliminate contact between wild deer and livestock.

3. Continue comprehensive surveillance of livestock and deer to determine the disease's prevalence, and to evaluate trends.

4. Disseminate information to hunters, farmers and the public regarding how to manage wild deer in the five-county area to eradicate bovine TB.

5. Create a bovine TB eradication coordinator in the Department of Community Health to work with agencies in overseeing eradication management tactics. (In February 1998, former Rep. Bob Bender was named to this post.)

Mandatory Feeding Ban

The Department of Agriculture banned the feeding of deer and elk in northeastern Michigan. The ban was deemed necessary to minimize concentration and crowding of deer to avoid possible transmission of bovine TB. The ban covered the critical TB area and a wide buffer zone around it. The area is bordered by Interstate 75 to the west, Michigan 55 to the south, Lake Huron to the east and the Straits of Mackinac to the north.

Since the late 1990s, deer baiting for hunting has continually been restricted. Traditionally, hunters had spread hundreds of tons of apples, sugar beets, cabbage and other assorted fruits and vegetables throughout Club Country each autumn.

Disease Control Permits

The Michigan DNR has also issued disease control permits to agriculture producers in Alcona, Alpena, Montmorency, Oscoda and Presque Isle counties. The permits expanded the existing permit system, which allowed agricultural producers to shoot deer causing crop damage or interfering with livestock operations.

That marked a working relationship between DNR employees and landowners to determine the number of permits and conditions for their issuance. All deer killed were collected and examined for TB.

Deer Population Reduction

The DNR estimates the Club Country held 40 to 60 whitetails per square mile in 1994 when TB in deer was discovered. However, some areas likely held as many as 100 deer per square mile, and concentrations of several hundred deer weren't uncommon at winter feeding stations.

Because of increased antlerless harvests, severe winters in 1996 and 1997, and a voluntary 50 percent reduction in winter feeding, the deer population numbered about 30 per square mile in the late 1990s.

Experience shows that efforts to control TB in domestic livestock have failed, and that killing all livestock on affected farms is the only solution. Obviously, it would be politically unpopular and probably impossible to kill every deer in northeastern Michigan. It's hoped that deer numbers can be held at about 30 per square mile or lower, especially in DMU 452. Special early and late seasons will be established in DMU 452 to assure adequate antlerless harvests, which are considered essential in preventing TB from spreading.

Research

In the first year of an ongoing three-year study into deer patterns at bait and winter feeding sites, 60 radio collars were placed on wild deer captured at four sites in the five-county area. Five other deer previously radio-collared were included in the study. As of November 1998, 30 of the original 65 radio-collared deer were alive. An additional 34 deer were radio-collared to start the study's second year.

The following observations were made at winter feeding sites:

1. An average of 13 deer per hour visited the sites.

2. Deer made an average of 21 nose-to-nose contacts per hour.

3. Deer made an average minimum of 19 contacts within three feet of each other per hour, in addition to nose-to-nose contacts.

Further, these observations were recorded at hunters' bait sites in autumn:

1. An average of two deer per hour visited the sites.

2. Deer averaged two nose-to-nose contacts per hour.

3. Deer made an average minimum of one contact within three feet of each other per hour, in addition to nose-to-nose contacts.

Radio-tracking data indicated deer in areas north of DMU 452 migrated an average distance of 6.4 miles, with a maximum range of 28 miles. Deer within DMU 452 appeared less mobile, migrating an average of 3.2 miles, with a maximum of 13 miles. Therefore, the risk of spreading bovine TB exists, but it's minimal if the proposed herd reduction and feeding ban are closely followed.

Goals

The overall goal is to eliminate bovine TB in Michigan's whitetails. This will take time. The manage-

While the immediate effects of TB in Michigan's deer will be nasty, the potential long-term biological, ecological and economic consequences could be devastating for a wide area. With everyone's cooperation, TB in Michigan whitetails can be eradicated promptly.

ment objectives are to:

1. Reduce the incidence of TB in deer to less than 1 percent in DMU 452 by Autumn 2003.

2. Eliminate TB-infected deer in areas outside of DMU 452 by the year 2003.

3. Eliminate TB-infected deer in DMU 452 by Autumn 2010.

Scientists are tackling this problem aggressively and confidently. According to a program update: "By halting supplemental feed, restricting bait, banning new captive deer/elk herds, and reducing the overall population in the five-county area, deer concentrations will be lowered, thereby reducing the risk of transmitting bovine TB among animals. With time, it is expected these measures will eliminate bovine TB from Michigan's wild deer and make this a short footnote in the history of Michigan's wild deer."

Conclusion

Certainly, no wildlife professionals predicted TB in Michigan Club Country deer. But, given the region's history, most biologists had predicted disaster of some sort. This is a lesson we learned long ago in Wildlife Management 101. It's unfortunate hunters and private landowners did not heed our warnings. Similar problems could arise wherever deer herds are managed at excessively high densities and supplemental feeding is allowed.

While the immediate effects of TB in Michigan's deer will be nasty, the potential long-term biological, ecological and economic consequences could be devastating for a wide area. With everyone's cooperation, TB in Michigan whitetails can be eradicated promptly.

In the future, maybe this episode will inspire Michigan Club Country landowners to work for deer habitat improvement instead of artificial feeding. And, just maybe, they'll begin to scientifically manage deer herds, which should have been done decades ago.

INDEX

ABOUT THE AUTHOR

John Ozoga and his wife, Janice, are natives of Crystal Falls, Mich., and currently reside in Munising, Mich. They have one daughter, three sons and three grandsons.

Ozoga holds bachelor and master of science degrees in wildlife management from Michigan State University. Most of his professional career was spent at the Cusino Wildlife Research Station in Michigan's Upper Peninsula, where he was a wildlife research biologist for 30 years. He retired from the Michigan Department of Natural Resources in 1994 after more than 33 years service.

As a researcher, Ozoga wrote or co-wrote more than 80 technical publications. Although his scientific work includes papers on small mammals, songbirds, foxes, coyotes, bears and elk, his research focused primarily on white-tailed deer ecology, physiology, reproduction, nutrition, behavior and population dynamics.

His scientific honors include the Outstanding Publication in Wildlife Ecology and Management Award, presented by the Wildlife Society.

Ozoga started publishing magazine and newspaper accounts of his research findings in the early 1980s. In 1988, he wrote the popular book *Whitetail Country*, and more recently the award-winning, four-book series *Seasons of the Whitetail*. The Safari Club International published a deer-management bulletin written by Ozoga in 1994 and, in 1998 named him Michigan's Outdoor Writer of the Year.

Ozoga's primary concern is educating the hunting and nonhunting public about white-tailed deer biology and the principles of sound deer management. To that end, he has published several hundred magazine and newspaper articles. His writings have appeared regularly in *Deer & Deer Hunting* since 1986, and in 1994 he became the magazine's research editor.

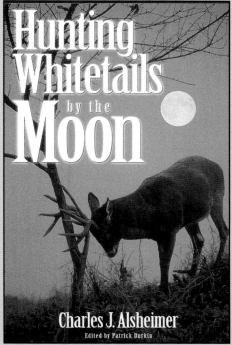

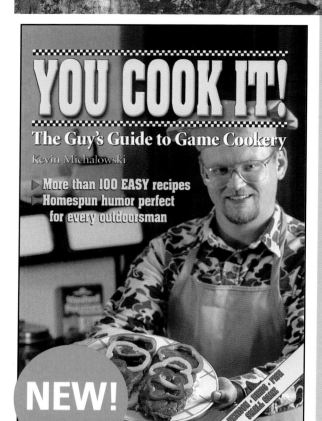